OF LAW AND MEN

Of Law and Men

PAPERS AND ADDRESSES OF

Felix Frankfurter

1939-1956

EDITED BY PHILIP ELMAN

ARCHON BOOKS • HAMDEN, CONNECTICUT

To

THE HARVARD LAW SCHOOL
IN GRATITUDE
AFTER FIFTY YEARS

Foreword

FROM TIME TO TIME it has fallen to me to say a parting word, what the Germans call a *Nachruf*, to a friend—now a revered master, now a contemporary, on rare occasions a young life snuffed out by war or the cruelty of nature. The dead should not cease to be in the minds of men. I feel this especially about men and women who have expended their lives on significant but unadvertised work, whether plowing the lonely furrow of scholarship, or foregoing the comforts of life for the drudgeries that accompany achievement in undramatic phases of government, or pioneering in the dark areas of our industrial society. These people have given proof, in diverse ways, of the grace and gallantry of the human spirit.

Feeling thus, I responded to the suggestion that these expressions should have the shelter of the covers of a book. Once this thought was urged upon me, it broadened to the proposal that I write the story of my own journey. Too often is it assumed that mere attainment of the Psalmist's years affords the Psalmist's justification for self-disclosure. The fact is that zestful as my years have been, I am not particularly interested in looking back. The present sufficiently absorbs my interest and energy. But I see no reason why utterances beyond those elicited on melancholy occasions should not be made part of this volume.

My life has been given to law—but not law as a critique of pure reason. For half a century I have been preoccupied with the study of law. For half of that time it was a scholar's study, subjected to the influences of fellow scholars and, particularly, the stimulus of questioning by critical young minds. The other half of my life in the law has been concerned with its concrete application in the context of a democratic society—law, that is, devoted to the protection of personal rights and the promotion of public ends.

All that appears in this volume was spoken or written after I came to the Supreme Court. This has restricted expression of views within the bounds that confine public nonjudicial speech by a member of the Court. Not even Jefferson and John Quincy Adams could have foreseen this country's present commitments throughout the world. Nor did Lincoln, when he urged ratification of the Thirteenth Amendment on Georgia, anticipate the extent to which the power of the States would later be restricted, as it has been, by the Fourteenth Amendment. De Tocqueville could not have appreciated the reach of his own prescience in realizing, more than a hundred years ago, that hardly any political question arises in the United States that does not sooner or later become a judicial question. Accordingly, one in my place should abstain from extrajudicial pronouncements within the wide areas of potential litigation. This is not merely because legal issues ought to be resolved only after full argument and due consideration within the Court. It is important not to give the appearance of a predisposed mind. And it is more important not to let the mind become predisposed. I hope, therefore, that I have not been guilty of straying outside the limits that judges must take care to observe in their extrajudicial utterances.

This volume is born of the generous friendship of Philip

Elman. I shall forbear to say more than to make acknowledgment of his skillful editing. What I said or wrote in these papers has been left unchanged, barring only that here and there obvious blemishes and repetitions have been removed.

FELIX FRANKFURTER

June 30, 1955
Washington, D. C.

Contents

I

LAW AND THE JUDICIAL PROCESS

One

John Marshall and the Judicial Function

(1955)

Commemorating the two-hundredth anniversary of the birth of Chief Justice Marshall, a conference on "Government under Law" was held in September 1955 at Cambridge, Massachusetts, under the auspices of the Harvard Law School. Mr. Justice Frankfurter delivered the opening address, which was printed in the December 1955 issue of the *Harvard Law Review* (Vol. 69, p. 217). The proceedings of the conference will be published in book form by Harvard University.

TWO HUNDRED YEARS AGO a great man was born who indisputably is the "one alone" to be chosen "if American law were to be represented by a single figure." John Marshall was the chief architect "of a new body of jurisprudence, by which guiding principles are raised above the reach of statute and State, and judges are entrusted with a solemn and hitherto unheard-of authority and duty." (Holmes, *Collected Legal Papers*, (1920), p. 270.) Such is the verdict of one whom so qualified a critic as Mr. Justice Cardozo deemed probably the greatest intellect in the history of the English-speaking judiciary.

Unlike other great pioneers in the law, Hardwicke in equity, Mansfield in commercial law, Stowell in prize law, Holmes in torts, the essential heritage of Marshall, because of the very nature of constitutional law, does not lie in specific precepts, definite rules more or less easy of application

3

in new circumstances. Of his opinions it is peculiarly true that their "radiating potencies" go far beyond the actual holdings of the decisions. See *Hawks* v. *Hamill*, 288 U.S. 52, 58 (1933). The tendencies propelled by his opinions give him his unique place in our history; through them he belongs among the main builders of our Nation. Although he led an important diplomatic mission and was not an otiose Secretary of State, the decisive claim to John Marshall's distinction as a great statesman is as a judge. And he is the only judge who has that distinction. It derives from the happy conjunction of Marshall's qualities of mind and character, the opportunities afforded by the Court over which he was called to preside, the duration of his service, and the time in which he served— the formative period in the country's history.

When Jefferson heard that Hamilton was urging John Marshall to enter Congress, he wrote to Madison, on June 29, 1792: "I am told that Marshall has expressed half a mind to come. Hence I conclude that Hamilton has plied him well with flattery & sollicitation, and I think nothing better could be done than to make him a judge." (6 *The Writings of Thomas Jefferson*, (Ford ed., 1895), pp. 95-97.) How ironically Fate outwitted Jefferson in his desire to sidetrack Marshall to what Jefferson conceived to be the innocuous role of a judge. (I am indebted to Professor Julian P. Boyd for calling my attention to this letter as well as for its exact phrasing, based on the recipient's copy in the Madison Papers, Library of Congress.)

When Marshall came to the Supreme Court, the Constitution was still essentially a virgin document. By a few opinions—a mere handful—he gave institutional direction to the inert ideas of a paper scheme of government. Such an achievement demanded an undimmed vision of the union of States as a Nation and the determination of an uncompromising devotion to such insight. Equally indispensable was the power to formulate views expressing this outlook with the persuasiveness of compelling simplicity.

It is shallow to deny that general ideas have influence or to minimize their importance. Marshall's ideas, diffused in all sorts of ways, especially through the influence of the legal profession, have become the presuppositions of our political institutions. He released an enduring spirit, a mode of approach for generations of judges charged with the awesome duty of subjecting the conduct of government and the claims of individual rights to the touchstone of a written document, binding the Government and safeguarding such rights. He has afforded this guidance not only for his own country. In the federalisms that have evolved out of the British Empire, Marshall's outlook in constitutional adjudications has been the lodestar. Unashamedly I recall the familiar phrase in which he expressed the core of his constitutional philosophy: "It is *a constitution* we are expounding." *M'Culloch* v. *Maryland*, 4 Wheat. 316, 407 (1819). It bears repeating because it is, I believe, the single most important utterance in the literature of constitutional law—most important because most comprehensive and comprehending.

I should like to follow James Bradley Thayer in believing that the conception of the Nation which Marshall derived from the Constitution and set forth in *M'Culloch* v. *Maryland* is his greatest single judicial performance. It *is* that, both in its persuasiveness and in its effect. As good a test as I know of the significance of an opinion is to contemplate the consequences of its opposite. The courage of *Marbury* v. *Madison*, 1 Cranch 137 (1803), is not minimized by suggesting that its reasoning is not impeccable and its conclusion, however wise, not inevitable. I venture to say this though fully aware that, since Marshall's time and largely, I suspect, through the momentum of the experience which he initiated, his conclusion in *Marbury* v. *Madison* has been deemed by great English-speaking courts an indispensable, implied characteristic of a

written constitution. Holmes could say, as late as 1913: "I do
not think the United States would come to an end if we lost
our power to declare an Act of Congress void." But he went
on to say: "I do think the Union would be imperiled if we
could not make that declaration as to the laws of the several
States. For one in my place sees how often a local policy prevails with those who are not trained to national views and
how often action is taken that embodies what the Commerce
Clause was meant to end." (Holmes, *Collected Legal Papers*,
(1920), pp. 295-96.) One can, I believe, say with assurance
that a failure to conceive the Constitution as Marshall conceived it in *M'Culloch* v. *Maryland*, to draw from it the national powers which have since been exercised and to exact
deference to such powers from the States, would have been
reflected by a very different United States than history knows.
Marshall surely was right when he wrote, a month after he
rejected the argument for Maryland: "If the principles which
have been advanced on this occasion were to prevail, the Constitution would be converted into the old Confederation."

Marshall's intrinsic achievements are too solid and his personal qualities too homespun to tolerate mythical treatment.
It is important not to make untouchable dogmas of the fallible reasoning of even our greatest judge, and not to attribute
godlike qualities to the builders of our Nation. Does it not
border on the ludicrous that by questioning whether Marshall
was an original thinker Holmes nearly barred his way to the
Supreme Court? So deeply had uncritical reverence for Marshall's place in our national pantheon lodged itself in the confident judgment of President Theodore Roosevelt. (See I *Correspondence of Theodore Roosevelt and Henry Cabot Lodge*,
(1925), pp. 517-19.) As though one should look among even
the greatest of judges for what Holmes called "originators
of transforming thought." (Holmes, *Collected Legal Papers*,
(1920), p. 269.) I venture to suggest that had they the mind
of such originators, the bench is not the place for its em-

ployment. Transforming thought implies too great a break with the past, implies too much discontinuity, to be imposed upon society by one who is entrusted with enforcing its law.

Marshall's creativeness has from time to time been discounted by attributing the ground he broke in his opinions to the arguments of the great lawyers who appeared before him, especially Webster. The latter was no mean appreciator of his own performance, but an examination of his argument in *Gibbons* v. *Ogden*, 9 Wheat. 1 (1824), hardly confirms his boast that Marshall's opinion "was little else than a recital of my argument." (Harvey, *Reminiscences and Anecdotes of Daniel Webster*, (1877), p. 142.) Powerful counsel no doubt have impact upon the strongest Court, and probably never in the history of the Supreme Court has such a galaxy of talent appeared before it as in Marshall's day. Not the least distinction of a great judge is his capacity to assimilate, to modify or to reject the discursive and inevitably partisan argument of even the most persuasive counsel and to transform their raw material into a judicial judgment. So it was with Marshall.

Again, it is not to be assumed that what Marshall wrote was wholly the product of his own brain, freed from infusion of his brethren's thinking. In his day there was the closest intimacy among the judges. It is inconceivable that they did not discuss their cases in their common boardinghouse. A man of Marshall's charm and power was bound to make himself deeply felt among his brethren. But the assumption that he dominated his colleagues leaves out of reckoning the strong personalities among them. Story had the deepest devotion to Marshall, but he also had views and vanity. Johnson's opinions reveal tough-mindedness, abounding intellectual energy, and a downright character. Likewise, we may be sure that Bushrod Washington was no mere echo. And so one may be confident in inferring that the novelty of the issues, the close social relations of the Justices, the ample opportunities they had for discussion among themselves, precluded Marshall's

path-breaking opinions from being exclusively solo performances. Then as now, constitutional decisions are the outcome
of the deliberative process, and as such, more or less, com-
posite products. But their expression is individual. The voice
of the Court cannot avoid imparting the distinction of its own
accent to a Court opinion. In the leading constitutional cases
Marshall spoke for the Court. But *he* spoke. The prestige of
his office, the esteem which he personally aroused, the deference he evoked, enabled Marshall to formulate in his own
way an agreement collectively reached. Thus, in his exposition of the Commerce Clause, Marshall indulged in observations not only beyond the necessities of the cases but outside
the demands of his own analysis.

To slight these phases of his opinions as dicta, though such
they were on a technical view, is to disregard significant
aspects of his labors and the ways in which constitutional law
develops. There can be little doubt that Marshall saw and
seized his opportunities to educate the country to a spacious
view of the Constitution, to accustom the public mind to
broad national powers, to counteract the commercial and
political self-centeredness of States. He was on guard against
every tendency to continue treating the new Union as though
it were the old Confederation. He imparted such a momentum
to his views that the Court and eventually the country were
moved in his general direction, beyond his own time and into
our own.

The role that Marshall played in the evolution of our Nation ought, I should think, to make it difficult for those who
believe that history is reducible to laws, to fit him into their
schemata. Surely the course of American history would have
been markedly different if the Senate had not rejected the
nomination of John Rutledge to succeed Jay as Chief Justice;
if the benign Cushing, a Federalist of different composition
from Marshall's, had not withdrawn after a week and had
continued as Chief Justice till his death in 1810; if Ellsworth's

resignation had come later; if John Adams had persuaded Jay to return as Chief Justice; or if some readily imaginable circumstance had delayed Ellsworth's replacement till John Adams was out of the White House so that the new Chief Justice would have been a Jeffersonian. (That it would have been Spencer Roane is an unsubstantiated tradition.) John Marshall is a conspicuous instance of Cleopatra's nose.

This does not make me an adherent of the hero theory of history. If I may quote Mr. Isaiah Berlin: "Historical movements exist, and we must be allowed to call them so. Collective acts do occur; societies do rise, flourish, decay, die. Patterns, 'atmospheres,' complex interrelationships of men or cultures are what they are, and cannot be analysed away into atomic constituents. Nevertheless, to take such expressions so literally that it becomes natural and normal to attribute to them causal properties, active powers, transcendent properties . . . is to be fatally deceived by myths. . . . There is no formula which guarantees a successful escape from either the Scylla of populating the world with imaginary powers and dominions, or the Charybdis of reducing everything to the verifiable behavior of identifiable men and women in precisely denotable places and times." (Berlin, *Historical Inevitability*, (1954), p. 16.) Certainly on this occasion it is appropriate to assert with emphasis that John Marshall was not the fated agency of inevitable economic and social forces to make his decisive contribution in the shaping of this country's destiny.

Temperament, experience, and association converged to his outlook in judicial action. Even more truly than Gibbon could say of himself, "the Captain of the Hampshire grenadiers . . . has not been useless to the historian of the Roman Empire" can it be claimed that Marshall's experience at Valley Forge was not without decisive influence in the work of the great Chief Justice. (*Autobiographies of Edward Gibbon*, (John Murray ed., 1896), p. 190.) Ties of friendship and effective participation in the struggle for the Constitution confirmed his national outlook. Local government had become associated in his mind with the petty bickerings of narrow ambition and dangerous indifference to rights of property and social cohesion. This revealed the need of a strong central government to whose authority the States must be obedient. Subordination of the States to the authority of the National Government within the scope of its powers was the deepest article of his faith, political and judicial. Experience of men and affairs in the Virginia House of Burgesses, in Congress, as a diplomat, and as Secretary of State, doubtless reinforced a temperament to which abstract theorizing was never congenial. He reflected the literary tradition of his time in his partiality for abstract language to support concrete results. But he had a hardheaded appreciation of the complexities of government, particularly in a federal system. His deep instinct for the practical saved him, on the whole, from rigidities to bind the changing future. Uncompromising as was his aim to promote adequate national power, he was not dogmatic in the choice of doctrine for attaining this end. And so at times, conspicuously in *Gibbons* v. *Ogden*, his views appear to reflect crosscurrents of doctrine, ambiguously expressed. In one striking instance, *Willson* v. *The Black Bird Creek Marsh Co.*, 2 Pet. 245 (1829), he did little more than decide, stating hardly any doctrine but hinting enough to foreshadow, certainly in direction, the vitally important accommodation between national and local needs formulated more than twenty years later in *Cooley* v. *Board of Wardens of the Port of Philadelphia*, 12 How. 299, 319 (1851).

There is a rather supercilious tendency to speak disparagingly of Marshall's work on the Court when dealing with lawyers' law. In contrast to Jefferson's view, which continues to have echoes, of regarding Marshall's associates as his tools in the constitutional cases, praise of his judicial statecraft is sometimes used to emphasize his inferiority in non-constitu-

tional adjudications. Story, Bushrod Washington, William
Johnson, Brockholst Livingston are counted as his superiors.
Joseph Story, to be sure, carried great learning, even if not
always lightly. Disregard of Bushrod Washington's judicial
qualities bespeaks unfamiliarity with Judge Hopkinson's and
Horace Binney's estimates of him, and Professor Donald G.
Morgan's recent book on Mr. Justice Johnson ought to bring
wider appreciation of one of the strongest minds in the
Court's history. But none of Marshall's associates will suffer
depreciation by recognizing his performance in cases that are
lawyers' law. After all, this constituted nine-tenths of the
Court's business during the thirty-four years of Marshall's
magistracy. He was not a bookish lawyer, though he was no
stranger to books. He could, as wise judges do, make them his
servants. He eschewed precedents, such as were then available, in his opinions for the Court. But he showed mastery in
treatment of precedents where they had been relied on for
an undesirable result. By way of example, I avouch his dissent in *The Venus*, 8 Cranch 253, 288 (1814), against the
strong views of Washington, J., supported by Story. Likewise, he was not overwhelmed by the parade of Story's learning in *The Nereide*, 9 Cranch 388 (1815), when such learning led to a harsh view of neutral rights. Though he respected
Lord Stowell as "a very great man," he cut free from that
master of prize law, deeming him to have a leaning, strong
even if unconscious, in favor of captors.

As good an insight as any into the quality of Marshall's
intellect is afforded by Francis Walker Gilmer, a brilliant
Virginia contemporary of high promise. Marshall's mind, he
wrote, "is not very richly stored with knowledge, but it is so
creative, so well organized by nature, or disciplined by early
education, and constant habits of systematick thinking, that
he embraces every subject with the clearness and facility of
one prepared by previous study to comprehend and explain

it." (Gilmer, *Sketches, Essays, and Translations*, pp. 23-24, quoted in 2 Beveridge, *John Marshall*, (1916), p. 178.)

Charged as I have been with opening a conference to commemorate the two-hundredth anniversary of the birth of John Marshall, I surely have been obedient to my duty in speaking of him. But once I leave the secure footing of that well-trodden ground, what else can be pertinent to an opening address of a three-day conference on Government under Law, systematically planned with definite parts appropriately assigned to learned inquirers into the perplexities of the problems summarized by this great theme?

Insofar as I have not already exhausted my function, my further relation to the resplendent show to follow is like unto that of the Greek chorus. In view of the preoccupation of this conference, of course I want to keep strictly within the law of my assignment. Accordingly, I have briefed myself on the proper task of the Greek chorus. While in early days the destiny of the chorus was "involved in that of the principal characters," when the Attic stage was at its highest perfection the chorus was "thrown much further into the background," and appears "not as a participant in the action, but merely as a sympathetic witness." The chorus was, so my authority continues, "removed from the stress and turmoil of the action into a calmer and more remote region, though it still preserves its interest in the events upon the stage." This clearly is my cue, rather than the later still more receding role of the chorus, whereby it "begins to lose even its interest in the action" and "sings odes of a mythological character, which have only the remotest connexion with the incidents of the plot." (Haigh, *Attic Theatre*, (2d ed., 1898), pp. 320-21.)

There is little danger that in my remaining observations I shall be intruding on the fertile areas of inquiry that belong to the distinguished speakers whom we are to hear these three days. I hope I shall be equally successful in not straying outside my confining judicial curtilage. One brought up in the traditions of James Bradley Thayer, echoes of whom were still resounding in this very building in my student days, is committed to Thayer's statesmanlike conception of the limits within which the Supreme Court should move, and I shall try to be loyal to his admonition regarding the restricted freedom of members of that Court to pursue their private views.

Marshall's significance could not be more fittingly celebrated than by scrutinizing, which is the aim of this conference, the state of "government under law," more particularly under the legal system to which Marshall so heavily contributed, a hundred and twenty years after he wrote his last opinion. Could he listen to these proceedings, nothing would be bound to strike him more than the enlarged scope of law since his day. He would, of course, think of law as legally enforceable rights. For, while he occasionally referred to "natural law," it was not much more than literary garniture, even as in our own day, and not a guiding means for adjudication. He would have sympathized, as other judges have, with Sir Frederick Pollock's remark: "In the Middle Ages natural law was regarded as the senior branch of divine law and therefore had to be treated as infallible (but there was no infallible way of knowing what it was)." (I *Holmes-Pollock Letters*, (Howe ed., 1941), p. 275.) Marshall would be amazed by the interpenetration of law in government, because during his whole era he was concerned with the Constitution as an instrument predominantly regulating the machinery of government, and more particularly, distributing powers between the central government and the States. The Constitution was not thought of as the repository of the supreme law limiting all government, with a court wielding the deepest-cutting power of deciding whether there is any authority in government at all to do what is sought to be done.

Thus, the gravamen of the attack in the Virginia and Kentucky Resolutions against the Alien and Sedition Acts of 1798 was that they infringed on the rights of the States and were promotive of "a general consolidated government." It deserves to be recalled that even Jefferson attributed to the States the power which he denied to the Federal Government. "Nor does the opinion of the unconstitutionality and consequent nullity of that law [the Sedition Act]," he wrote to Abigail Adams, "remove all restraint from the overwhelming torrent of slander which is confounding all vice and virtue, all truth and falsehood in the US. The power to do that is fully possessed by the several state legislatures. . . . While we deny that Congress have a right to controul the freedom of the press, we have ever asserted the right of the states, and their exclusive right, to do so." (I am indebted for the exact text of this letter, dated September 11, 1804, to the kindness of Professor Julian P. Boyd, in one of whose forthcoming volumes of *The Papers of Thomas Jefferson* it will duly appear in its entirety.)

The only two Marshallian constitutional opinions that concern individual rights as such, *Fletcher* v. *Peck*, 6 Cranch 87 (1810), and the *Dartmouth College Case*, 4 Wheat. 518 (1819), rather than the delimitation of power between two governments, are, in the perspective of time, not of great importance. This came to pass partly because of easy legislative correction, partly because the doctrine of strict construction devised in the *Charles River Bridge Case*, 11 Pet. 420 (1837), took the sting out of the decision of the *Dartmouth College Case*. Moreover, insofar as the latter case forbade legislative transfer of the property of the college to the trustees, it is a safe assumption that the Due Process Clauses would condemn such an attempt. See Chief Justice Doe's opinion in *Dow* v. *Northern R. Co.*, 67 N.H. 1, 27-53, 36 Atl. 510, 524-37 (1887); Doe, "A New View of the Dartmouth College Case,"

6 Harv. L. Rev. 161, 213 (1892); and Jeremiah Smith in
1 Proc. N.H. Bar Ass'n 287, 302 (N.S. 1901).

The vast change in the scope of law between Marshall's
time and ours is at bottom a reflection of the vast change in
the circumstances of society. The range of business covered
by Marshall's Court, though operating under a written Constitution, was in the main not very different from the concerns of the English courts, except that the latter dealt much
more with property settlements. The vast enveloping present-
day role of law is not the design of a statesman nor attributable to the influence of some great thinker. It is a reflection
of the great technological revolution which brought in its
train what a quiet writer in *The Economist* could call "the
tornado of economic and social change of the last century."
Law has been an essential accompaniment of the shift from
"watch-dog government"—the phrase is George Kennan's—
to the service state. For government has become a service
state, whatever the tint of the party in power and whatever
time-honored slogans it may use to enforce and promote
measures that hardly vindicate the slogans. Profound social
changes continue to be in the making, due to movements
of industrialization, urbanization, and permeating egalitarian
ideas.

With crude accuracy I have just summarized the situation
in the countries of the English-speaking world, about which
alone I may speak. But when these transforming economic
and social forces got under full swing in the United States,
lawyers and courts found available in the Fourteenth Amendment resources for curbing legislative responses to new pressures. That Amendment was gradually invoked against the
substance of legislation and not merely to support claims
based on traditionally fair procedure.

I have thus reached the slippery slope of due process. But
not even to take a glance at it in a reconnaissance, however

sketchy, of government under law, would indeed be to play
Hamlet without Hamlet.

It has been frequently stated that when a question arises in
due course of a litigation, whether a constitutional provision
has been infringed, the established courts of justice "must of
necessity determine that question." See Lord Selborne in
The Queen v. *Burah*, 3 A.C. 889, 904 (1878), quoted approv-
ingly by Lord Wright in *James* v. *Commonwealth*, [1936]
A.C. 578, 613; and see also *Swart, N.O. and Nicol, N.O.* v.
de Kock and Garner, 1951 (3) S.A. 589, 601-02 and 611.
This is only qualifiedly true regarding our Constitution.
Thus, the explicit provision requiring one State to surrender
to another a fugitive from justice (Art. IV, § 2, cl. 2) is
"merely declaratory of a moral duty" and is not, because of
the subject matter, enforceable in the courts. *Kentucky* v.
Dennison, 24 How. 66 (1861). Likewise, the "guarantee to
every state" of "a Republican Form of Government," must,
because of the subject-matter, look elsewhere than to the
courts for observance. *Pacific States Tel. & Tel. Co.* v.
Oregon, 223 U.S. 118 (1912). There are not a few other instances in which judicial relief was barred because "political
questions" were deemed to be involved.

It is not for me to find the common denominator of these
judicial abstentions, or to give the contour and content of
what questions are "political," in the sense of precluding judicial examination. But I do venture to believe that no judge
charged with the duty of enforcing the Due Process Clauses
of the Fifth and Fourteenth Amendments, and the Equal Protection of the Laws Clause of the Fourteenth Amendment,
can free himself from the disquietude that the line is often
very thin between the cases in which the Court felt compelled
to abstain from adjudication because of their "political" nature, and the cases that so frequently arise in applying the
concepts of "liberty" and "equality."

In his First Inaugural Jefferson spoke of the "sacred principle" that "the will of the majority is in all cases to prevail." [1] Jefferson himself hardly meant all by "all." (See Jefferson's answers to Démeunier's first queries, reprinted in 10 *The Papers of Thomas Jefferson*, (Boyd ed., 1954), p. 18.) In any event, one need not give full adherence to his view to be deeply mindful of the fact that judicial review is a deliberate check upon democracy through an organ of government not subject to popular control. In relation to the judiciary's task in the type of cases I am now discussing, I am raising difficulties which I think must in all good conscience be faced, unless perchance the Court is expected to register a particular view and unless the profession that the judiciary is the disinterested guardian of our Constitution be pretense.

It may be that responsibility for decision dulls the capacity of discernment. The fact is that one sometimes envies the certitude of outsiders regarding the compulsions to be drawn from vague and admonitory constitutional provisions. Only for those who have not the responsibility of decision can it be easy to decide the grave and complex problems they raise, especially in controversies that excite public interest. This is so because they too often present legal issues inextricably and deeply bound up in emotional reactions to sharply conflicting economic, social, and political views. It is not the duty of judges to express their personal attitudes on such issues, deep as their individual convictions may be. The opposite is the truth; it is their duty not to act on merely personal views. But "due process," once we go beyond its strictly procedural

[1] The following is the sentence in which the quoted phrase occurs: "All, too, will bear in mind this sacred principle, that though the will of the majority is in all cases to prevail, that will to be rightful must be reasonable; that the minority possess their equal rights, which equal law must protect, and to violate would be oppression." A little later in that address Jefferson included in what he deemed "the essential principles of our Government," "absolute acquiescence in the decisions of the majority, the vital principle of republics, from which is no appeal but to force, the vital principle and immediate parent of despotism. . . ." 1 *Messages and Papers of the Presidents*, (Richardson ed., 1899), pp. 322, 323.

aspect, and the "equal protection of the laws" enshrined in
the Constitution, are precisely defined neither by history nor
in terms. It deserves to be noted that so far as gaining light
from pertinent data on the intention of Congress on specific
issues in formulating the Fourteenth Amendment, the Supreme Court found that "[a]t best, they are inconclusive."
Brown v. *Board of Education*, 347 U.S. 483, 489 (1954). This
finding of darkness was reached not for want of searching
inquiry by Court and counsel.

No doubt, these provisions of the Constitution were not
calculated to give permanent legal sanction merely to the
social arrangements and beliefs of a particular epoch. Like all
legal provisions without a fixed technical meaning, they are
ambulant, adaptable to the changes of time. That is their
strength; that also makes dubious their appropriateness for
judicial enforcement—dubious because their vagueness readily
lends itself to make of the Court a third chamber with drastic
veto power. This danger has been pointed out by our greatest
judges too often to be dismissed as a bogey. Holding democracy in judicial tutelage is not the most promising way to
foster disciplined responsibility in a people. See *AFL* v.
American Sash & Door Co., 335 U.S. 538, 555-557 (1949)
(concurring opinion).

It is, of course, no longer to be questioned that claims
under the Fourteenth Amendment are subject to judicial
judgment. This makes it all the more important to realize
what is involved in the discharge of this function of the
Court, particularly since this is probably the largest source of
the Court's business. It is important, that is, fully to appreciate the intrinsic nature of the issues when the Court is called
upon to determine whether the legislature or the executive
has regulated "liberty" or "property" "without due process
of law" or has denied "equal protection of the laws"; to appreciate the difficulties in making a judgment upon such issues,
difficulties of a different order from those normally imposed

upon jural tribunals; and, not least, to appreciate the qualifications requisite for those who exercise this extraordinary authority, demanding as it does a breadth of outlook and an invincible disinterestedness rooted in temperament and confirmed by discipline. Of course, individual judgment and feeling cannot be wholly shut out of the judicial process. But if they dominate, the judicial process becomes a dangerous sham. The conception by a judge of the scope and limits of his function may exert an intellectual and moral force as much as responsiveness to a particular audience or congenial environment.

We are dealing with constitutional provisions the nature of which can be best conveyed compendiously by Judge Learned Hand's phrase that they "represent a mood rather than a command, that sense of moderation, of fair play, of mutual forbearance, without which states become the prey of faction." *Daniel Reeves, Inc.* v. *Anderson*, 43 F. 2d 679, 682 (1930). Alert search for enduring standards by which the judiciary is to exercise its duty in enforcing those provisions of the Constitution that are expressed in what Ruskin called "chameleon words," needs the indispensable counterpoise of sturdy doubt that one has found those standards. Yesterday the active area in this field was concerned with "property." Today it is "civil liberties." Tomorrow it may again be "property." Who can say that in a society with a mixed economy, like ours, these two areas are sharply separated, and that certain freedoms in relation to property may not again be deemed, as they were in the past, aspects of individual freedom?

Let me sharpen these difficulties by concreteness. In *Plessy* v. *Ferguson*, 163 U.S. 537, 559 (1896), Mr. Justice Harlan floated an oft-quoted epigram, but in a few short years he did not apply it, proving once more that sonorous abstractions do not solve problems with intractable variables. See *Cumming* v. *Richmond County Board of Education*, 175 U.S. 528

(1899), and its influence on *Gong Lum* v. *Rice,* 275 U.S. 78, 85 (1927). Thinking of "equality" in abstract terms led Mr. Justice Harlan to be blind to the meaning of "yellow-dog contracts" as a serious curtailment of liberty in the context of antiunion strategy, *Adair* v. *United States,* 208 U.S. 161 (1908); Richard Olney, "Discrimination against Union Labor," 42 Am. L. Rev. 161 (1908), and to be equally blind to the fact that important differences between industry and agriculture may justify differentiation in legislation. See *Connolly* v. *Union Sewer Pipe Co.,* 184 U.S. 540 (1902), and compare with *Tigner* v. *Texas,* 310 U.S. 141 (1940).

Take the other side of the medal. It is too easy to attribute judicial review resulting in condemnation of restrictions on activities pertaining to property to "economic predilection" of particular judges. The Due Process Clauses extend to triune interests—life, liberty and property—and "property" cannot be deleted by judicial fiat rendering it nugatory regarding legislation touching property. Moreover, protection of property interests may, as already indicated, quite fairly be deemed, in appropriate circumstances, an aspect of liberty. Regulation of property may be struck down on assumptions or beliefs other than narrow economic views. And so we find that Justices who were the most tolerant of legislative power dealing with economic interests have found in due process a protection even against an exercise of the so-called police power. It was true of Mr. Justice Holmes in *Pennsylvania Coal Co.* v. *Mahon,* 260 U.S. 393 (1922), and of Mr. Justice Brandeis in *Thompson* v. *Consolidated Gas Utilities Corp.,* 300 U.S. 55 (1937).

Let us turn to the much-mooted "clear and present danger" doctrine. It is at least interesting that that phrase originated in one (*Schenck* v. *United States,* 249 U.S. 47, 52 (1919)) of a series of cases in which convictions for heavy sentences were sustained against defendants who had invoked the right of free speech in circumstances which led Mr. Justice Holmes to characterize them as "poor fools whom I should have been inclined to pass over if I could." (2 *Holmes-Pollock Letters,* (Howe ed., 1941), p. 11.) "Clear and present danger" thus had a compulsion for Mr. Justice Holmes against recognizing Debs's freedom to an utterance that in retrospect hardly seems horrendous. *Debs* v. *United States,* 249 U.S. 211 (1919). Would it carry equal compulsion with other judges? One can be confident, in any event, that Mr. Justice Holmes would not have deemed his doctrine a bar to the power of a State to safeguard the fair conduct of a trial for a capital offense from being thwarted by intrusion of utterances from without. See *Maryland* v. *Baltimore Radio Show Inc.,* 338 U.S. 912 (1950), denying certiorari to 193 Md. 300, 67 A. 2d 497 (1949). There is the best of reasons for believing that Mr. Justice Brandeis would not have carried his natural devotion to the place of freedom of speech in a democracy to such a doctrinaire denial of an equally indispensable need of a free society—trial in court, not outside it.

Concerned as I am with the evolution of social policy by way of judicial application of Delphic provisions of the Constitution, recession of judicial doctrine is as pertinent as its expansion. The history of the constitutional position of the right to strike affords an illuminating instance. After invalidating a law withdrawing the use of the injunction against strikes, *Truax* v. *Corrigan,* 257 U.S. 312 (1921), the Court came to conceive of the conduct of a strike as an aspect of the constitutionally protected freedom of discussion, *Thornhill* v. *Alabama,* 310 U.S. 88 (1940), but soon retreated from this position and recognized that picketing, as the weapon of strikes, is not merely a means of communication, *Giboney* v. *Empire Storage & Ice Co.,* 336 U.S. 490 (1949). No matter how often the Court insists that it is not passing on policy when determining constitutionality, the emphasis on constitutionality and its fascination for the American public seriously confound problems of constitutionality with the merits of a policy. Industrial relations are not alone in presenting problems that suffer in their solution from having public opinion too readily assume that because some measure is found to be constitutional it is wise and right, and, contrariwise, because it is found unconstitutional it is intrinsically wrong. That such miseducation of public opinion, with its effect upon action, has been an important consequence of committing to the Court the enforcement of "the mood" represented by these vague constitutional provisions, can hardly be gainsaid by any student of their history.

Much as the constitution-makers of other countries have drawn upon our experience, it is precisely because they have drawn upon it that they have, one and all, abstained from including a "due process" clause. They have rejected it in conspicuous instances after thorough consideration of our judicial history of "due process." See Wallace Mendelson, "Foreign Reactions to American Experience with 'Due Process of Law,'" 41 Va. L. Rev. 493 (1955). It is particularly noteworthy that such was the course of events in framing the constitution of India. Sir B. N. Rau, one of the most penetrating legal minds of our time, had a major share in its drafting, and for the purpose he made a deep study of the workings of the Due Process Clause during an extensive stay here.

Is it the tenor of these remarks that courts should have no concern with other than material interests, that they must be unmindful of the imponderable rights and dignities of the individual which are, I am sure I shall have your agreement in saying, the ideals which the Western world holds most high? Of course not. Recognition of them should permeate the law, and it does so effectively even in courts that do not have veto power over legislation. They constitute presuppositions where parliaments have not spoken unequivocally and courts are left with the jural task of construction in its fair sense.

Thus, while the Chief Justice of Canada could say: "We

have not a Bill of Rights such as is contained in the United States Constitution and decisions on that part of the latter are of no assistance," he reached the same result in *Saumur* v. *City of Quebec*, [1953] 2 S.C.R. 299, as a matter of construction, that was reached under the Due Process Clause in *Lovell* v. *City of Griffin*, 303 U.S. 444 (1938). Again, only the other day the Supreme Court of Canada rejected the view that the mere claim of immunity by a minister of the Crown from producing in court a document relevant to its proceeding is conclusive. It deemed such a claim "not in harmony with the basic conceptions of our polity." The reason given by Mr. Justice Rand deserves to be quoted: "What is secured by attributing to the courts this preliminary determination of possible prejudice is protection against executive encroachments upon the administration of justice; and in the present trend of government little can be more essential to the maintenance of individual security. In this important matter, to relegate the courts to such a subserviency as is suggested would be to withdraw from them the confidence of independence and judicial appraisal that so far appear to have served well the organization of which we are the heirs." *Regina* v. *Snider*, [1954] S.C.R. 479, 485, 486. So, likewise, the Appellate Division of the Supreme Court of South Africa ruled that when an Act conferred autocratic powers upon a minister—it was the Suppression of Communism Act—it must, in the absence of explicit direction by Parliament, be construed with the least interference with the liberty of the subject. *R.* v. *Ngwevela*, 1954 (1) S.A. 123.

While the subjection to parliamentary criticism is the only remedy for much in Great Britain that with us becomes the stuff of lawsuits, the English executive is amenable to challenge in court for exceeding statutorily defined legal powers. In construing such authority, English courts enforce the right to a hearing as a presupposition of English law, unless Parliament has clearly enough indicated the contrary. See S. A.

de Smith, "The Right to a Hearing in English Administrative Law," 68 Harv. L. Rev. 569 (1955); so, likewise in Canada, *L'Alliance des Professeurs Catholiques* v. *Labour Relations Board,* [1953] 2 S.C.R. 140; and in New Zealand, *New Zealand Dairy Board* v. *Okitu Co-operative Dairy Co.,* [1953] N.Z.L.R. 366. The English courts have also been resourceful, through the use they make of *certiorari,* in setting aside executive action when based on reasons not justifiable in law. For application of this principle in the United States see *Perkins* v. *Elg,* 307 U.S. 325 (1939), and *Securities and Exchange Commission* v. *Chenery Corp.,* 318 U.S. 80 (1943). This increasing tendency of courts to scrutinize the legal grounds given by administrative agencies for their actions may well promote greater responsibility in the agencies' exercise of authority and in their justification of that exercise.

If government under law were confined to what is judicially enforced, law in government would be very restricted, no matter how latitudinarian one's conception of what is fitting for judicial examination of governmental action. For one thing, courts have a strong tendency to abstain from constitutional controversies. *E.g., Peters* v. *Hobby,* 349 U.S. 331 (1955). Thereby, they may avoid conflict, at least prematurely if not permanently, with the other branches of the government and they may avoid also the determination of conflict between the Nation and the States. Moreover, settlement of complicated public issues, particularly on the basis of constitutional provisions conveying indeterminate standards, is subject to the inherent limitations and contingencies of the judicial process. For constitutional adjudications involve adjustment of vast and incommensurable public interests through episodic instances, upon evidence and information limited by the narrow rules of litigation, shaped and intellectually influenced by the fortuitous choice of particular counsel.

Mr. Justice Brandeis made a fair estimate in saying that by

applying its restrictive canons for adjudication, the Court has in the course of its history "avoided passing upon a large part of all the constitutional questions pressed upon it for decision." *Ashwander* v. *Tennessee Valley Authority*, 297 U.S. 288, 346 (1936). This is true not only of our Supreme Court, which cannot render advisory opinions however compelling the appeal for legal guidance even at times of national emergency. (See Chief Justice Jay's reply to President Washington's inquiry, conveyed by Thomas Jefferson, in 3 *The Correspondence and Public Papers of John Jay*, (Johnston ed., 1891), pp. 486-89.) Insistence on an immediate, substantial, and threatened interest in raising such constitutional issues is a characteristic of all high courts with power to pass upon them. See the recent Australian case, *Australian Boot Trade Employees' Federation* v. *Commonwealth*, (1954) 90 C.L.R. 24; see also *Musgrove* v. *Chun Teeong Toy*, [1891] A.C. 272, 283. But even where advisory opinions are constitutionally authorized, tribunals are reluctant to pronounce in situations that are hypothetical or abstract or otherwise not conducive to judicial disposition. See Lord Haldane, in *Attorney General for British Columbia* v. *Attorney General for Canada*, [1914] A.C. 153, 162; Lord Sankey, in *In re the Regulation and Control of Aeronautics*, [1932] A.C. 54, 66. It is, I believe, not inaccurate to say that most of the occasions when the Supreme Court has come into virulent conflict with public opinion were those in which the Court disregarded its settled tradition against needlessly pronouncing on constitutional issues. (The *Dred Scott Case*, 19 How. 393 (1857), does not stand alone; see the *Income Tax Cases*, 157 U.S. 429 and 158 U.S. 601 (1895), controlling until the Sixteenth Amendment of February 25, 1913; *Adkins* v. *Children's Hospital*, 261 U.S. 525, 543 (1923), overruled by *West Coast Hotel Co.* v. *Parrish*, 300 U.S. 379 (1937).)

The confining limits within which courts thus move in expounding law is not the most important reason for a con-

ception of government under law far transcending merely
law that is enforced in the courts. The day has long gone
by when Austin's notions exhaust the content of law. Law
is not set above the government. It defines its orbit. But government is not law except insofar as law infuses government.
This is not word-playing. Also indispensable to government
is ample scope for individual insight and imaginative origina-
tion by those entrusted with the public interest. If society is
not to remain stagnant, there is need of action beyond uniformities found recurring in instances which sustain a generalization and demand its application. But law is not a code
of fettering restraints, a litany of prohibitions and permissions.
It is an enveloping and permeating habituation of behavior,
reflecting the counsels of reason on the part of those entrusted
with power in reconciling the pressures of conflicting interests. Once we conceive of "the rule of law" as embracing the
whole range of presuppositions on which government is conducted and not as a technical doctrine of judicial authority,
the relevant question is not, has it been achieved, but, is it
conscientiously and systematically pursued.[2]

What matters most is whether the standards of reason and
fair dealing are bred in the bones of people. Hyde Park represents a devotion to free speech far more dependable in its
assurances, though unprotected by formal constitutional requirement, than reliance upon the litigious process for its
enjoyment. Again, widespread popular intolerance of the

[2] In what I have said of course I do not mean to give the remotest support to the notion that the law is "a brooding omnipresence in the sky."
I reject it as completely as did Mr. Justice Holmes in *Southern Pacific Co.*
v. *Jensen*, 244 U.S. 205, 222 (1917) (dissenting opinion). It might further
avoid confusion to restrict the term "law," particularly in a judge's mouth,
to the commands of society which it is the duty of courts to enforce, and
not apply it to those decencies of conduct which should control other
branches of government but are without judicial sanction. But perhaps law
has so established itself as a portmanteau word that clarity does not require
too pedantically restrictive a use of it as long as no doubt is left regarding
the circumscribed scope of the judiciary's function.

third degree, such as manifested itself in the well-known Savidge affair, reflects a more deeply grounded rule of law than is disclosed by the painful story of our continuing judicial endeavor to root out this evil through decisions in occasional dramatic cases. (For the Savidge case, see 220 *Hans. Deb.* (Commons), cols. 5, 805 *et seq.* (July 20, 1928); Inquiry in regard to the Interrogation by the Police of Miss Savidge (1928, Cmd. 3147). As to our experience, see, *e.g.*, "Report on the Third Degree" by Chafee, Pollak and Stern in 4 *National Commission on Law Observance and Enforcement, Reports,* p. 13 (1931), and the series of well-known cases in the Supreme Court Reports.) Let me give another illustration. "Crichel Down" will, in its way, serve to summarize the duty of obedience to standards of fair dealing and avoidance even of the appearance of official arbitrariness. As such it will affect the future conduct of English government as much as some of the leading cases which have been important factors in the development of a democratic society. See Public Inquiry ordered by the Ministry of Agriculture into the disposal of land at Crichel Down (1954, Cmd. 9176); R. Douglas Brown, *The Battle of Crichel Down.* You will note that the instances I have given of manifestations of law responsive to the deep feelings of a people are drawn from a nation that does not rely on a written constitution. I need not add that the distinctive historical development in Great Britain, in the context of its progressive cultural and economic homogeneity, has made possible accommodation between stability and change, defining the powers of government and the limits within which due regard for individual rights require it to be kept, without embodying it in a single legal document enforceable in courts of law.

I hope, however, that you will not deem me unduly romantic in deriving comfort from the undertaking given the other day by the Kabaka, as a condition of his return to his people in Buganda, when he promised that he "will well and truly govern Buganda according to law." (The [London] *Times*, Aug. 13, 1955, p. 6, col. 5) I find reason for my comfort in the fascinating account by Professor Max Gluckman of Manchester University of the extent to which law permeates the lives of the Barotse tribes of Northern Rhodesia, law in the sense in which this conference is discussing it and not something religious in nature. (Gluckman, *The Judicial Process among the Barotse of Northern Rhodesia*, (1955).)

If what I have brought you, in my endeavor to give you as frankly as I may the distillation of sixteen years of reflection from within the tribunal peculiarly concerned with government under law, is charged with being an old-fashioned liberal's view of government and law, I plead guilty. For the charge implies allegiance to the humane and gradualist tradition in dealing with refractory social and political problems, recognizing them to be fractious because of their complexity and not amenable to quick and propitious solutions without resort to methods which deny law as the instrument and offspring of reason.

I have not been able to submit to you large generalizations that illumine or harmoniously assimilate discrete instances. Still less have I been able to fashion criteria for easier adjudication of the specific cases that will trouble future judges. They are bound to be troubled, whether they will be faced with variant aspects of old problems—old conflicts between liberty and authority, between the central government and its constituent members—or new problems inevitably thrown up by the everlasting flux of life.

Believing it still important to do so, I have tried to dispel the age-old illusion that the conflicts to which the energy and ambition and imagination of the restless human spirit give rise can be subdued, even if not settled, by giving the endeavors of reason we call law a mechanical or automatic or enduring configuration. Law cannot be confined within any such mold because life cannot be so confined. Man's most

piercing discernment of the future cannot see very far beyond his day, even when guided by the prophet's insight and
the compassionate humility of a Lincoln. And I am the last
to claim that judges are apt to be endowed with these gifts.
But a fair appraisal of Anglo-American judicial history ought
to leave us not without encouragement that modest goals,
uncompromisingly pursued, may promote what I hope you
will let me call civilized ends without the need of defining
them.

In what I have been saying you have no doubt heard under-
tones of a judge's perplexities—particularly of a judge who
has to construe, as it is called, vague and admonitory constitutional provisions. But I am very far from meaning to
imply a shriveled conception of government under law. Quite
the contrary. The intention of my emphasis has been not on
the limited scope of judicial enforcement of laws. My concern
is an affirmation—my plea is for the pervasiveness throughout
the whole range of government of the spirit of law, at least
in the sense of excluding arbitrary official action. But however limited the area of adjudication may be, the standards of
what is fair and just set by courts in controversies appropriate
for their adjudication are perhaps the single most powerful
influence in promoting the spirit of law throughout government. These standards also help shape the dominant civic
habits and attitudes which ultimately determine the ethos of
a society.

In exercising their technical jurisdiction, courts thus release
contagious consequences. Nothing is farther from my mind
than to suggest that judges should exceed the professional
demands of a particular decision. If judges want to be preach-
ers, they should dedicate themselves to the pulpit; if judges
want to be primary shapers of policy, the legislature is their
place. Self-willed judges are the least defensible offenders
against government under law. But since the grounds of decisions and their general direction suffuse the public mind and

the operations of government, judges cannot free themselves
from the responsibility of the inevitable effect of their opinions in constricting or promoting the force of law throughout
government. Upon no functionaries is there a greater duty
to promote law.

Two

The Judicial Process and the Supreme Court

(1954)

Mr. Justice Frankfurter read this paper before the American Philosophical Society on April 22, 1954, at its annual meeting in Philadelphia. It was printed in the Society's *Proceedings* for August 1954 (Vol. 98, p. 233).

IF ONE IS to talk at all before an audience as learned as this, he had best talk about that of which he is least ignorant. And so I have chosen the topic I have, circumscribed as one in my position is to talk about it. But this is not to be a technical professional paper. What I shall say derives from the assumption that I am talking about complicated and subtle problems to those who are not professionally concerned with them, nor professionally trained to their understanding, and yet feel free to make judgments, because as citizens they are deeply involved in these problems. Broadly speaking, the chief reliance of law in a democracy is the habit of popular respect for law. Especially true is it that law as promulgated by the Supreme Court ultimately depends upon confidence of the people in the Supreme Court as an institution. Indispensable, therefore, for the country's welfare is an appreciation of what the nature of the enterprise is in which that Court is engaged —an understanding of what the task is that has been committed to the succession of nine men.

I said I shall speak "circumscribed" as I am in doing so. I am circumscribed not only by the very limited freedom of speech that his position imposes on a member of the Court. I am no less circumscribed by want of those qualities that are not the normal endowment of judges, nor cultivated in them by training. Those who know tell me that the most illuminating light on painting has been furnished by painters, and that the deepest revelations on the writing of poetry have come from poets. It is not so with the business of judging. The power of searching analysis of what it is that they are doing seems rarely to be possessed by judges, either because they are lacking in the art of critical exposition or because they are inhibited from practicing it. The fact is that pitifully little of significance has been contributed by judges regarding the nature of their endeavor, and, I might add, that which is written by those who are not judges is too often a confident caricature rather than a seer's vision of the judicial process of the Supreme Court.

We have, of course, one brave and felicitous attempt—Mr. Justice Cardozo's little classic. I have read and reread, and reread very recently, that charming book and yield to no one in my esteem for it. And yet you must not account it as immodesty or fractiousness if I say that the book would give me very little help in deciding any of the difficult cases that come before the Court. Why should a book about the judicial process by one of the great judges of our time shed relatively little light on the actual adjudicatory process of the Supreme Court? For the simple reason that *The Nature of the Judicial Process* derived from Cardozo's reflections while in Albany, before he came to Washington. The judicial business out of which Cardozo's experience came when he wrote the book was the business of the New York Court of Appeals, and that is very different business from the most important aspects of the litigation on which the Supreme Court must pass.

Let me indulge in one of the rare opportunities for the valid use of statistics in connection with the work of the Supreme Court. The reports of the New York decisions for the year during which Judge Cardozo delivered the lectures which comprise his book show that only about one out of a hundred cases before the New York Court of Appeals raised questions comparable to those that gave him most trouble in Washington. The year that he left Albany for Washington, 1932, only two opinions out of a hundred in the New York Reports raise the kind of questions that are the greatest concern for the Supreme Court. Cardozo wrote something like five hundred opinions on the New York Court of Appeals. In them he was concerned with matters that would not have been foreign, say, to Lord Mansfield or Lord Ellenborough, and would have been quite familiar to Cardozo's contemporaries on the English Supreme Court of Judicature.

After Cardozo came to Washington, he wrote 128 opinions for the Court during the tragically short period that fate allowed him there. He wrote twenty-one dissents. Of these 149 opinions only ten dealt with matters comparable to those which came before him while on the New York Court of Appeals. No one was more keenly aware than he of the differences between the two streams of litigation; no one more keenly alive than he to the resulting differences in the nature of the judicial process in which the two courts were engaged. Let me quickly add that such were the genius and the learning and, perhaps most important of all, the priestlike disinterestedness of his mind, that, even during his few brief years as a Justice, Cardozo became an outstanding contributor to the history of Supreme Court adjudication. What is relevant to our immediate purpose is realization of the important fact that the problems dealt with in Cardozo's illuminating little book, and in two other little books which played on the same theme, derive from an experience in the raw materials of the adjudicatory process very different from those that are the most anxious concern of the Supreme Court of the United States.

It is time for me to be explicit. I am advised by an arithmetically minded scholar that the Constitution of the United States is composed of some 6,000 words. Not every provision of that document that becomes controversial can come before the Supreme Court for adjudication. The questions that are not meet for judicial determination have elicited their own body of literature. A hint of the nature of such questions is given by their fair characterization as an exercise of judicial self-limitation. This area constitutes one very important and very troublesome aspect of the Court's functioning—its duty not to decide.

Putting to one side instances of this judicial self-restraint, De Tocqueville showed his characteristic discernment when he wrote: "Scarcely any political question arises in the United States that is not resolved sooner or later into a judicial question." (1 *Democracy in America,* (Bradley ed., 1948), p. 280.) Those provisions of the Constitution that do raise justiciable issues vary in their incidence from time to time. The construction of all of them, however, is related to the circumambient condition of our Constitution—that our nation is a federalism. The most exacting problems that in recent years have come before the Court have invoked two provisions expressed in a few undefined words—the clause giving Congress power to regulate commerce among the States and the Due Process Clauses of the Fifth and Fourteenth Amendments.

A federalism presupposes the distribution of governmental powers between national and local authority. Between these two authorities there is shared the power entirely possessed by a unitary state. In addition to the provisions of our Constitution making this distribution of authority between the two governments, there is also in the United States Constitution a withdrawal of power from both governments, or, at least, the exercise of governmental power is subject to limitations protective of the rights of the individual. Of the two types of constitutional provision calling for construction from case to case, the limitation in the interest of the individual presents the most delicate and most pervasive of all issues to come before the Court, for these cases involve no less a task than the accommodation by a court of the interest of an individual over against the interest of society.

Human society keeps changing. Needs emerge, first vaguely felt and unexpressed, imperceptibly gathering strength, steadily becoming more and more exigent, generating a force which, if left unheeded and denied response so as to satisfy the impulse behind it at least in part, may burst forth with an intensity that exacts more than reasonable satisfaction. Law as the response to these needs is not merely a system of logical deduction, though considerations of logic are far from irrelevant. Law presupposes sociological wisdom as well as logical unfolding. The nature of the interplay of the two has been admirably conveyed, if I may say so, by Professor Alfred North Whitehead:

It is the first step in sociological wisdom, to recognize that the major advances in civilization are processes which all but wreck the societies in which they occur:—like unto an arrow in the hand of a child. The art of free society consists first in the maintenance of the symbolic code; and secondly in fearlessness of revision, to secure that the code serves those purposes which satisfy an enlightened reason. Those societies which cannot combine reverence to their symbols with freedom of revision, must ultimately decay either from anarchy, or from the slow atrophy of a life stifled by useless shadows. (Whitehead, *Symbolism*, (1927), p. 88.)

The Due Process Clauses of our Constitution are the vehicles for giving response by law to this felt need by allowing accommodations or modifications in the rules and standards that govern the conduct of men. Obviously, therefore, due process as a concept is neither fixed nor finished.

The judgment of history on the inherently living and therefore changing applicability of due process was thus pronounced by Mr. Justice Sutherland, one of the most traditionally minded of judges:

> Regulations, the wisdom, necessity and validity of which, as applied to existing conditions, are so apparent that they are now uniformly sustained, a century ago, or even half a century ago, probably would have been rejected as arbitrary and oppressive. (*Village of Euclid* v. *Ambler Realty Co.,* 272 U.S. 365, 387.)

A more expansive attempt at indicating the viable function of the guarantee of due process was made in a recent opinion:

> The requirement of "due process" is not a fair-weather or timid assurance. It must be respected in periods of calm and in times of trouble; it protects aliens as well as citizens. But "due process," unlike some legal rules, is not a technical conception with a fixed content unrelated to time, place and circumstances. Expressing as it does in its ultimate analysis respect enforced by law for that feeling of just treatment which has been evolved through centuries of Anglo-American constitutional history and civilization, "due process" cannot be imprisoned within the treacherous limits of any formula. Representing a profound attitude of fairness between man and man, and more particularly between the individual and government, "due process" is compounded of history, reason, the past course of decisions, and stout confidence in the strength of the democratic faith which we profess. Due process is not a mechanical instrument. It is not a yardstick. It is a process. It is a delicate process of adjustment inescapably involving the exercise of judgment by those whom the Constitution entrusted with the unfolding of the process. (*Joint Anti-Fascist Refugee Committee* v. *McGrath,* 341 U.S. 123, 162-163, concurring opinion.)

This conception of due process meets resistance from what has been called our pigeonholing minds, which seek to rest uninquiringly on formulas—phrases which, as Holmes pointed out long ago, "by their very felicity delay further analysis," and often do so for a long time. This is, of course, a form of intellectual indulgence, sometimes called the law of imitation. "[T]raditions which no longer meet their original end" must be subjected to the critique of history whereby we are enabled "to make up our minds dispassionately whether the survival which we are enforcing answers any new purpose when it has ceased to answer the old." (Holmes, *Collected Legal Papers*, (1920), p. 225.)

But a merely private judgment that the time has come for a shift of opinion regarding law does not justify such a shift. Departure from an old view, particularly one that has held unquestioned sway, "must be duly mindful of the necessary demands of continuity in a civilized society. A reversal of a long current of decisions can be justified only if rooted in the Constitution itself as an historic document designed for a developing nation." (*Graves v. N. Y. ex rel. O'Keefe*, 306 U.S. 466, 487-488, concurring opinion.) It makes an important difference, of course, if the validity of an old doctrine on which decisions were based was always in controversy and so did not embed deeply and widely in men's feelings justifiable reliance on the doctrine as part of the accepted outlook of society. What is most important, however, is that the Constitution of the United States, except in what might be called the skeleton or framework of our society—the anatomical as against the physiological aspects,—"was designed for a developing nation." As to those features of our Constitution which raise the most frequent perplexities for decision by the Court, they were drawn in many particulars with purposeful vagueness so as to leave room for the unfolding but undisclosed future.

At this point one wishes there were time to document these generalizations with concrete instances which would help to define the problem and illustrate generalities from which the Court starts and differences of opinion which naturally enough arise in their application. Such documentation would expose divergencies by which common starting points lead to different destinations because of differences in emphasis and valuation in the process of reasoning. They would also shed some light on the interplay between language and thought. Differences in style eventually may embody differences of content, just as a sonnet may sometimes focus thought more trenchantly than a diffuse essay.

The other major source of puzzling problems is the Commerce Clause. With us the Commerce Clause is perhaps the most fruitful and important means for asserting national authority against the particularism of state policy. The role of the Court in striking the balance between the respective spheres of federal and state power was thus adumbrated by the Court:

The interpenetrations of modern society have not wiped out state lines. It is not for us to make inroads upon our federal system either by indifference to its maintenance or excessive regard for the unifying forces of modern technology. Scholastic reasoning may prove that no activity is isolated within the boundaries of a single State, but that cannot justify absorption of legislative power by the United States over every activity. On the other hand, the old admonition never becomes stale that this Court is concerned with the bounds of legal power and not with the bounds of wisdom in its exercise by Congress. When the conduct of an enterprise affects commerce among the States is a matter of practical judgment, not to be determined by abstract notions. The exercise of this practical judgment the Constitution entrusts primarily and very largely to the Congress, subject to the latter's control by the electorate. Great power was thus given to the Congress: the power of legislation and thereby the power of passing judgment upon the needs of a complex society. Strictly confined though far-reaching power was given to this Court: that of determining whether the Congress has exceeded limits allowable in reason for the judgment which it has exercised. To hold that Congress could not deem the activities here in question to affect what men of practical affairs would call commerce, and to deem them related to such commerce merely by gossamer threads and not by solid ties, would be to disrespect the judgment that is open to men who have the constitutional power and responsibility to legislate for the Nation. (*Polish National Alliance* v. *Labor Board,* 322 U.S. 643, 650-651.)

The problems which the Commerce Clause raises as a result of the diffusion of power between a national government and its constituent parts are shared in variant forms by Canada, Australia, and India. While the distribution of powers between each national government and its parts varies, leading at times to different legal results, the problems faced by the United States Supreme Court under the Commerce Clause are not different in kind, as are the problems of judicial review under the Due Process Clause, from those which come before the Supreme Court of Canada and the High Court of Australia.

Judicial judgment in these two classes of the most difficult cases must take deep account, if I may paraphrase Maitland, of the day before yesterday in order that yesterday may not paralyze today, and it must take account of what it decrees for today in order that today may not paralyze tomorrow.

A judge whose preoccupation is with such matters should be compounded of the faculties that are demanded of the historian and the philosopher and the prophet. The last demand upon him—to make some forecast of the consequences of his action—is perhaps the heaviest. To pierce the curtain of the future, to give shape and visage to mysteries still in the womb of time, is the gift of imagination. It requires poetic sensibilities with which judges are rarely endowed and which their education does not normally develop. These judges, you will infer, must have something of the creative artist in them; they must have antennae registering feeling and judgment beyond logical, let alone quantitative, proof.

The decisions in the cases that really give trouble rest on judgment, and judgment derives from the totality of a man's

nature and experience. Such judgment will be exercised by
two types of men, broadly speaking, but of course with varying emphasis—those who express their private views or revelations, deeming them, if not *vox dei*, at least *vox populi;* or
those who feel strongly that they have no authority to
promulgate law by their merely personal view and whose
whole training and proved performance substantially insure
that their conclusions reflect understanding of, and due regard for, law as the expression of the views and feelings that
may fairly be deemed representative of the community as a
continuing society.

Judges are men, not disembodied spirits. Of course a judge
is not free from preferences or, if you will, biases. But he may
deprive a bias of its meretricious authority by stripping it of
the uncritical assumption that it is founded on compelling
reason or the coercive power of a syllogism. He will be alert
to detect that though a conclusion has a logical form it in
fact represents a choice of competing considerations of policy,
one of which for the time has won the day.

An acute historian recently concluded that those "who
have any share of political power . . . usually obtain it because they are exceptionally able to emancipate their purposes
from the control of their unformulated wishes and impressions." (Richard Pares, "Human Nature in Politics—III," *The
Listener*, Dec. 17, 1953, p. 1037.) For judges, it is not merely
a desirable capacity "to emancipate their purposes" from their
private desires; it is their duty. It is a cynical belief in too
many quarters, though I believe this cult of cynicism is receding, that it is at best a self-delusion for judges to profess
to pursue disinterestedness. It is asked with sophomoric bright-
ness, does a man cease to be himself when he becomes a Justice? Does he change his character by putting on a gown? No,
he does not change his character. He brings his whole experience, his training, his outlook, his social, intellectual, and moral
environment with him when he takes a seat on the supreme

bench. But a judge worth his salt is in the grip of his function. The intellectual habits of self-discipline which govern his mind are as much a part of him as the influence of the interest he may have represented at the bar, often much more so. For example, Mr. Justice Bradley was a "corporation lawyer" par excellence when he went on the Court. But his decisions on matters affecting corporate control in the years following the Civil War were strikingly free of bias in favor of corporate power.

To assume that a lawyer who becomes a judge takes on the bench merely his views on social or economic questions leaves out of account his rooted notions regarding the scope and limits of a judge's authority. The outlook of a lawyer fit to be a Justice regarding the role of a judge cuts across all his personal preferences for this or that social arrangement. The conviction behind what John Adams wrote in the provision of the Massachusetts Declaration of Rights regarding the place of the judiciary in our governmental scheme, and the considerations which led the framers of the Constitution to give federal judges life tenure and other safeguards for their independence, have, I believe, dominated the outlook and therefore the action of the generality of men who have sat on the Supreme Court. Let me recall the Massachusetts Declaration:

It is essential to the preservation of the rights of every individual, his life, liberty, property, and character, that there be an impartial interpretation of the laws, and administration of justice. It is the right of every citizen to be tried by judges as free, impartial, and independent as the lot of humanity will admit. . . . (Article XXIX.)

Need it be stated that true humility and its offspring, disinterestedness, are more indispensable for the work of the Supreme Court than for a judge's function on any other bench? These qualities alone will not assure another indis-

pensable requisite. This is the capacity for self-searching.
What Jacques Maritain said in another connection applies
peculiarly to members of the Supreme Court. A Justice of
that Court cannot adequately discharge his function "without
passing through the door of the knowing, obscure as it may
be, of his own subjective." (Maritain, *Creative Intuition in
Art and Poetry*, (1953), p. 114.)

This is not to say that the application of this view of the
judge's function—that he is there not to impose his private
views upon society, that he is not to enforce personalized
justice—assures unanimity of judgments. Inevitably there are
bound to be fair differences of opinion. And it would be pretense to deny that in the self-righteous exercise of this role
obscurantist and even unjustifiable decisions are sometimes
rendered. Why should anyone be surprised at this? The very
nature of the task makes some differences of view well-nigh
inevitable. The answers that the Supreme Court is required
to give are based on questions and on data that preclude automatic or even undoubting answers. If the materials on which
judicial judgments must be based could be fed into a machine
so as to produce ineluctable answers, if such were the nature
of the problems that come before the Supreme Court and
such were the answers expected, we would have IBM ma-
chines doing the work instead of judges.

How amazing it is that, in the midst of controversies on every
conceivable subject, one should expect unanimity of opinion
upon difficult legal questions! In the highest ranges of thought,
in theology, philosophy and science, we find differences of view
on the part of the most distinguished experts,—theologians, philosophers and scientists. The history of scholarship is a record of
disagreements. And when we deal with questions relating to
principles of law and their application, we do not suddenly rise
into a stratosphere of icy certainty. (Address by Mr. Chief Justice Hughes, 13 American Law Institute Proceedings, (1936),
pp. 61, 64.)

The core of the difficulty is that there is hardly a question of any real difficulty before the Court that does not entail more than one so-called principle. Anybody can decide a question if only a single principle is in controversy. Partisans and advocates often cast a question in that form, but the form is deceptive. In a famous passage Mr. Justice Holmes has exposed this misconception:

All rights tend to declare themselves absolute to their logical extreme. Yet all in fact are limited by the neighborhood of principles of policy which are other than those on which the particular right is founded, and which become strong enough to hold their own when a certain point is reached. . . . The boundary at which the conflicting interests balance cannot be determined by any general formula in advance, but points in the line, or helping to establish it, are fixed by decisions that this or that concrete case falls on the nearer or farther side. (*Hudson County Water Co.* v. *McCarter*, 209 U.S. 349, 355.)

This contest between conflicting principles is not limited to law. In a recent discussion of two books on the conflict between the claims of literary individualism and dogma, I came across this profound observation: "But when, in any field of human observation, two truths appear in conflict it is wiser to assume that neither is exclusive, and that their contradiction, though it may be hard to bear, is part of the mystery of things." ("Literature and Dogma," *Times Literary Supplement* [London], Jan. 22, 1954, p. 51.) But judges cannot leave such contradiction between two conflicting "truths" as "part of the mystery of things." They have to adjudicate. If the conflict cannot be resolved, the task of the Court is to arrive at an accommodation of the contending claims. This is the core of the difficulties and misunderstandings about the judicial process. This, for any conscientious judge, is the agony of his duty.

Three

The Reading of Statutes

(1947)

Mr. Justice Frankfurter delivered the Sixth Annual Benjamin N. Cardozo Lecture on March 18, 1947, before the Association of the Bar of the City of New York. This lecture, under the title "Some Reflections on the Reading of Statutes," was printed in the May 1947 issue of the *Columbia Law Review* (Vol. 47, p. 527) and in the *Record of the Association of the Bar of the City of New York* for June 1947 (Vol. 2, p. 213).

A SINGLE VOLUME of 320 octavo pages contains all the laws passed by Congress during its first five years, when measures were devised for getting the new government under way; 26 acts were passed in the 1789 session, 66 in 1790, 94 in 1791, 38 in 1792, 63 in 1793. For the single session of the 70th Congress, to take a pre-Depression period, there are 993 enactments in a monstrous volume of 1,014 pages—quarto not octavo—with a comparable range of subject matter. Do you wonder that one for whom the statutes at large constitute his staple reading should have sympathy, at least in his moments of baying at the moon, with the touching Congressman who not so long ago proposed a "Commission on Centralization" to report whether "the Government has departed from the concept of the founding fathers" and what steps should be taken "to restore the Government to its original purposes and sphere of activity"? Inevitably the work of the Supreme

Court reflects the great shift in the center of gravity of law-making. Broadly speaking, the number of cases disposed of by opinions has not changed from term to term. But even as late as 1875 more than 40 per cent of the controversies before the Court were common-law litigation, fifty years later only 5 per cent, while today cases not resting on statutes are reduced almost to zero. It is therefore accurate to say that courts have ceased to be the primary makers of law in the sense in which they "legislated" the common law. It is certainly true of the Supreme Court that almost every case has a statute at its heart or close to it.

This does not mean that every case before the Court involves questions of statutory construction. If only literary perversity or jaundiced partisanship can sponsor a particular rendering of a statute there is no problem. When we talk of statutory construction we have in mind cases in which there is a fair contest between two readings, neither of which comes without respectable title deeds. A problem in statutory construction can seriously bother courts only when there is a contest between probabilities of meaning.

Though it has its own preoccupations and its own mysteries, and above all its own jargon, judicial construction ought not to be torn from its wider, nonlegal context. Anything that is written may present a problem of meaning, and that is the essence of the business of judges in construing legislation. The problem derives from the very nature of words. They are symbols of meaning. But unlike mathematical symbols, the phrasing of a document, especially a complicated enactment, seldom attains more than approximate precision. If individual words are inexact symbols, with shifting variables, their configuration can hardly achieve invariant meaning or assured definiteness. Apart from the ambiguity inherent in its symbols, a statute suffers from dubieties. It is not an equation or a formula representing a clearly marked process, nor is it an expression of individual thought to which is imparted the definiteness a single authorship can give. A statute is an instrument of government partaking of its practical purposes but also of its infirmities and limitations, of its awkward and groping efforts. With one of his flashes of insight, Mr. Justice Johnson called the science of government "the science of experiment." [1] The phrase, uttered a hundred and twenty-five years ago, has a very modern ring, for time has only served to emphasize its accuracy. To be sure, laws can measurably be improved with improvement in the mechanics of legislation, and the need for interpretation is usually in inverse ratio to the care and imagination of draftsmen. The area for judicial construction may be contracted. A large area is bound to remain.

The difficulties are inherent not only in the nature of words, of composition, and of legislation generally. They are often intensified by the subject matter of an enactment. The imagination which can draw an income tax statute to cover the myriad transactions of a society like ours, capable of producing the necessary revenue without producing a flood of litigation, has not yet revealed itself.[2] Moreover, government sometimes solves problems by shelving them temporarily. The legislative process reflects that attitude. Statutes as well as constitutional provisions at times embody purposeful ambiguity or are expressed with a generality for future unfolding. "The prohibition contained in the Fifth Amendment refers to infamous crimes—a term obviously inviting interpretation in harmony with conditions and opinions prevailing from time to time." [3] And Mr. Justice Cardozo once remarked, "a great principle of constitutional law is not susceptible of comprehensive statement in an adjective." [4]

[1] *Anderson* v. *Dunn*, 6 Wheat. 204, 226 (U.S. 1821).

[2] 1 Report of Income Tax Codification Committee, Cmd. 5131, pp. 16-19 (England 1936).

[3] See Mr. Justice Brandeis in *United States* v. *Moreland*, 258 U.S. 433, 451 (1922).

[4] *Carter* v. *Carter Coal Co.*, 298 U.S. 238, 327 (1936).

The intrinsic difficulties of language and the emergence after enactment of situations not anticipated by the most gifted legislative imagination reveal doubts and ambiguities in statutes that compel judicial construction. The process of construction, therefore, is not an exercise in logic or dialectic: the aids of formal reasoning are not irrelevant; they may simply be inadequate. The purpose of construction being the ascertainment of meaning, every consideration brought to bear for the solution of that problem must be devoted to that end alone. To speak of it as a practical problem is not to indulge a fashion in words. It must be that, not something else; not, for instance, an opportunity for a judge to use words as "empty vessels into which he can pour anything he will"— his caprices, fixed notions, even statesmanlike beliefs in a particular policy. Nor, on the other hand, is the process a ritual to be observed by unimaginative adherence to well-born professional phrases. To be sure, it is inescapably a problem in the keeping of the legal profession and subject to all the limitations of our adversary system of adjudication. When the judge, selected by society to give meaning to what the legislature has done, examines the statute, he does so not in a laboratory or in a classroom. Damage has been done or exactions made, interests are divided, passions have been aroused, sides have been taken. But the judge, if he is worth his salt, must be above the battle. We must assume in him not only personal impartiality but intellectual disinterestedness. In matters of statutory construction also it makes a great deal of difference whether you start with an answer or with a problem.

Everyone has his own way of phrasing the task confronting judges when the meaning of a statute is in controversy. Judge Learned Hand speaks of the art of interpretation as "the proliferation of purpose." Who am I not to be satisfied with Learned Hand's felicities? And yet that phrase might mislead judges intellectually less disciplined than Judge Hand.

It might justify interpretations by judicial libertines, not merely judicial libertarians. My own rephrasing of what we are driving at is probably no more helpful, and is much longer than Judge Hand's epigram. I should say that the troublesome phase of construction is the determination of the extent to which extraneous documentation and external circumstances may be allowed to infiltrate the text on the theory that they were part of it, written in ink discernible to the judicial eye.

Chief Justice White was happily endowed with the gift of finding the answer to problems by merely stating them. Often have I envied him this faculty but never more than in recent years. No matter how one states the problem of statutory construction, for me at least it does not carry its own answer. Though my business throughout most of my professional life has been with statutes, I come to you empty-handed. I bring no answers. I suspect the answers to the problems of an art are in its exercise. Not that one does not inherit, if one is capable of receiving it, the wisdom of the wise. But I confess unashamedly that I do not get much nourishment from books on statutory construction, and I say this after freshly re-examining them all, scores of them.

When one wants to understand or at least get the feeling of great painting, one does not go to books on the art of painting. One goes to the great masters. And so I have gone to great masters to get a sense of their practice of the art of interpretation. However, the art of painting and the art of interpretation are very different arts. Law, Holmes told us, becomes civilized to the extent that it is self-conscious of what it is doing. And so the avowals of great judges regarding their process of interpretation and the considerations that enter into it are of vital importance, though that ultimate something called the judgment upon the avowed factors escapes formulation and often, I suspect, even awareness. Nevertheless, an examination of some 2,000 cases, the bulk of which directly or indirectly involves matters of construction, ought to shed light on the encounter between the judicial and the legislative processes, whether that light be conveyed by hints, by explicit elucidation, or, to mix the metaphor, through the ancient test, by their fruits.

And so I have examined the opinions of Holmes, Brandeis, and Cardozo and sought to derive from their treatment of legislation what conclusions I could fairly draw, freed as much as I could be from impressions I had formed in the course of the years.

Holmes came to the Supreme Court before the great flood of recent legislation, while the other two, especially Cardozo, appeared at its full tide. The shift in the nature of the Court's business led to changes in its jurisdiction, resulting in a concentration of cases involving the legislative process. Proportionately to their length of service and the number of opinions, Brandeis and Cardozo had many more statutes to construe. And the statutes presented for their interpretation became increasingly complex, bringing in their train a quantitatively new role for administrative regulations. Nevertheless, the earliest opinions of Holmes on statutory construction, insofar as he reveals himself, cannot be distinguished from Cardozo's last opinion, though the latter's process is more explicit.

A judge of marked individuality stamps his individuality on what he writes, no matter what the subject. What is, however, striking about the opinions of the three Justices in this field is the essential similarity of their attitude and of their appraisal of the relevant. Their opinions do not disclose a private attitude for or against extension of governmental authority by legislation, or toward the policy of particular legislation, which consciously or imperceptibly affected their judicial function in construing laws. It would thus be a shallow judgment that found in Mr. Justice Holmes's dissent in the *Northern Securities* case [5] an expression of his disapproval of

[5] *Northern Securities Co.* v. *United States*, 193 U.S. 197, 400 (1904).

the policy behind the Sherman Law. His habit of mind—to be as accurate as one can—had a natural tendency to confine what seemed to him familiar language in a statute to its familiar scope. But the proof of the pudding is that his private feelings did not lead him to invoke the rule of indefiniteness to invalidate legislation of which he strongly disapproved,[6] or to confine language in a constitution within the restrictions which he gave to the same language in a statute.[7]

The reservations I have just made indicate that such differences as emerge in the opinions of the three Justices on statutory construction are differences that characterize all of their opinions, whether they are concerned with interpretation or constitutionality, with admiralty or patent law. They are differences of style.

If it be suggested that Mr. Justice Holmes is often swift, if not cavalier, in his treatment of statutes, there are those who level the same criticism against his opinions generally. It is merited in the sense that he wrote, as he said, for those learned in the art. I need hardly add that for him "learned" was not a formal term comprehending the whole legal fraternity. When dealing with problems of statutory construction also he illumined whole areas of doubt and darkness with insights enduringly expressed, however briefly. To say "We agree to all the generalities about not supplying criminal laws with what they omit, but there is no canon against using common sense in construing laws as saying what they obviously mean"[8] is worth more than most of the dreary writing on how to construe penal legislation. Again when he said that "the meaning of a sentence is to be felt rather than to be proved,"[9] he expressed the wholesome truth that the final

[6] Cf. *Nash* v. *United States*, 229 U.S. 373 (1913) and *International Harvester Co.* v. *Kentucky*, 234 U.S. 216 (1914).

[7] Cf. *Towne* v. *Eisner*, 245 U.S. 418 (1918) and *Eisner* v. *Macomber*, 252 U.S. 189 (1920).

[8] *Roschen* v. *Ward*, 279 U.S. 337, 339 (1929).

[9] *United States* v. *Johnson*, 221 U.S. 488, 496 (1911).

rendering of the meaning of a statute is an act of judgment. He would shudder at the thought that by such a statement he was giving comfort to the school of visceral jurisprudence. Judgment is not drawn out of the void but is based on the correlation of imponderables all of which need not, because they cannot, be made explicit. He was expressing the humility of the intellectual that he was, whose standards of exactitude distrusted pretensions of certainty, believing that legal controversies that are not frivolous almost always involve matters of degree, and often degree of the nicest sort. Statutory construction implied the exercise of choice, but precluded the notion of capricious choice as much as choice based on private notions of policy. One gets the impression that in interpreting statutes Mr. Justice Holmes reached meaning easily, as was true of most of his results, with emphasis on the language in the totality of the enactment and the felt reasonableness of the chosen construction. He had a lively awareness that a statute was expressive of purpose and policy, but in his reading of it he tended to hug the shores of the statute itself, without much re-enforcement from without.

Mr. Justice Brandeis, on the other hand, in dealing with these problems as with others, would elucidate the judgment he was exercising by proof or detailed argument. In such instances, especially when in dissent, his opinions would draw on the whole arsenal of aids to construction. More often than either Holmes or Cardozo, Brandeis would invoke the additional weight of some "rule" of construction. But he never lost sight of the limited scope and function of such "rules." Occasionally, however, perhaps because of the nature of a particular statute, the minor importance of its incidence, the pressure of judicial business, or even the temperament of his law clerk, whom he always treated as a co-worker, Brandeis disposed of a statute even more dogmatically, with less explicit elucidation, than did Holmes.

For Cardozo, statutory construction was an acquired taste.

He preferred common-law subtleties, having great skill in bending them to modern uses. But he came to realize that problems of statutory construction had their own exciting subtleties and gave ample employment to philosophic and literary talents. Cardozo's elucidation of how meaning is drawn out of a statute gives proof of the wisdom and balance which, combined with his learning, made him a great judge. While the austere style of Brandeis seldom mitigated the dry aspect of so many problems of statutory construction, Cardozo managed to endow even these with the glow and softness of his writing. The differences in the tone and color of their style as well as in the moral intensity of Brandeis and Cardozo became apparent when they wrote full-dress opinions on problems of statutory construction. Brandeis almost compels by demonstration; Cardozo woos by persuasion.

From the hundreds of cases in which our three Justices construed statutes one thing clearly emerges. The area of free judicial movement is considerable. These three remembered that laws are not abstract propositions. They are expressions of policy arising out of specific situations and addressed to the attainment of particular ends. The difficulty is that the legislative ideas which laws embody are both explicit and immanent. And so the bottom problem is: What is below the surface of the words and yet fairly a part of them? Words in statutes are not unlike words in a foreign language in that they too have "associations, echoes, and overtones." [10] Judges must retain the associations, hear the echoes, and capture the overtones. In one of his very last opinions, dealing with legislation taxing the husband on the basis of the combined income of husband and wife, Holmes wrote: "The statutes are the outcome of a thousand years of history. . . . They form a system with echoes of different moments, none of which is entitled to prevail over the other." [11]

[10] Barker, *The Politics of Aristotle* lxiii (1946).
[11] *Hoeper* v. *Tax Comm'n*, 284 U.S. 206, 219 (1931).

What exactions such a duty of construction places upon judges, and with what freedom it entrusts them! John Chipman Gray was fond of quoting from a sermon by Bishop Hoadley that "Whoever hath an *absolute authority* to *interpret* any written or spoken laws, it is he who is truly the lawgiver to all intents and purposes, and not the person who first wrote or spoke them." [12] By admitting that there is some substance to the good Bishop's statement, one does not subscribe to the notion that they are lawgivers in any but a very qualified sense.

Even within their area of choice the courts are not at large. They are confined by the nature and scope of the judicial function in its particular exercise in the field of interpretation. They are under the constraints imposed by the judicial function in our democratic society. As a matter of verbal recognition certainly, no one will gainsay that the function in construing a statute is to ascertain the meaning of words used by the legislature. To go beyond it is to usurp a power which our democracy has lodged in its elected legislature. The great judges have constantly admonished their brethren of the need for discipline in observing the limitations. A judge must not rewrite a statute, neither to enlarge nor to contract it. Whatever temptations the statesmanship of policy-making might wisely suggest, construction must eschew interpolation and evisceration. He must not read in by way of creation. He must not read out except to avoid patent nonsense or internal contradiction. "If there is no meaning in it," said Alice's King, "that saves a world of trouble, you know, as we needn't try to find any." Legislative words presumably have meaning and so we must try to find it.

This duty of restraint, this humility of function as merely the translator of another's command is a constant theme of our Justices. It is on the lips of all judges, but seldom, I venture to believe, has the restraint which it expresses, or the

[12] Gray, *Nature and Sources of the Law* 102, 125, 172 (2d ed., 1921).

duty which it enjoins, been observed with so consistent a realization that its observance depends on self-conscious discipline. Cardozo put it this way: "We do not pause to consider whether a statute differently conceived and framed would yield results more consonant with fairness and reason. We take this statute as we find it." [13] It was expressed more fully by Mr. Justice Brandeis when the temptation to give what might be called a more liberal interpretation could not have been wanting. "The particularization and detail with which the scope of each provision, the amount of the tax thereby imposed, and the incidence of the tax, were specified, preclude an extension of any provision by implication to any other subject. . . . What the Government asks is not a construction of a statute, but, in effect, an enlargement of it by the court, so that what was omitted, presumably by inadvertence, may be included within its scope." [14] An omission at the time of enactment, whether careless or calculated, cannot be judicially supplied however much later wisdom may recommend the inclusion.

The vital difference between initiating policy, often involving a decided break with the past, and merely carrying out a formulated policy, indicates the relatively narrow limits within which choice is fairly open to courts and the extent to which interpreting law is inescapably making law. To say that, because of this restricted field of interpretive declaration, courts make law just as do legislatures is to deny essential features in the history of our democracy. It denies that legislation and adjudication have had different lines of growth, serve vitally different purposes, function under different conditions, and bear different responsibilities. The judicial process of dealing with words is not at all Alice in Wonderland's way of dealing with them. Even in matters legal some words and phrases, though very few, approach mathematical symbols

---

[13] *Anderson* v. *Wilson*, 289 U.S. 20, 27 (1933).
[14] *Iselin* v. *United States*, 270 U.S. 245, 250, 251 (1926).

and mean substantially the same to all who have occasion to use them. Other law terms like "police power" are not symbols at all but labels for the results of the whole process of adjudication. In between lies a gamut of words with different denotations as well as connotations. There are varying shades of compulsion for judges behind different words, differences that are due to the words themselves, their setting in a text, their setting in history. In short, judges are not unfettered glossators. They are under a special duty not to overemphasize the episodic aspects of life and not to undervalue its organic processes—its continuities and relationships. For judges at least it is important to remember that continuity with the past is not only a necessity but even a duty.

There are not wanting those who deem naïve the notion that judges are expected to refrain from legislating in construing statutes. They may point to cases where even our three Justices apparently supplied an omission or engrafted a limitation. Such an accusation cannot be rebutted or judged in the abstract. In some ways, as Holmes once remarked, every statute is unique. Whether a judge does violence to language in its total context is not always free from doubt. Statutes come out of the past and aim at the future. They may carry implicit residues or mere hints of purpose. Perhaps the most delicate aspect of statutory construction is not to find more residues than are implicit nor purposes beyond the bound of hints. Even for a judge most sensitive to the traditional limitation of his function, this is a matter for judgment not always easy of answer. But a line does exist between omission and what Holmes called "misprision or abbreviation that does not conceal the purpose." [15] Judges may differ as to the point at which the line should be drawn, but the only sure safeguard against crossing the line between adjudication and legislation is an alert recognition of the necessity not to cross it and instinctive, as well as trained, reluctance to do so.

[15] *St. Louis-San Francisco Ry.* v. *Middlekamp*, 256 U.S. 226, 232 (1921).

In those realms where judges directly formulate law because the chosen lawmakers have not acted, judges have the
duty of adaptation and adjustment of old principles to new
conditions. But where policy is expressed by the primary
lawmaking agency in a democracy, that is by the legislature,
judges must respect such expressions by adding to or subtracting from the explicit terms which the lawmakers use no more
than is called for by the shorthand nature of language. An admonition like that of Justice Brandeis in the *Iselin* case that
courts should leave even desirable enlargement to Congress
will not by itself furnish the meaning appropriate for the
next statute under scrutiny. But as is true of other important
principles, the intensity with which it is believed may be decisive of the outcome.

Let me descend to some particulars.

The text: Though we may not end with the words in construing a disputed statute, one certainly begins there. You
have a right to think that a hoary platitude, but it is a platitude not acted upon in many arguments. In any event, it
may not take you to the end of the road. The Court no doubt
must listen to the voice of Congress. But often Congress cannot be heard clearly because its speech is muffled. Even when
it has spoken, it is as true of Congress as of others that what
is said is what the listener hears. Like others, judges too listen
with what psychologists used to call the apperception mass,
which I take it means in plain English that one listens with
what is already in one's head. One more caution is relevant
when one is admonished to listen attentively to what a statute
says. One must also listen attentively to what it does not say.

We must, no doubt, accord the words the sense in which
Congress used them. That is only another way of stating the
central problem of decoding the symbols. It will help to determine for whom they were meant. Statutes are not archaeo-
logical documents to be studied in a library. They are written
to guide the actions of men. As Mr. Justice Holmes re-

marked upon some Indian legislation, "The word was addressed to the Indian mind." [16] If a statute is written for ordinary folk, it would be arbitrary not to assume that Congress intended its words to be read with the minds of ordinary men. If they are addressed to specialists, they must be read by judges with the minds of the specialists.

And so we assume that Congress uses common words in their popular meaning, as used in the common speech of men. The cases speak of the "meaning of common understanding," "the normal and spontaneous meaning of language," "the common and appropriate use," "the natural, straightforward and literal sense," and similar variants. In *McBoyle* v. *United States*,[17] Mr. Justice Holmes had to decide whether an airplane is a "motor vehicle" within the meaning of the Motor Vehicle Theft Act. He thus disposed of it: "No doubt etymologically it is possible to use the word to signify a conveyance working on land, water or air, and sometimes legislation extends the use in that direction. . . . But in everyday speech 'vehicles' calls up a picture of a thing moving on land."

Sometimes Congress supplies its own dictionary. It did so in 1871 in a statute defining a limited number of words for use as to all future enactments. It may do so, as in recent legislation, by a section within the statute containing detailed definitions. Or there may be indications from the statute that words in it are the considered language of legislation. "If Congress has been accustomed to use a certain phrase with a more limited meaning than might be attributed to it by common practice, it would be arbitrary to refuse to consider that fact when we come to interpret a statute. But, as we have said, the usage of Congress simply shows that it has spoken with careful precision, that its words mark the exact spot at which it stops." [18] Or words may acquire scope and function

[16] *Fleming* v. *McCurtain*, 215 U.S. 56, 60 (1909).
[17] 283 U.S. 25, 26 (1931).
[18] *Boston Sand & Gravel Co.* v. *United States*, 278 U.S. 41, 48 (1928).

from the history of events which they summarize or from the purpose which they serve.

However colloquial and uncertain the words had been in the beginning, they had won for themselves finally an acceptance and a definiteness that made them fit to play a part in the legislative process. They came into the statute . . . freighted with the meaning imparted to them by the mischief to be remedied and by contemporaneous discussion. . . . In such conditions history is a teacher that is not to be ignored.[19]

Words of art bring their art with them. They bear the meaning of their habitat whether it be a phrase of technical significance in the scientific or business world, or whether it be loaded with the recondite connotations of feudalism. Holmes made short shrift of a contention by remarking that statutes used "familiar legal expressions in their familiar legal sense." [20] The peculiar idiom of business or of administrative practice often modifies the meaning that ordinary speech assigns to language. And if a word is obviously transplanted from another legal source, whether the common law or other legislation, it brings the old soil with it.

The context: Legislation is a form of literary composition. But construction is not an abstract process equally valid for every composition, not even for every composition whose meaning must be judicially ascertained. The nature of the composition demands awareness of certain presuppositions. For instance, the words in a constitution may carry different meanings from the same words in a statute precisely because "it is *a constitution* we are expounding." The reach of this consideration was indicated by Mr. Justice Holmes in language that remains fresh no matter how often repeated:

[W]hen we are dealing with words that also are a constituent act, like the Constitution of the United States, we must realize

[19] Mr. Justice Cardozo in *Duparquet Co.* v. *Evans,* 297 U.S. 216, 220, 221 (1936).
[20] *Henry* v. *United States,* 251 U.S. 393, 395 (1920).

that they have called into life a being the development of which could not have been foreseen completely by the most gifted of its begetters. It was enough for them to realize or to hope that they had created an organism; it has taken a century and has cost their successors much sweat and blood to prove that they created a nation. The case before us must be considered in the light of our whole experience and not merely in that of what was said a hundred years ago.[21]

And so, the significance of an enactment, its antecedents as well as its later history, its relation to other enactments, all may be relevant to the construction of words for one purpose and in one setting but not for another. Some words are confined to their history; some are starting points for history. Words are intellectual and moral currency. They come from the legislative mint with some intrinsic meaning. Sometimes it remains unchanged. Like currency, words sometimes appreciate or depreciate in value.

Frequently the sense of a word cannot be got except by fashioning a mosaic of significance out of the innuendoes of disjointed bits of statute. Cardozo phrased this familiar phenomenon by stating that "the meaning of a statute is to be looked for, not in any single section, but in all the parts together and in their relation to the end in view." [22] And to quote Cardozo once more on this phase of our problem: "There is need to keep in view also the structure of the statute, and the relation, physical and logical, between its several parts." [23]

The generating consideration is that legislation is more than composition. It is an active instrument of government which, for purposes of interpretation, means that laws have ends to be achieved. It is in this connection that Holmes said, "words

[21] *Missouri* v. *Holland*, 252 U.S. 416, 433 (1920).
[22] *Panama Refining Co.* v. *Ryan*, 293 U.S. 388, 433, 439 (1935) (dissenting).
[23] *Duparquet Co.* v. *Evans*, 297 U.S. 216, 218 (1936).

are flexible." [24] Again it was Holmes, the last judge to give quarter to loose thinking or vague yearning, who said that "the general purpose is a more important aid to the meaning than any rule which grammar or formal logic may lay down." [25] And it was Holmes who chided courts for being "apt to err by sticking too closely to the words of a law where those words import a policy that goes beyond them." [26] Note, however, that he found the policy in "those words"!

You may have observed that I have not yet used the word "intention." All these years I have avoided speaking of the "legislative intent" and I shall continue to be on my guard against using it. The objection to "intention" was indicated in a letter by Mr. Justice Holmes which the recipient kindly put at my disposal:

> Only a day or two ago—when counsel talked of the intention of a legislature, I was indiscreet enough to say I don't care what their intention was. I only want to know what the words mean. Of course the phrase often is used to express a conviction not exactly thought out—that you construe a particular clause or expression by considering the whole instrument and any dominant purposes that it may express. In fact intention is a residuary clause intended to gather up whatever other aids there may be to interpretation beside the particular words and the dictionary.

If that is what the term means, it is better to use a less beclouding characterization. Legislation has an aim; it seeks to obviate some mischief, to supply an inadequacy, to effect a change of policy, to formulate a plan of government. That aim, that policy is not drawn, like nitrogen, out of the air; it is evinced in the language of the statute, as read in the light of other external manifestations of purpose. That is what the judge must seek and effectuate, and he ought not to be led off the trail by tests that have overtones of subjective design.

[24] *International Stevedoring Co.* v. *Haverty*, 272 U.S. 50, 52 (1926).
[25] *United States* v. *Whitridge*, 197 U.S. 135, 143 (1905).
[26] *Olmstead* v. *United States*, 277 U.S. 438, 469 (1928) (dissenting).

We are not concerned with anything subjective. We do not delve into the mind of legislators or their draftsmen, or committee members. Against what he believed to be such an attempt Cardozo once protested:

The judgment of the court, if I interpret the reasoning aright, does not rest upon a ruling that Congress would have gone beyond its power if the purpose that it professed was the purpose truly cherished. The judgment of the court rests upon the ruling that another purpose, not professed, may be read beneath the surface, and by the purpose so imputed the statute is destroyed. Thus the process of psychoanalysis has spread to unaccustomed fields. There is a wise and ancient doctrine that a court will not inquire into the motives of a legislative body. . . .[27]

The difficulty in many instances where a problem of meaning arises is that the enactment was not directed toward the troubling question. The problem might then be stated, as once it was by Mr. Justice Cardozo, "which choice is it the more likely that Congress would have made?" [28] While in its context the significance and limitations of this question are clear, thus to frame the question too often tempts inquiry into the subjective and might seem to warrant the court in giving answers based on an unmanifested legislative state of mind. But the purpose which a court must effectuate is not that which Congress should have enacted, or would have. It is that which it did enact, however inaptly, because it may fairly be said to be imbedded in the statute, even if a specific manifestation was not thought of, as is often the very reason for casting a statute in very general terms.

Often the purpose or policy that controls is not directly displayed in the particular enactment. Statutes cannot be read intelligently if the eye is closed to considerations evidenced in affiliated statutes, or in the known temper of legislative opinion. Thus, for example, it is not lightly to be presumed

[27] *United States* v. *Constantine*, 296 U.S. 287, 298, 299 (1936) (dissenting).
[28] *Burnet* v. *Guggenheim*, 288 U.S. 280, 285 (1933).

that Congress sought to infringe on "very sacred rights." [29]
This improbability will be a factor in determining whether
language, though it should be so read if standing alone, was
used to effect such a drastic change.

More frequently still, in the interpretation of recent regu-
latory statutes, it becomes important to remember that the
judicial task in marking out the extent to which Congress has
exercised its constitutional power over commerce is not that
of devising an abstract formula. The task is one of accommodation as between assertions of new federal authority and historic functions of the individual states. Federal legislation of
this character cannot therefore be construed without regard
to the implications of our dual system of government. In such
cases, for example, it is not to be assumed as a matter of course
that when Congress adopts a new scheme for federal industrial regulation, it deals with all situations falling within the
general mischief which gave rise to the legislation. The underlying assumptions of our dual form of government, and the
consequent presuppositions of legislative draftsmanship which
are expressive of our history and habits, cut across what might
otherwise be the implied range of legislation. The history of
congressional legislation regulating not only interstate commerce as such but also activities intertwined with it, justify
the generalization that, when the Federal Government takes
over such local radiations in the vast network of our national
economic enterprise and thereby radically readjusts the balance of state and national authority, those charged with the
duty of legislating are reasonably explicit and do not entrust
its attainment to that retrospective expansion of meaning
which properly deserves the stigma of judicial legislation.

How then does the purpose which a statute expresses reveal
itself, particularly when the path of purpose is not straight
and narrow? The English courts say: Look at the statute and

---

[29] *Milwaukee Social Democrat Publishing Co.* v. *Burleson*, 255 U.S. 407,
438 (1921) (Justice Holmes, dissenting).

look at nothing else. Lord Reading so advised the House of Lords when a bill was before it as to which the attorney general had given an interpretative explanation during its passage in the House of Commons:

> Neither the words of the Attorney General nor the words of an ex-Lord Chancellor, spoken in this House, as to the meaning intended to be given to language used in a Bill, have the slightest effect or relevance when the matter comes to be considered by a Court of Law. The one thing which stands out beyond all question is that in a Court of Law you are not allowed to introduce observations made either by the Government or by anybody else, but the Court will only give consideration to the Statute itself. That is elementary, but I think it is necessary to bring it home to your Lordships because I think too much importance can be attached to language which fell from the Attorney General.[30]

How narrowly the English courts confine their search for understanding an English enactment is vividly illustrated by the pronouncements of Lord Haldane, surely one of the most broad-minded of all modern judges. He said in *Viscountess Rhondda's Claim:* [31]

> My Lords, the only other point made on the construction of the Act was that this Committee might be entitled to look at what passed while the Bill was still a Bill and in the Committee stage in the House. It was said that there amendments were moved and discussions took place which indicated that the general words of s. 1 were not regarded by your Lordships' House as covering the title to a seat in it. But even assuming that to be certain, I do not think, sitting as we do with the obligation to administer the principles of the law, that we have the least right to look at what happened while the Bill was being discussed in Committee and before the Act was passed. Decisions of the highest authority show that the interpretation of an Act of Par-

[30] 94 H.L. Deb. 232 (5th ser. 1934).
[31] [1922] 2 A.C. 339, 383.

liament must be collected from the words in which the Sovereign
has made into law the words agreed upon by both Houses. The
history of previous changes made or discussed cannot be taken
to have been known or to have been in view when the Royal
assent was given. The contrary was suggested at the Bar, though
I do not think the point was pressed, and I hope that it will not
be thought that in its decision this Committee has given any
countenance to it. To have done so would, I venture to say, have
been to introduce confusion into well-settled law. In *Millar v.
Taylor* the principle of construction was laid down in words,
which have never, so far as I know, been seriously challenged,
by Willes J. as long ago as in 1769: "The sense and meaning of
an Act of Parliament must be collected from what it says when
passed into a law; and not from the history of changes it under-
went in the house where it took its rise. That history is not known
to the other house or to the sovereign."

These current English rules of construction are simple.
They are too simple. If the purpose of construction is the
ascertainment of meaning, nothing that is logically relevant
should be excluded. The rigidity of English courts in interpreting language merely by reading it disregards the fact that
enactments are, as it were, organisms which exist in their environment. One wonders whether English judges are confined
psychologically as they purport to be legally. The judges
deem themselves limited to reading the words of a statute.
But can they really escape placing the words in the context
of their minds, which after all are not automata applying
legal logic but repositories of all sorts of assumptions and
impressions? Such a modest if not mechanical view of the
task of construction disregards legal history. In earlier centuries the judges recognized that the exercise of their judicial function to understand and apply legislative policy is not
to be hindered by artificial canons and limitations. The well-
known resolutions in *Heydon's Case*,[32] have the flavor of

[32] 3 Co. 7a, 76 Eng. Rep. 637 (1584).

Elizabethan English but they express the substance of a current volume of U.S. Reports as to the considerations relevant to statutory interpretation. To be sure, early English legislation helped ascertainment of purpose by explicit recitals; at least to the extent of defining the mischief against which the enactment was directed. To take a random instance, an act in the reign of Edward VI reads: " 'Forasmuch as intolerable Hurts and Troubles to the Commonwealth of this Realm doth daily grow and increase through such Abuses and Disorders as are had and used in common Alehouses and other Houses called Tipling houses': (2) it is therefore enacted by the King our Sovereign Lord, etc." [33] Judicial construction certainly became more artificial after the practice of elucidating recitals ceased. It is to be noted that Macaulay, a great legislative draftsman, did not think much of preambles. He believed that too often they are jejune because legislators may agree on what ought to be done, while disagreeing about the reasons for doing it. At the same time he deemed it most important that in some manner governments should give reasons for their legislative course.[34] When not so long ago the parliamentary mechanism was under scrutiny of the Lord Chancellor's Committee, dissatisfaction was expressed with the prevailing practice of English courts not to go outside the statutes. It was urged that the old practice of preambles be restored or that a memorandum of explanation go with proposed legislation.[35]

At the beginning, the Supreme Court reflected the early English attitude. With characteristic hardheadedness Chief Justice Marshall struck at the core of the matter with the observation: "Where the mind labours to discover the design of the legislature, it seizes everything from which aid can be

[33] 6 Edw. VI, c. 25 (1552).
[34] *Lord Macaulay's Legislative Minutes*, 145 et seq. (Dharker ed., 1946).
[35] Laski, Note to the *Report of the Committee on Minister's Powers*, Cmd. 4060, Annex V, 135 (1932).

derived." [36] This commonsensical way of dealing with statutes fell into disuse, and more or less catchpenny canons of construction did service instead. To no small degree a more wooden treatment of legislation was due, I suspect, to the fact that the need for keeping vividly in mind the occasions for drawing on all aids in the process of distilling meaning from legislation was comparatively limited. As the area of regulation steadily widened, the impact of the legislative process upon the judicial brought into being, and compelled consideration of, all that convincingly illumines an enactment, instead of merely that which is called, with delusive simplicity, "the end result." Legislatures themselves provided illumination by general definitions, special definitions, explicit recitals of policy, and even directions of attitudes appropriate for judicial construction. Legislative reports were increasingly drawn upon, statements by those in charge of legislation, reports of investigating committees, recommendations of agencies entrusted with the enforcement of laws, et cetera. When Mr. Justice Holmes came to the Court, the U.S. Reports were practically barren of references to legislative materials. These swarm in current volumes.

The change I have summarized was gradual. Undue limitations were applied even after courts broke out of the mere language of a law. We find Mr. Justice Holmes saying, "It is a delicate business to base speculations about the purposes or construction of a statute upon the vicissitudes of its passage." [37] And as late as 1925 he referred to earlier bills relating to a statute under review, with the reservation "If it be legitimate to look at them." [38]

Such hesitations and restraints are in limbo. Courts examine the forms rejected in favor of the words chosen. They look at later statutes "considered to throw a cross light" upon an

[36] *United States* v. *Fisher*, 2 Cranch 358, 386 (U.S. 1805).
[37] *Pine Hill Coal Co.* v. *United States*, 259 U.S. 191, 196 (1922).
[38] *Davis* v. *Pringle*, 268 U.S. 315, 318 (1925).

earlier enactment.[39] The consistent construction by an administrative agency charged with effectuating the policy of an enactment carries very considerable weight. While assertion of authority does not demonstrate its existence, long-continued, uncontested assertion is at least evidence that the legislature conveyed the authority. Similarly, while authority conferred does not atrophy by disuse, failure over an extended period to exercise it is some proof that it was not given. And since "a page of history is worth a volume of logic," [40] courts have looked into the background of statutes, the mischief to be checked and the good that was designed, looking sometimes far afield and taking notice also as judges of what is generally known by men.

Unhappily, there is no table of logarithms for statutory construction. No item of evidence has a fixed or even average weight. One or another may be decisive in one set of circumstances, while of little value elsewhere. A painstaking, detailed report by a Senate Committee bearing directly on the immediate question may settle the matter. A loose statement even by a chairman of a committee, made impromptu in the heat of debate, less informing in cold type than when heard on the floor, will hardly be accorded the weight of an encyclical.

Spurious use of legislative history must not swallow the legislation so as to give point to the quip that only when legislative history is doubtful do you go to the statute. While courts are no longer confined to the language, they are still confined by it. Violence must not be done to the words chosen by the legislature, unless, indeed, no doubt can be left that the legislature has in fact used a private code, so that what appears to be violence to language is merely respect to special usage. In the end, language and external aids, each

---

[39] *United States* v. *Aluminum Co. of Amer.*, 148 F. 2d 416, 429 (C.C.A. 2d 1945).

[40] *New York Trust Co.* v. *Eisner*, 256 U.S. 345, 349 (1921).

accorded the authority deserved in the circumstances, must
be weighed in the balance of judicial judgment. Only if its
premises are emptied of their human variables, can the process
of statutory construction have the precision of a syllogism.
We cannot avoid what Mr. Justice Cardozo deemed inherent
in the problem of construction, making "a choice between
uncertainties. We must be content to choose the lesser." [41]
But to the careful and disinterested eye, the scales will hardly
escape appearing to tip slightly on the side of a more probable meaning.

Nor can canons of construction save us from the anguish
of judgment. Such canons give an air of abstract intellectual
compulsion to what is in fact a delicate judgment, concluding
a complicated process of balancing subtle and elusive elements. All our three Justices have at one time or another
leaned on the crutch of a canon. But they have done so only
rarely, and with a recognition that these rules of construction
are not in any true sense rules of law. So far as valid, they
are what Mr. Justice Holmes called them, axioms of experience.[42] In many instances, these canons originated as observations in specific cases from which they were abstracted, taken
out of the context of actuality, and, as it were, codified in
treatises. We owe the first known systematic discussion of
statutory interpretation in England to the scholarship of Professor Samuel E. Thorne, Yale's law librarian. According to
Professor Thorne, it was written probably prior to 1567. The
latest American treatise on the subject was published in 1943.
It is not unfair to say that in the four intervening centuries
not much new wisdom has been garnered. But there has been
an enormous quantitative difference in expounding the wisdom. "A Discourse upon the Exposicion & Understandinge of
Statutes" is a charming essay of not more than thirty pages.
Not even the freest use of words would describe as charming

[41] *Burnet* v. *Guggenheim,* 288 U.S. 280, 288 (1933).
[42] *Boston Sand & Gravel Co.* v. *United States,* 278 U.S. 41, 48 (1928).

the latest edition of Sutherland's *Statutory Construction*, with its three volumes of more than 1,500 pages.

Insofar as canons of construction are generalizations of experience, they all have worth. In the abstract, they rarely arouse controversy. Difficulties emerge when canons compete in soliciting judgment, because they conflict rather than converge. For the demands of judgment underlying the art of interpretation, there is no vade-mecum.

But even generalized restatements from time to time may not be wholly wasteful. Out of them may come a sharper rephrasing of the conscious factors of interpretation; new instances may make them more vivid but also disclose more clearly their limitations. Thereby we may avoid rigidities which, while they afford more precise formulas, do so at the price of cramping the life of law. To strip the task of judicial reading of statutes of rules that partake of the mysteries of a craft serves to reveal the true elements of our problem. It defines more accurately the nature of the intellectual responsibility of a judge and thereby subjects him to more relevant criteria of criticism. Rigorous analysis also sharpens the respective duties of legislature and courts in relation to the making of laws and to their enforcement.

The quality of legislative organization and procedure is inevitably reflected in the quality of legislative draftsmanship. Representative Monroney told the House last July that "ninety-five percent of all the legislation that becomes law passes the Congress in the shape that it came from our committees. Therefore if our committee work is sloppy, if it is bad, if it is inadequate, our legislation in ninety-five percent of the cases will be bad and inadequate as well." [43] And Representative Lane added that ". . . in the second session of the 78th Congress 953 bills and resolutions were passed, of which only 86 were subject to any real discussion." [44] But what

[43] 92 Cong. Rec. 10040 (1946).
[44] 92 Cong. Rec. 10054 (1946).

courts do with legislation may in turn deeply affect what
Congress will do in the future. Emerson says somewhere that
mankind is as lazy as it dares to be. Loose judicial reading
makes for loose legislative writing. It encourages the practice
illustrated in a recent cartoon in which a senator tells his colleagues: "I admit this new bill is too complicated to understand. We'll just have to pass it to find out what it means."
A modern Pascal might be tempted at times to say of legislation what Pascal said of students of theology when he charged
them with "a looseness of thought and language that would
pass nowhere else in making what are professedly very fine
distinctions." And it is conceivable that he might go on and
speak, as did Pascal, of the "insincerity with which terms are
carefully chosen to cover opposite meanings." [45]

But there are more fundamental objections to loose judicial
reading. In a democracy the legislative impulse and its expression should come from those popularly chosen to legislate,
and equipped to devise policy, as courts are not. The pressure
on legislatures to discharge their responsibility with care, understanding, and imagination should be stiffened, not relaxed.
Above all, they must not be encouraged in irresponsible or
undisciplined use of language. In the keeping of legislatures
perhaps more than any other group is the well-being of their
fellow men. Their responsibility is discharged ultimately by
words. They are under a special duty therefore to observe
that "exactness in the use of words is the basis of all serious
thinking. You will get nowhere without it. Words are
clumsy tools, and it is very easy to cut one's fingers with
them, and they need the closest attention in handling; but
they are the only tools we have, and imagination itself cannot work without them. You must master the use of them, or
you will wander forever guessing at the mercy of mere im-

[45] Pater, Essay on Pascal in *Miscellaneous Studies,* 48, 51 (1895).

pulse and unrecognized assumptions and arbitrary associations, carried away with every wind of doctrine." [46]

Perfection of draftsmanship is as unattainable as demonstrable correctness of judicial reading of legislation. Fit legislation and fair adjudication are attainable. The ultimate reliance of society for the proper fulfillment of both these august functions is to entrust them only to those who are equal to their demands.

[46] Allen, Essay on Jeremy Bentham in *The Social and Political Ideas of the Revolutionary Era*, 181, 199 (Hearnshaw ed., 1931).

Four

___

The Treatment of Criminals:
Questions That Remain Unanswered

___

(1945)

Mr. Justice Frankfurter wrote this foreword to *After-Conduct of Discharged Offenders*, a report prepared by Sheldon and Eleanor T. Glueck for the Department of Criminal Science, Faculty of Law of the University of Cambridge. The Gluecks' work was published in 1945 by Macmillan and Co., Ltd., London, and St. Martin's Press, Inc., New York, as Volume V of *English Studies in Criminal Science*.

FROM TIME TO TIME some criminal episode dramatizes the high rate of crime in the United States. The press exploits the incident with talk about a "crime wave," leaving out of account the long-standing inadequacies of American criminal justice, and encouraging both the sentimentalism and the vindictiveness that are characteristic of American public opinion regarding criminals. At such times sleazy explanations for our high incidence of crime readily gain popular acceptance. The admixture of races in our population is blamed although the crime rate in homogeneous old-stock communities is nothing to boast of. The Puritan tradition of resistance to authority is offered as another explanation, although crime flourishes where the Puritan tradition is least rooted. America's youth as a nation is frequently blamed. But Canada, too, has claims

72

to the indulgence of immaturity, and yet her criminal statistics do not tell as melancholy a tale as do ours.

When such inadequate causes are assigned, it is not surprising that the favorite remedies suggested are equally inadequate and produce little improvement, so far as crime is
concerned, when adopted. Dissatisfaction with the processes
of American criminal justice has resulted largely only in mechanical tinkering with the machinery of the law. I do not
mean to belittle the need for improving such machinery. But
to speak of the law in terms of machinery is to employ a dangerous metaphor. The problems raised by crime go far deeper
than what is ordinarily implied by proper standards in the
administration of the criminal law. And though the crime
rate of Great Britain is lower and its administration of the
criminal law less garish, in Britain as in the United States the
phenomena of crime present social problems the elements of
which have hardly begun to be analyzed.

"What have we better than a blind guess to show that the
criminal law in its present form does more good than harm?
I do not stop to refer to the effect which it has had in de-
grading prisoners and in plunging them further into crime,
or to the question whether fine and imprisonment do not
fall more heavily on a criminal's wife and children than on
himself. I have in mind more far-reaching questions. Does
punishment deter? Do we deal with criminals on proper principles?" These questions were put by Mr. Justice Holmes
nearly half a century ago.[1] They could be put with equal relevance today—with equal relevance, but with a realization that
their relevance is receiving a growing acceptance and that
their answers are being pursued with devotion by men
equipped with scientific skill. The best of the legal profession is no longer content to repeat the formula of intellectual
abdication attributed to a great medieval judge that the Devil

[1] *Collected Legal Papers*, (1920), pp. 188-89.

himself knoweth not the mind of men, nor is it content to leave illumination of the dark recesses of a criminal's being to a rare great artist—a Shakespeare or a Dostoevski. To be sure, the secrets of personality can no more be unlocked by the mere accumulation of observed facts than can those of nature. Without the exercise of imagination no new insights can be gained. But the imaginative insight of a Shakespeare is no substitute for the systematic, scientific pursuits of a Freud. Mr. Justice Holmes's accusatory questions will be answered, or rather, properly framed for answer, only when enough men of talent spend their lives in the effort.

The authors of the pages that follow, Sheldon and Eleanor Glueck, have been among the most fruitful workers in this resistant vineyard. And so I could not but respond to the wish that I should send this book forth with a word of blessing. Not less notable than the new perspective given by this book to obdurate social problems, is the enterprise of the Faculty of Law at the University of Cambridge, through its Department of Criminal Science, grappling with these problems while Great Britain is a beleaguered island. This is indeed a striking piece of evidence of faith in the freedom which is espoused and of determination to use that freedom for progressively civilized ends.

In reporting their investigation of the antecedents of a thousand adolescents, and of five hundred male and five hundred female adult offenders, and of the careers of these persons after the heavy hand of the law was lifted from them, the Gluecks have not arrived at the Heavenly City of ultimate answers to the questions raised by crime. But they have blazed significant trails. No doubt many of the things that they report have long been suspected. But it means much to have speculation supplanted by facts and to prove quantitatively that which was previously merely surmised. Like so many of the conquests of science, the results of the inquiries reported by the Gluecks have merely pushed back the boundaries of darkness. We still do not know what is chargeable to nature and irremediable by man. Nor do we know to what extent what is good in nature is thwarted by man's institutions—what potentialities can be realized that are now frustrated. One may well assume that the biological factors are of importance in the maladjustments that beget crime. But awareness of that truth hardly tells us what are the biological factors, their extent and their significance.

We have lived to see biological fictions and fantasies employed as justification for the most brutal practices. This has made us more wary than ever of untested biological explanations. On the other hand, this report of the Gluecks makes it abundantly clear that criminal acts are apt to be the product of the interplay of complex pressures and resistance that are but ill described and dealt with as though they constituted a single dominating spring of action called criminal intent.

Doctrines or judgments are no stronger than the facts on which they are based. The labors which this report reflects help to undermine still further a number of presuppositions of our present system of criminal justice. The characteristic of law in a progressive society is an adjustment between continuity and change. Our criminal codes should not too rapidly accommodate themselves to the latest guidance of scientific inquiry. But it is equally fatal to be heedless of such guidance. Whatever our metaphysical notions about the freedom of the will may be, we can no longer rest content with the adequacy of the conception of criminal intent as an expression of a full and free choice between doing a proscribed act and not doing it. Again, the inadequacy of our traditional methods for determining the appropriate treatment for offenders, once wrongdoing is established, can no longer be disregarded. The conclusion of this report on the deficiencies of our procedure in imposing punishment has been given weighty support, in essence, by a committee of the federal judiciary of the United States. (See Report [1942] to the

Judicial Conference of the Committee on Punishment for Crime.)

Social phenomena like crime are imbedded in the texture of our society. To be understood they cannot be severed from the total environment. Only complacency will assume that the maladjustments which underlie crime are all reflected in our criminal statistics. And so, just as the study of disease illumines physiological processes that are not pathological, critical and persistent inquiry into the social pathology that is crime ought greatly to further understanding of the interplay between society and the individual in its many manifestations that happily are not the concern of the criminal courts.

Five

The Problem of Capital Punishment

(1950)

In the summer of 1950, while vacationing in England, Mr. Justice Frankfurter was invited to appear as a witness before the Royal Commission on Capital Punishment. A verbatim transcript of his testimony, given in London on July 21, 1950, was published by His Majesty's Stationery Office, and is reprinted below with minor deletions. The Commission presented its final report to Parliament in September 1953 (Cmd. 8932).

SIR ERNEST GOWERS (Chairman): We are very grateful to you for giving up some of your valuable time to help us. We have arranged for a verbatim record to be made of what you say to us. That is for our own benefit and not necessarily for publication. Have you any feelings about whether some of it might be published eventually as part of our proceedings? Perhaps you would like to reserve your answer until you see the transcript?

MR. JUSTICE FRANKFURTER: I am in hopes of not saying anything one in my position should not say, and you are free to use any of it. I gladly entrust myself to your judgment. I should like to make one brief statement. I do not want to appear here under false pretences. I deem it an honour to be allowed to come before you and to contribute what I can to your inquiry. But I am not an authority on criminology, and the light which I can shed on your problems is extremely

77

limited. The use that I can, perhaps, be to you is to indicate the line of inquiry that can be pursued by you regarding relevant American experience.

SIR ERNEST GOWERS: Thank you very much. The first topic in the list of subjects sent to you was degrees of murder. I believe that the typical law in the United States is that there are degrees of murder—first and second degree—that only murders of the first degree are punishable with death and also that even those who are guilty of murder in the first degree may escape the death penalty if the jury find that there were extenuating circumstances?

MR. JUSTICE FRANKFURTER: That is a fair summary. I had occasion a few years ago to make a study of the individual legislation of the various States regarding murder, and, perhaps, this is as good a time as any to speak of the general considerations that should be kept in mind about the American experience. You know, of course, that there are 48 States, each one having its own body of substantive and procedural law with reference to the crimes within the jurisdiction of those States. On the whole, the great range of crimes is a matter for State enforcement within State competence, and outside the competence of the Federal Government, each State having its own system of laws and procedures and judicial system. Any generalisation about America is bound to be inaccurate or inadequate, unless one qualifies it constantly by bearing in mind that what one says about America may be true of two-thirds of the States, or one-third, or some proportion of the States.

It may not be without interest if you will let me put to you a summary I made of the state of the law of the 48 States in regard to the death penalty itself, and you will see the surprising variations. In four States—only four States—the death penalty is mandatory, beyond discretionary authority either of jury or court, and it is interesting to see how unrelated geographically the States are to one another. The States are Connecticut, Massachusetts, Vermont and North Carolina. In six States the death penalty is abolished. There, again, you get surprising geographic puzzles. The States are Maine, Michigan, Minnesota, Rhode Island, North Dakota and Wisconsin.

In 38 States the death penalty is not mandatory. In 3 of those States the juries are authorised to recommend mercy, but the recommendation is not binding. In 15 States, the jury must specify whether the sentence should be death, or a life sentence; in other words, there is no verdict unless the jury says life or death. In 8 States the jury may deviate from the death penalty, and if it does not, then the death penalty automatically follows. If the jury says nothing it means death. In 2 States, the jury must designate a death sentence, or it is a life sentence. And then you get 9 States in which the jury may qualify their verdict "without capital punishment." It is not binding, in the sense that the judge is free not to follow it, and very recently we had an interesting case before the Supreme Court. Questions arising under these State laws rarely come before the Court, for they can come only if a substantial claim under the Federal Constitution is made. This was rather a fascinating case from the point of view of penological procedure. It was a case where a jury in New York strongly urged mitigation of sentence by the court, and the court, after privately consulting the probation officers, disregarded the jury's recommendation, but the defendant was given no chance to put his side of the case for mitigation. The question was whether under our Constitution, requiring "due process of law," he had a right to be heard on the question of mitigation, or whether if the court chose not to do so, that was its concern, and not within the ambit of the Federal Constitution.[1]

[1] *Williams* v. *New York*, 337 U.S. 241 (1949).

Then there are 2 States, and surprisingly enough to me, 2 Southern States, in which a recommendation by a majority of the jury suffices. It is one answer to a problem that came before the Supreme Court under Federal legislation. We had a case arising in the Federal courts in Hawaii as to the way in which the court must charge the jury in relation to the manner in which they may recommend mercy. That was the *Andres* case.[2] In these two Southern States they solved the problem by saying that if a majority recommends, then it is a life, and not a death, sentence.

I venture to set this out at the beginning as an illustration of what a crazy quilt pattern American law in this field is.

MR. LEON RADZINOWICZ: You have mentioned that in the 38 States where capital punishment is not mandatory, the jury may in some cases recommend mercy. Would you be so kind as to tell us more about how this system works?

MR. JUSTICE FRANKFURTER: I cannot possibly tell you. I do not know what happens in Wisconsin or Idaho. In years gone by I have tried to get students of mine, and more latterly colleagues, to study these things, so that you can get some illumination. Take Michigan. For 100 years she has had no capital punishment. There have been vigorous efforts to restore capital punishment in that State, but they have failed. Nobody, so far as I know, has studied or explored the history of that in Michigan in order to get some light on it. There are other States which had abolished capital punishment and have now restored it. I know of nothing which makes Michigan unique as to the incidence of murder or that should set it apart. Take Maine. Maine abolished capital punishment because there was a miscarriage of justice, the hanging of the wrong person. They abolished capital punishment, and kept it abolished. Why American sociologists or penologists have not made it their business to find out the incidence of murder in Maine as compared with murder in, say, Massachusetts,

[2] *Andres* v. *United States,* 333 U.S. 740 (1948).

and the comparative environments of the two States, I do not know.

MR. RADZINOWICZ: In the light of your great experience, do you approve of the system under which the jury has the power virtually to suspend capital punishment?

MR. JUSTICE FRANKFURTER: If I am to answer that at all, which I do with great diffidence because I do not feel very confident about my competence to do so, I think I ought to disclose my personal prejudice. I am strongly against capital punishment for reasons that are not related to concern for the murderer or the risk of convicting the innocent, and for reasons and considerations that might not be applicable to your country at all. When life is at hazard in a trial, it sensationalises the whole thing almost unwittingly; the effect on juries, the Bar, the public, the judiciary, I regard as very bad. I think scientifically the claim of deterrence is not worth much. Whatever proof there may be in my judgment does not outweigh the social loss due to the inherent sensationalism of a trial for life. I am speaking about my country, not yours. Any opinion I may give is subject to one's bias on the question of capital punishment; so, naturally, I view every system that mitigates the imposition of capital punishment with favour.

MR. RADZINOWICZ: Would you be in favour of reducing the scope of capital punishment?

MR. JUSTICE FRANKFURTER: I myself would abolish it.

MR. RADZINOWICZ: If you do not abolish it, but try to reduce its scope, there are two alternatives, I suppose—one is to give power to the jury; the other is to recast the law of murder; or there might be a combination of the two. Do you feel that this system of giving extensive power to the jury is the best way to reduce the scope of capital punishment?

MR. JUSTICE FRANKFURTER: I do not know whether this Commission has read the opinions or the judgments in the

Fisher case.[3] The *Fisher* case brings out the difficulties because that case turned on the adequacy of the charge that
the court gave to the jury in ascertaining what is and what
is not deliberation. My quarrel with my brethren—I wrote
a dissenting opinion in that case—was that I felt the judge's
charge was mumbo-jumbo; in that from what the judge told
the jury the most high-minded conscientious jury of men
and women would find it very hard to know whether there
was or was not deliberation within the criteria he expressed;
and I think there is a good deal of that in charging juries,
with us. On the whole, if the jury system—and I think in
the United States the jury system is in greater favour than
I gather it is with you—if the jury system has this social advantage of being a participating influence in the administration of justice, I should want to use it here in this type of
case. On the whole, not only do they express a rough kind
of popular feeling about conduct, but for the most part I
think we can trust twelve people on a jury at least as well
as judges as to motives, for judges are rather removed from
every-day actualities and on the whole are bound to be so
by their calling.

SIR ERNEST GOWERS: Is it possible to explain premeditation
clearly and logically without mumbo-jumbo entering into it?

MR. JUSTICE FRANKFURTER: I think it is. I think—you will
not mind my saying so—I think I would be very happy to
entrust the author of *Plain Words*[4] with that task. Take the
Fisher case. May I recall its facts very briefly? That was a
"murder in the cathedral." A poor devil, a coloured fellow,
who had hardly any schooling worth the name and was
brought up in the most squalid circumstances, was a "char-
man." The librarian—a very pathetic and tragic figure she
must have been; life had not dealt very fairly with her—I do
not know whether she was a southerner or not, but she com-

---

[3] *Fisher* v. *United States*, 328 U.S. 463 (1946).
[4] The author of *Plain Words* is Sir Ernest Gowers.

plained to the superintendent that he had not tidied her room, and Fisher had been spoken to, and that created a disturbance in him. A day or two later the librarian said to him, "You dirty nigger," and he exploded, and in no time she was killed. In all seriousness, I think that under the duty that the statute laid on that trial judge, if you had been in the judge's shoes, you would have explained to the jury when they retired that "deliberation" meant something, and particularly it meant something since the gradations of murder in the United States had changed the common law to make a different requirement—that Congress in 1897 said that murder in the first degree required deliberation and premeditation. Under the statute, the jury must be able to find that there was some opportunity for him, however fleetingly and momentarily, to reflect on what he was doing, and if the words, "You dirty nigger," pulled the trigger, as it were, and did not allow time for reflection, it was their duty not to find murder in the first degree. All this should have been—and I submit could have been—made crystal clear to the jury.

There are two questions. The first is, is it desirable to have grading, and to introduce the element of deliberation? But assuming there is that provision in the legislation, judges are duty bound to carry it out. I do not think it is too difficult a task to make clear to the jury that Congress meant to create two categories, and that it required something that had to be satisfied; and I would rather have the judgment of those twelve men on whether there was that something than entrust the decision to my own calling, including myself, because the more intellectual you are, the more likely are you to go into undue subleties.

I think the charges given by trial judges in the United States are too often not very helpful. I used to read regularly —I stopped recently, time being an outrageous thief of one's energy—the reports of the Court of Criminal Appeal in England, and I have been struck in the course of years with what

I regard, with all respect, as great wisdom in their insistence on proper directions by the judges to juries in this country. I think our judges are apt to direct in very abstract, and therefore not very illuminating and not guiding, terms. And here again is a marked element that differentiates your law from what may be compendiously, but not accurately, called American law: in many States, but not in all, and not in the Federal Courts, judges *must* direct in abstract terms. There was a period when our people became so suspicious of the bench that in a number of States they took away the power of judges to charge the jury on the facts, so that in some States the judges do not even charge orally, but give juries something in writing and tell them to go to the jury-room and read over abstract rulings on what is and what is not "malice" or "intent." In short, you cannot generalise about American law, but can only speak of the specific American jurisdiction.

SIR ALEXANDER MAXWELL: Are there cases where some section of responsible public opinion is shocked by inconsistency between the decisions of juries, where in one case the jury have made a recommendation for mercy and in another they have not?

MR. JUSTICE FRANKFURTER: I am not aware of such instances. There are, as you well know, periodic newspaper crime waves in the United States. Popular feeling is excited to fluctuate between being sentimental and being harsh. If you ask me what I regard as the basic cause for justifiable dissatisfaction with the administration of criminal justice in the United States, I would say that it is enveloped in sensationalism. The prosecution of crime ought to be dealt with, as closely as possible, in the same way a physical illness is dealt with. A criminal trial should have the austerity and objectivity of the operating room in a hospital. I am not suggesting that crime is a disease; I do not belong to that school of thought. But I am suggesting that the administration of justice should be what I envy yours as being—dignified, quiet, and substantially free from sensationalism—though I should be romantic about your press if I said it was wholly free of sensationalism regarding crime.

MR. RADZINOWICZ: Are those recommendations for a reduced sentence made by the majority or unanimity of the jury?

MR. JUSTICE FRANKFURTER: It varies. In the States where the jury has the duty of recommending, they must be told that the recommendation is itself part of the verdict, and there is not a verdict brought in unless they bring in a verdict not only as to guilt, not only as to commission of the crime by the accused, but also as to the assessment of punishment, because that is part of the verdict, and if they cannot agree on that, there is no verdict. That is true of the States where they have the power to assess the punishment, and that must be done by the jury unanimously, except in those few States in which, by a specific statute, less than a majority may bring in a verdict of guilty.

DR. ELIOT SLATER: It has been said to us by witnesses that the task of making such a recommendation would be too difficult for the jury—that they are not in a position to cope with it intellectually, and that they would be ruled by very emotional and sentimental considerations. I think that has been said?

SIR ERNEST GOWERS: Yes, and moreover that they do not know material facts because of the operation of the rules of evidence?

SIR ALEXANDER MAXWELL: This difficulty occurs to us, that at the time the jury bring in their verdict of guilty, they do not know the man's past record. If, at the same time, they have to consider the question of clemency, are they not hampered by the fact that they have no indication before them as to whether he has been guilty of crimes of violence before?

MR. JUSTICE FRANKFURTER: Let me answer as best I can,

in parts. Perhaps you will permit me a preliminary remark. As to impossibility, all I can say is that nothing is more true of my profession than that the most eminent among them, for 100 years, have testified with complete confidence that something is impossible which, once it is introduced, is found to be very easy of administration. The history of legal procedure is the history of rejection of reasonable and civilised standards in the administration of law by most eminent judges and leading practitioners. That is true of your country and mine. That is true of civil law and criminal law. The reason is a very simple one, and was given by one of the great lawyers of my country. He said in effect: "Of course, we oppose all reform; we grew up under the old system, and look at us as proof of its efficiency." Every effort to effect improving changes is resisted on the assumption that man's ultimate wisdom is to be found in the legal system as at the date at which you try to make a change.

Take the whole business of the form of indictment. When I came to the Bar an indictment often was pages and pages long, because that form had passed the test of judicial approval. If you left out a few words of what were deemed sanctioned words it was like touching the Ark of the Covenant. And yet today the simple form of indictment satisfies good sense and all the requirements of due notice to an accused.

As to the point Sir Alexander Maxwell makes, that raises far-reaching questions. I, myself, think that the bench—we lawyers who become judges—are not very competent, are not qualified by experience, to impose sentences where any discretion is to be exercised. I do not think it is in the domain of the training of lawyers to know what to do with a fellow after you find out he is a thief. I do not think legal training gives you any special competence. I, myself, hope that one of these days, and before long, we will divide the functions of criminal justice. I think the lawyers are the people who are competent to ascertain whether or not a crime has been committed. The whole scheme of common law judicial machinery—the rules of evidence, the ascertainment of what is relevant and what is irrelevant and what is fair, the whole question of whether you can introduce prior crimes in order to prove intent—I think lawyers are peculiarly fitted for that task. But all the questions that follow upon ascertainment of guilt, I think, require very different and much more diversified talents than the lawyers and judges of my country and your country are normally likely to possess. In the existing system, to be sure, there does not come before the jury, in deciding whether a fellow who committed a homicide should be found guilty of murder in the first or second degree, his full past record. But with reference to the particular transaction on which the jury has to pass, a good many facts incidentally come out, either through the defendant, when he takes the stand, or through other witnesses, when he doesn't. May I say, with all respect, I do not understand the view that juries are not qualified to discriminate between situations calling for mitigated sentences?

SIR ERNEST GOWERS: Who decides what charge is to be brought—whether the offender is charged with murder in the first degree or the second degree, or manslaughter, or what?

MR. JUSTICE FRANKFURTER: The prosecution of crime, the vindication of the criminal law, is with us in the hands of public prosecutors, who have various names—district attorneys, United States attorneys—and in States where the grand jury is still in existence, and as to Federal crimes, where prosecution must be by indictment, the public prosecutors advise the grand jury.

SIR ERNEST GOWERS: Of that you have had some direct experience?

MR. JUSTICE FRANKFURTER: Yes.

SIR ERNEST GOWERS: Did you find you were faced with

rather troublesome problems in deciding what charge to bring?

MR. JUSTICE FRANKFURTER: My experience was as a Federal prosecutor, and murder is not a crime that often comes within the Federal jurisdiction; it comes very rarely, because it only takes place either on so-called Federal reservations, such as West Point, or the territories, like Alaska or Hawaii, or the high seas, so that is not a problem within my immediate experience. But, of course, even Federal prosecutors at times must choose under what statute to lay the prosecution, a professional problem that must also confront, I suspect, your Director of Public Prosecutions. Of course a prosecutor has a problem under these American homicide statutes—shall I charge him as a co-conspirator?—shall I bring an accusation against him as a habitual offender? But on the whole the homicides that one worries about are, in more recent years, gang crimes, murders for profit in holdups. I do not think these raise serious difficulties.

SIR ERNEST GOWERS: I asked you that because it has been brought so much as an argument against the system of degrees of murder in evidence by witnesses in this country that it would create most troublesome problems for the prosecutor in deciding on the charge to bring?

MR. JUSTICE FRANKFURTER: My guess is that the ordinary prosecutor would lay the indictment as murder in the first degree and the jury could then find a lesser included crime. I should be surprised if this aspect were shown to present a serious difficulty.

DR. SLATER: How does the trial work out? Is it like a battle, or a court of inquiry?

MR. JUSTICE FRANKFURTER: We have the adversary system and therefore it is too much like a battle. Especially is this so, almost inevitably, when life is at stake. It is largely a battle dependent on the fairness and skill of the presiding judge. But, as I indicated earlier, in too many States our judges have very limited control over the jury. They cannot instruct them or guide them on the facts. They are really umpires at a fight. Also you must remember that in most States the judges—the State court judges—are elected. There is less than a handful of States in which judges have a life tenure and the effect of that on the administration of justice is often far-reaching.

SIR ERNEST GOWERS: Elected by whom?

MR. JUSTICE FRANKFURTER: By the people, mostly for relatively short tenures. I can quite understand that you are, as I gather, surprised at that situation. Men go on the bench for six years, and then go back to the Bar. So often I feel about those aspects of America what Dr. Johnson said about the performing dog: the wonder is the dog performs at all.

DR. SLATER: What is the position of the psychiatric witness in the ordinary court in the States?

MR. JUSTICE FRANKFURTER: Do you mean, is he treated with great respect? One of the real abuses, squalid aspects, of our administration of justice, especially until relatively recently, was the psychiatric expert. The defence, particularly if it had money, went out and bought experts, and then the State bought experts, and the thing was as unseemly as it could be. A considerable change, I believe, is taking place, in a relatively short time. In most States the situation was more or less the same, but it did not become lurid, except where the defendant is a rich man, like the famous Harry Thaw case. But I do think you can gain light on this subject from what has been done in two or three States—especially Massachusetts and California. I think in Massachusetts the insanity expert has shrivelled up as a result of the Briggs Law, whereby automatically the Department of Mental Health makes an examination of those accused. The expectation has been fulfilled that the quality of the Briggs Law examination expert is such that the report carries such weight that, although the defendant is entitled to have his own experts, they are either not drawn upon or the disinterested Briggs examination controls.

DR. SLATER: The disagreeable side has been cut out by the law?

MR. JUSTICE FRANKFURTER: Yes, you really get a disinterested judgment so far as psychiatry is concerned. One of the things I was going to suggest to the Commission was that they should have, at least, a statement from a man who probably had experience such as nobody else has had—Dr. Winfred Overholser. For many years he was Commissioner of the department of mental diseases in Massachusetts. He is now head of St. Elizabeths, the biggest psychiatric hospital of the Federal Government. Then California has adopted a pioneer procedure in separating the determination of insanity from the determination of guilt. There is a separate initial inquiry, as to whether a man is sane or insane, and if they find him sane, then the question of guilt for the commission of the offence goes before another jury. I am told—though I have no first-hand knowledge—that that is a system which has given great satisfaction. You see what it does—it takes away the opportunity of confusing the jury by saying: he did not do it—but anyhow he is insane.

SIR ERNEST GOWERS: Can you generalise about the practice of examining before trial those who are charged with murder with a view to finding out whether they are insane or not?

MR. JUSTICE FRANKFURTER: I do not speak by the book but I should be surprised if such pre-trial examination is not the exception rather than the rule. My impression is that where that practice prevails it has been found very fruitful.

SIR ERNEST GOWERS: If there was reason to suspect the prisoner's sanity, I suppose it would be done as a matter of course?

MR. JUSTICE FRANKFURTER: It would be, yes.

SIR ERNEST GOWERS: Supposing the accused shows signs of insanity and is examined by orders of the District Attorney, or of whoever it may be, by a psychiatrist, and the psychiatrist pronounces him insane, what happens then?

MR. JUSTICE FRANKFURTER: He is committed to an institution for the criminally insane.

SIR ERNEST GOWERS: The question has to go before the judge, I suppose?

MR. JUSTICE FRANKFURTER: That report goes before the judge.

SIR ERNEST GOWERS: And the jury?

MR. JUSTICE FRANKFURTER: That varies too. If the psychiatrist reports that the accused is insane, the judge may at once commit him to the hospital for the criminally insane.

SIR ERNEST GOWERS: Supposing he is not found insane, in the sense of being unfit to plead, but has to stand his trial, and he then pleads that he was insane at the time of the crime. Sometimes he may plead that he did not do it, but that if he did do it, he was insane at the time. There, in England, we get to the M'Naghten Rules,[5] and so do you, do you not?

MR. JUSTICE FRANKFURTER: Yes.

SIR ERNEST GOWERS: Are they strictly applied?

MR. JUSTICE FRANKFURTER: If I may use your phrase "by and large," I should think by and large there is hostility to the M'Naghten Rules.

SIR ERNEST GOWERS: Hostility?

MR. JUSTICE FRANKFURTER: Even when formally recognised, the M'Naghten Rules can be sufficiently, I was about to say, manipulated so that they can be professed in terms and departed from in practice.

SIR ERNEST GOWERS: We have been told by some English

[5] The test of criminal responsibility laid down in *M'Naghten's Case*, 10 Cl. & Fin. 200, 210, 8 Eng. Rep. 718, 722 (1843), is that "to establish a defence on the ground of insanity, it must be clearly proved that at the time of the committing of the act, the party accused was labouring under such a defect of reason, from disease of the mind, as not to know the nature and quality of the act he was doing; or, if he did know it, that he did not know he was doing what was wrong."

witnesses that they are sometimes grossly manipulated to such an extent that if they do not seem to fit in with the merits of the case the judge and jury in practice ignore them. Would you say that was true in America?

MR. JUSTICE FRANKFURTER: Except where they are candidly departed from, as they are, I believe, in a number of jurisdictions.

SIR ERNEST GOWERS: The most obvious case would be a man who is clearly insane, who will never be executed, but about whom it might be said with truth that the M'Naghten Rules did not fit him, because at the moment he committed the crime he did know what he was doing, and that it was wrong. Would you say that in such a case he would probably be found whatever is the equivalent of "guilty but insane"?

MR. JUSTICE FRANKFURTER: I should say so. I think the M'Naghten Rules are discredited, roughly speaking, by the generality of opinion and by the generality of practice.

SIR ERNEST GOWERS: They have been definitely superseded?

MR. JUSTICE FRANKFURTER: Certainly in some States.

SIR ERNEST GOWERS: What sanction have they where they have not been superseded? Merely the sanction of long practice?

MR. JUSTICE FRANKFURTER: Unless legislation is explicit. They were taken over almost wholesale by various States and rule unless they have been explicitly repealed or modified by judicial formulation.

SIR ERNEST GOWERS: Would you like to tell us anything more about the Briggs Law, which we touched on earlier? You spoke of it with favour.

MR. JUSTICE FRANKFURTER: With great favour. In the first place because it takes out of the arena parties in combat, sometimes with pecuniary interests. The area of interest should be as narrow as possible in the administration of criminal justice, and the area of disinterestedness as great as possible. Whoever now administers the Briggs Law could be very helpful to the Commission, because there you have a confined procedure which has been operating for 30 odd years and from all accounts the workings of it have been very favourable. Massachusetts is perhaps—I am not a native of Massachusetts, though I have lived there for a quarter of a century—is in some ways as good as any jurisdiction for you to draw upon, because its standards of criminal justice are probably as good as there are in the United States. The traditions are longer, the judiciary is a strong one, with a life tenure. The standards and the general atmosphere in which the criminal law moves in Massachusetts are perhaps more akin to yours than those of any other State.

SIR ERNEST GOWERS: This is an examination which is always made as a matter of course of every person who is accused of murder?

MR. JUSTICE FRANKFURTER: Such is my understanding. I may be wrong.

SIR ERNEST GOWERS: At whose instance? At the instance of the District Attorney? Who is appointed to do it? Is there a panel?

MR. JUSTICE FRANKFURTER: The Department for Mental Diseases, the experts attached to that.

SIR ERNEST GOWERS: They would be State servants?

MR. JUSTICE FRANKFURTER: Yes. State officials, but not State partisans. The thing that has impressed me so much is that by the sheer force of respect that is accorded to these disinterested people, partisan spirit has tended to disappear from treatment of the issue of insanity, so that you no longer have the abuse of having two eminent professors, each expounding his great virtues and his great experience, each testifying to contradictory views as dogma, which is not only not edifying with reference to the administration of justice, but I think rather disquieting for public opinion in regard to scientists generally.

MR. RADZINOWICZ: The defence has the right to call independent medical evidence?

MR. JUSTICE FRANKFURTER: It has the right to call its own experts. I doubt whether that right could be shut off. It is reserved to it. In practice it has become unimportant, because the examination made by what your Chairman calls State servants is such that respect is accorded to it.

SIR ERNEST GOWERS: Is there not liable to be a feeling that these psychiatrists, being State officials, will naturally be on the side of the prosecution?

MR. JUSTICE FRANKFURTER: That was a strong argument urged at the time the remedy was proposed, and that is an instance where judgment by speculation was replaced by judgment by experience.

SIR ERNEST GOWERS: There is nothing in it?

MR. JUSTICE FRANKFURTER: I think not. At all events Massachusetts experience disproves it and I doubt whether Massachusetts would be unique in this. These are people who have sanctions that operate against them: they have their professional reputation at stake; they are probably connected with some university; they have no interest in it one way or another. They may be wrong, as who may not be wrong, but at all events the motives are withdrawn to the same extent that your higher civil servants are propelled by disinterestedness.

MR. RADZINOWICZ: As the Chairman has told you, in England the M'Naghten Rules are very often disregarded or very loosely interpreted. Am I right in saying that this is true also of the United States?

MR. JUSTICE FRANKFURTER: I believe that is a fair statement of our situation.

MR. RADZINOWICZ: I also understand that you feel that the M'Naghten Rules are somewhat out of date; is that right?

MR. JUSTICE FRANKFURTER: That is my view, that the M'Naghten Rules were rules which the judges, in response to questions by the House of Lords, formulated in the light of the then existing psychological knowledge. Practically what it has meant is psychology translated into law. I do not see why the rules of law should be arrested at the state of psychological knowledge of the time when they were formulated.

MR. RADZINOWICZ: What do you envisage as the alternative? Assuming that they correspond to the state of knowledge then existing, what should we do about it? Should we drop them altogether and adopt a broad criterion of medical insanity? Or should we evolve M'Naghten Rules which would be more flexible? What is your view?

MR. JUSTICE FRANKFURTER: I do not know that I have the right to speak with any kind of weight on that subject, but perhaps it is blameless of me to say that if you find rules that are, broadly speaking, discredited by those who have to administer them, which is, I think, the real situation, certainly with us—they are honoured in the breach and not in the observance—then I think the law serves its best interests by trying to be more honest about it. There are, I believe, considerable communities of agreement in practice between you and American jurisdictions, which have exploded the relevance of the formula of the M'Naghten Rules except in so far as you manipulate them; and I should think it is not beyond the wit of lawyers and of disinterested specialists to form a different set of rules more in conformity with the largest agreement among the most sensible students of psychology, in its broadest sense, as well as the actualities of criminal justice. I know the danger and the arguments against leaving too much discretion, but I submit with all due respect that at present the discretion is being exercised but not candidly.

MR. RADZINOWICZ: As you know, in this country we have another resource. After conviction the Home Secretary, in considering whether to recommend the exercise of the Royal

Prerogative of Mercy, may hold an inquiry into the mental state of the offender. The mental condition of the offender is then again reviewed from a point of view which can be progressively broadened. Is it not better to retain the M'Naghten Rules as a general criterion and to supplement them by the working of this agency?

MR. JUSTICE FRANKFURTER: I am not justified in making any comment on your situation, but I think that to have rules which cannot rationally be justified except by a process of interpretation which distorts and often practically nullifies them, and to say the corrective process comes by having the Governor of a State charged with the responsibility of deciding when the consequences of the rule should not be enforced, is not a desirable system. Take New York; the Governor of New York has I do not know how many, but surely hundreds of applications for pardon each year. Every conscientious Governor of New York, and that means every Governor, feels his personal responsibility, since he must sign the paper that makes a man go to his death or long incarceration. To throw upon the Governor of New York the job of going through the records and deciding whether this man or that was mentally responsible seems to me to be putting a burden upon the Governor of a State that ought not to be put upon him.

SIR ERNEST GOWERS: I am not sure what your answer was to this question; I am not sure that Mr. Radzinowicz asked the question quite in this form. Which is the better remedy—to re-write the M'Naghten Rules in accordance with modern medical knowledge, bringing in perhaps what we call for convenience the doctrine of the "irresistible impulse," or to abandon the Rules altogether and put the question to the jury, "Was this man so mad that he ought to be held irresponsible?" without any formula at all, which is in effect what they do in Scotland?

MR. JUSTICE FRANKFURTER: I would certainly not adhere to the M'Naghten Rules. I start with that, because I am a great believer in being as candid as possible about my institutions. They are in large measure abandoned in practice, and therefore I think the M'Naghten Rules are in large measure shams. That is a strong word, but I think the M'Naghten Rules are very difficult for conscientious people and not difficult enough for people who say, "We'll just juggle them." What would you put in their place? It would be arrogant were I to propose an off-hand answer, but I dare to believe that we ought not to rest content with the difficulty of finding an improvement in the M'Naghten Rules. Unless one must conclude that there is no irreducible minimum of agreement among people who are by life-long study concerned with the states of mind of human beings, and more particularly those that eventuate in homicide, I think probably the safest thing to do would be to do what they do in Scotland, because it is what it gets down to in the end anyhow.

SIR ERNEST GOWERS: I wonder whether you can help us by expressing any views on the question whether, assuming capital punishment must remain in this country, for a time at any rate, hanging is as good a way of despatching the criminal as any other?

MR. JUSTICE FRANKFURTER: I do not think I have an opinion that is worth anything on that subject, always assuming that you do it as discreetly as you do it, that is, that it is a very private business. The time of hanging is not known by the public here, is that true?

SIR ERNEST GOWERS: No, it is known, and sometimes there are crowds. The flag is no longer hoisted and the bell is no longer tolled, but the time is known and the notice is posted on the prison gate.

MR. JUSTICE FRANKFURTER: I knew the notice was posted, but I assumed it was of the result of hanging and not of its time.

SIR ERNEST GOWERS: It is known, is it not, Sir Alexander Maxwell?

SIR ALEXANDER MAXWELL: Yes. The date is known and everybody knows it is generally 9 o'clock.

MR. JUSTICE FRANKFURTER: I do not think that is very good myself. At least it would not be very good in the United States, so far as its effect on public respect and emotions is concerned.

SIR ERNEST GOWERS: Has either the electric chair or the gas chamber shown itself to be open to any marked objections?

MR. JUSTICE FRANKFURTER: I do not recall anything of that sort, so far as my limited reading goes. We had a very interesting case two or three years ago, a case that told on my conscience a good deal. This was the case of poor Willie Francis, a young coloured fellow convicted of murder. There was no question about his guilt. He went to the electric chair and there was some mischance by which the current or something went wrong, something mechanical; there was no negligence. His counsel then tried to prevent execution and said that on various grounds it would be "cruel and unusual punishment," and, as such, violation of due process. Various objections were put forward and questions arose as to whether it would be a denial of due process, that is, contrary to fundamental principles common to the English-speaking world, to try to execute a man after the first attempt had failed. The Court held that if that is what Louisiana wants to do, that is for Louisiana to do, so far as the United States Constitution goes.[6] I was very much bothered by the problem, it offended my personal sense of decency to do this. Something inside of me was very unhappy, but I did not see that it violated due process of law. This problem has arisen several times in your history. It was raised in the House of Commons by Harcourt, who had been Home Secretary in the '80's or '90's, and he was outraged by it. I believe it is the law of

[6] *Francis* v. *Resweber*, 329 U.S. 459 (1947).

England, is it not, that if there are two mischances you cannot do it the third time, but you can go wrong twice—or is it thrice?

SIR ALEXANDER MAXWELL: I do not think there is any law, but I do seem to remember a case in which the Home Secretary ordered a reprieve because something had gone wrong.

MR. JUSTICE FRANKFURTER: There was a full-dress debate in Harcourt's time. It was a very interesting debate, and there was the same feeling of revulsion. Sir William Harcourt, I think it was, made a powerful speech, he was outraged by it, as also were others, and there was a reprieve because the third time the rope went wrong again. I mention that because that is the only incident that has come to my knowledge, and I spent quite a good deal of time trying to find out whether there was any dissatisfaction about the electric chair. I think that is accepted now. Hanging is still the mode of execution in some States. I do not know how many States still have hanging. I think on the whole American feeling is strongly against hanging.

SIR ERNEST GOWERS: What about the gas chamber?

MR. JUSTICE FRANKFURTER: I do not know about that. How many States have that, do you happen to know?

SIR ERNEST GOWERS: Electrocution is used by 22. Eleven use hanging, 8 use lethal gas and in Utah the man has the choice between hanging and shooting. Do you know why electrocution was first substituted for hanging?

MR. JUSTICE FRANKFURTER: It was deemed to be quicker, more merciful and to give less opportunity for mischance. It was contested as to its validity, as a matter of due process or in relation to the *ex post facto* clause of our Constitution. Everything seems to come before the Supreme Court, from the validity of a treaty of peace to whether or not electrocution instead of hanging is such a disadvantageous change in the termination of a life that a prisoner had a right to object to it.

SIR ERNEST GOWERS: There is something rather repulsive about hanging?

MR. JUSTICE FRANKFURTER: Yes, there is.

SIR ERNEST GOWERS: Has any suggestion been made in the United States that, as an alternative to being executed, the condemned man should be allowed to commit suicide?

MR. JUSTICE FRANKFURTER: No.

SIR ERNEST GOWERS: Would it be regarded as very shocking if the warder said to the man, "It is time to come along to the scaffold but if you care to drink this instead . . ."?

MR. JUSTICE FRANKFURTER: If it were known that he said that?

SIR ERNEST GOWERS: Yes.

MR. JUSTICE FRANKFURTER: I think the notion of being yourself the agency in taking life is bad.

SIR ERNEST GOWERS: Even though you know you are going to be pushed over the edge, you shall not do it?

MR. JUSTICE FRANKFURTER: I do not believe this Commission will recommend that.

MRS. CAMERON: There is the question of alternative punishment. You said earlier on that the abolitionist States—you were thinking of the State of Maine—had to face particular problems created by that, which is presumably the alternative, where the man is confined for a long time. A number of witnesses we have heard here have defended the *status quo* by suggesting that it was more humane to execute than to keep a man in jail for more than ten years at a time. I personally find that hard to believe, but it has been brought up again and again, and this has tended to lead to the conclusion that it would need an immense reform of the prison system to create conditions of imprisonment in which a man could survive and be kept from society for many years without very grave deterioration. Was that the problem which you had in mind when you spoke of the problem of the abolitionist States?

MR. JUSTICE FRANKFURTER: I do not think so in the abolitionist States, except when once in a while there is some atrocious murder and they proposed this. In the first place they have gone on the assumption that for reasons which are good and sufficient they do not want capital punishment. In the second place I think the suggestion that after all it is better to be dead than to be ten years languishing in jail is always made by people who are outside the jail. It is not made by the people who are confronting death.

MRS. CAMERON: We have heard it from the people employed in prisons, or, at least, they have said that prisoners deteriorate appallingly after ten years.

MR. JUSTICE FRANKFURTER: It all depends what you do with them. There is a women's prison in Massachusetts run by Miriam van Waters, who proves what wise prison administration can be. She has murderers in her penal colony and she has had trouble with conventional minds because she did not want them to deteriorate and therefore took appropriate measures against such tendencies. This question raises the whole question of our prison administration.

SIR ERNEST GOWERS: Has there been much movement in the States away from the conception of prisons as penal institutions towards the conception of them as curative institutions?

MR. JUSTICE FRANKFURTER: I think there has been a considerable practical movement of trying to make the inmates of prisons members of society with confined freedom. I should think one of the most important and, on the whole, encouraging sociological reforms has been of prison administration in the United States. Professor Liepmann, who was Professor of Criminology in the pre-Hitler days at Hamburg, knew our situation and spent two years examining it. I saw him when he started and I saw him when he left, and I asked him to make some general observation. He said this, which I think is very important. "In the United States you can find the very best and the very worst" and I suspect that that is still true. When I was a prosecutor I had to go to a jail in New Jersey to examine a witness prior to trial, and it was a revolting sight—ball and chain, not figuratively, but literally. I am speaking of 1908, but since then one of the best prison systems in the United States is, I believe, in New Jersey. I think one can generalise and say, "Yes, there has been, and is need of, great practical improvement," but not say, "Oh well, it must be all curative, the punishment." I should say the best thing is a fair balance, bearing in mind that after all society has to be secured, but it is not secured if you take a lot of people and make them worse by putting them into prison.

SIR ERNEST GOWERS: We are greatly indebted to you for having found the time, among your many engagements in this country, to give us such interesting and valuable evidence.

(*The witness withdrew.*)

Six

Advice to a Young Man Interested in Going into Law

(1954)

In May 1954 a twelve-year-old boy living in Alexandria, Virginia, sent a letter to Mr. Justice Frankfurter in which he wrote that he was "interested in going into law as a career" and requested advice as to "some ways to start preparing myself while still in junior high school." He received this reply.

My dear Paul:

No one can be a truly competent lawyer unless he is a cultivated man. If I were you, I would forget all about any technical preparation for the law. The best way to prepare for the law is to come to the study of the law as a well-read person. Thus alone can one acquire the capacity to use the English language on paper and in speech and with the habits of clear thinking which only a truly liberal education can give. No less important for a lawyer is the cultivation of the imaginative faculties by reading poetry, seeing great paintings, in the original or in easily available reproductions, and listening to great music. Stock your mind with the deposit of much good reading, and widen and deepen your feelings by experiencing vicariously as much as possible the wonderful mysteries of the universe, and forget all about your future career.

> With good wishes,
> Sincerely yours,
> [*Signed*] Felix Frankfurter

Master M. Paul Claussen, Jr.

II

THE JUDICIAL PROCESS IN ACTION

One

A Note on Judicial Biography

(1948)

A round table on judicial biography was a feature of the annual meeting of the American Political Science Association in December 1948 at Chicago, Illinois. Professor Charles Fairman, who presided, invited Mr. Justice Frankfurter to contribute to the symposium. He received this response, which later was printed in the Spring 1949 issue of the *Indiana Law Journal* (Vol. 24, p. 367).

MY DEAR FAIRMAN:

Your kind desire to have a word from me for your round table on judicial biography stirs in me the nostalgic desire for academic freedom. (Not that I am implying a grievance against the restraints of the bench, for the Thirteenth Amendment protects me against involuntary servitude.) As it is, let me take shelter behind thoughts I was free to utter when academic freedom was mine. I find that nearly twenty years ago I ventured these observations:

. . . the work of the Supreme Court is the history of relatively few personalities. However much they may have represented or resisted their *Zeitgeist*, symbolized forces outside their own individualities, they were also individuals. The fact that they were "*there*" and that others were not, surely made decisive differences. To understand what manner of men they were is crucial to an understanding of the Court. Yet how much real insight have we about the seventy-four men who constitute the Supreme Court's

roll of judges? How much is known about the inner forces that
directed their action and stamped the impress of their unique
influence upon the Court? Only of Marshall have we an adequate
biography; Story's revealing correspondence takes us behind his
scholarly exterior; very recently not a little light has been shed
on the circumstances and associations that helped to mold Field's
outlook. About most of the Justices we have only mortuary
estimates. ("Mr. Justice Brandeis and the Constitution," reprinted
in *Law and Politics*, (1939), pp. 113-14.)

Since this was written, a half a dozen or so additional Supreme Court biographies have been published. It would be
invidious for me to speak of their inadequacies or their merits.
Suffice it to say most worlds of exciting judicial biography
still remain to be conquered. Indeed, my lips may be judicially sealed regarding living biographers, but I may be par-
doned—or not—for confessing that time has lessened for me
the significance of Beveridge's *Marshall*. I do not remotely
imply that this is due to disagreements I may have with Beveridge's views. The excellence of a biography is hardly to be
measured by the extent to which it echoes a reader's opinion.
A biography is to be judged by the insight it gives into the
complexities of character, not by the satisfaction it affords the
reader's presuppositions.

I suppose judicial biography has all the difficulties that confront biographers of those who are thinkers rather than doers.
But there are additional difficulties as to judges. A member of
the Supreme Court is at once a soloist and part of an orchestra.
While dissenting opinions seem like solo performances, even
that is not always true, and, in any event, the private re-
hearsals, as it were, behind the impenetrable draperies of judicial secrecy may tell much more about the soloist and the rest
of the orchestra than the public performance even remotely
reveals.

Judges like other people have their inborn qualities, deflected and disciplined, enriched or narrowed, by their edu-

cation, their reading, their experience, their associations, their depth and drive of creative reflection, their capacity for rigorous, undeceiving self-analysis.

Judges are seldom men of great literary talent and not always are they copious letter writers yielding self-revelation—self-revelation that is either the product of a Socratic kind of self-knowledge or the unintended self-revelation which gives a picture of oneself as one would like to appear to oneself as well as to others. One can infer much of Holmes's outlook on life as well as on law from his opinions. But how much greater our opportunity for knowing him by reason of his voluminous correspondence and that awing list of books covering his reading for half a century. Reading maketh a man only in part—yet how illuminating it would be to have a list of the books read by the justices, as well as to know who were their intimates before they went on the bench and after.

But the fullest knowledge of the elements that play upon a judge do not automatically reveal or explain him, any more than even Lowes's penetrating *Road to Xanadu* accounts for the creativeness of Coleridge. Still less do the variegated and illusive aspects of human personality lend themselves to tidy but tight categories. Perhaps you will tell us in your Life of Bradley why that "corporation lawyer" should have entertained such drastic but wise views of constitutional law against what were deemed to be the interests of property while Harlan, who thought himself a tribune of the people, gave comfort to those interests.

I have said very little, but enough, I hope, to make you realize why I covet your academic freedom to discuss these exciting problems. They are problems that go to the root of the judicial function and to our capacity to produce men adequately equipped to discharge it. But even one who is ex officio compelled to deny himself freedom of speech may say wholeheartedly that the great art of judicial biography requires deep understanding of the judicial process, delicate analysis of character, and the creative humility of the artist.

My best wishes for the success of your round-table discussion. May it stimulate great biographies.

Very sincerely yours,
[*Signed*] Felix Frankfurter

Two

Chief Justices I Have Known

(1953)

This informal talk was given by Mr. Justice Frankfurter before a group of students and professors at the University of Virginia Law School in Charlottesville on May 12, 1953. A transcript of his remarks, which had been tape recorded, appeared in the *Virginia Law Review* for November 1953 (Vol. 39, p. 883) and is reprinted here, with minor editorial revisions.

I'M TOLD YOU CAN'T teach an old dog new tricks, but my problem tonight is not to try to indulge in new tricks but to see if I can recall an old trick—talking to a group of people. I must see if I can do what I used to do for twenty-five years—sit in a room and talk with students, fellow students, the difference between whom and myself was merely that I had traveled the road once, or several times, before they did.

Here I am without a note, and therefore we'll just have a chat. This room is larger than the one in which I used to meet with students at the Harvard Law School, but we'll contract the walls and imagine we are sitting around that room, where for twenty-five years I received such stimulus and delight as only the young can give to a teacher. It's about as pleasurable a thing as can come to a man in a lifetime.

I've been told to talk to you about chief justices I've known, and I'll talk just as it lies in my mind.

It is 164 years since the Supreme Court of the United States

was established by an act of Congress. During those years
there have been, including Fred M. Vinson, the present in-
cumbent, thirteen chief justices. It seems almost incredible,
old as I am, that I've known six of them. The mystery is
easily resolved by the fact that the term of office of chief justices, if nature is kind, as happily it has been to some of the
greatest of them, is longer than that of any other official in
our government.

I shall speak to you about five of the chief justices. I shall
not say anything, of course, of the chief justice whom I've
known longest in service, the present occupant of the seat.
But I shall speak of one—Fuller—whom I knew only rather
remotely, somewhat platonically as it were, because I never
had any personal relations with him. But I saw him on and
off, first when I was a student at the Harvard Law School,
and eventually when I appeared before him in that wonderful old courtroom in the Capitol, which I think it was almost
a desecration of tradition to leave.

The five chief justices of whom I will speak are Fuller,
White, Taft, Hughes, and Stone. But, of course, in order that
what I say may have something more than merely episodic
significance, a few preliminary remarks ought to be made.

The one judicial figure whom even the least informed
knows of in the history of the United States is the great Chief
Justice John Marshall, of your Commonwealth. It is an interesting fact that although, for essential purposes, the history of
our constitutional law almost begins with him, and the significant history of the Supreme Court of the United States
begins with him, he was the fourth chief justice. His three
predecessors all had very short tenure.

The first was a great man, John Jay. It is not without significance in attempting to understand the then position of the
chief justice of the United States, that John Jay resigned the
chief justiceship to become governor of New York—not that
I underrate the importance of the governorship of New York,

either then or now. But it is certainly true that since Marshall's time only a madman would resign the chief justiceship to become governor, let me say, even of Virginia.

Jay's successor, John Rutledge of South Carolina, had the singular distinction of serving only a few months as chief justice by interim appintment. He was rejected by the Senate of the United States, and therefore was not able to continue to occupy the post.

The third chief justice was another eminent man in our history, Oliver Ellsworth, who was the architect of the act that created the federal judicial system. His structure remained, for all practical purposes, unaltered from 1789 to 1869. He was chief justice for only four years. Ill health put an end to his service.

Then came John Marshall. I should say the three greatest chief justices we've had were John Marshall, Roger Taney, and Charles E. Hughes. It is an interesting fact that the first two of these, between them and in immediate succession, served for almost one-half of the 164 years the Court has been in existence. Marshall from 1801 to 1835, and Taney from 1836 to 1864. I emphasize the duration of their service because the length of time during which a chief justice presides over the Court has, of course, a great deal to do with his place in history. Time is one of the most important factors in the realization of a man's potentialities.

Coming to the chief justices whom I have seen in action, about whom professionally I may be allowed to have some judgment, let me come down to 1888 when Grover Cleveland appointed a man who was not known generally to the country at all. I suppose Melville Weston Fuller was a man about whom there was nothing in what newspapermen call the morgues of the leading newspapers in the country. He had no record to speak of, except a professional one. His appointment is a striking illustration of the contingencies of life. And I think he—and I shall speak of others—illustrates the importance of not having a fixed, specific ambition in life. The chances of realizing a specific ambition, the laws of chance, are so much against you that, if I may say so, I do not think any of you should harbor an ambition to become chief justice of the United States. The likelihood that you will realize it—I do not know what the mathematicians, if there be any in this audience, would say—is worth nothing, and the likelihood that you will have an embittered life is very considerable. The thing to do is to have ambition in a certain direction but not to fix it on a point of arrival, an ambition going to general purpose in life and not to the particular form in which that purpose is to be realized.

When Chief Justice Waite died, if a poll had been taken among lawyers and judges to determine the choice of a successor, I do not suppose a single vote would have been cast for Melville W. Fuller, certainly outside Chicago. Indeed, he was not Grover Cleveland's first choice. It was widely believed that a man named Edward J. Phelps of Vermont would become chief justice. He was a leader of the bar. He was a well-known man. He had been minister to Great Britain. But 1888 was a time when the so-called Irish vote mattered more than it has seemed to matter in recent years. Edward J. Phelps, as has been true of other ministers and ambassadors to Great Britain, had made some speeches in England in which he said some nice things about the British people. Patrick Collins, a Democratic leader, then an influential member of the House of Representatives and later mayor of Boston, felt that that wouldn't do. A man who says nice things about the British, he evidently thought, couldn't possibly make a good chief justice of the United States. And since Patrick Collins was a powerful influence in the Democratic party, he advised President Cleveland that if he sent Phelps's name to the Senate, the chances of confirmation might not be very bright. Phelps's name was not sent to the Senate.

Melville Fuller was born in Maine, educated at Bowdoin, and the Harvard Law School. As a young man, after a little political activity in Augusta, Maine, he tried his luck in the beckoning West. He went to Chicago, where he was active as a Democrat. In that way it chanced that Grover Cleveland came to know and respect him. After some maneuvering, Cleveland named Fuller, to the great surprise of the press of the country and even of the profession. Fuller was confirmed, but with a very large vote in opposition. One of the opponents of confirmation was Senator Hoar of Massachusetts, then on the powerful Judiciary Committee, who afterward did the handsome thing by saying how wrong he had been, just as in our day Senator Norris, who had opposed the confirmation of Harlan F. Stone, later publicly expressed his regret.

The point about Fuller was, or rather is, that he was a practicing lawyer, and a lawyer only. I need hardly tell this audience that to me being a lawyer, with the full implications of responsibility and opportunity that the word carries, in a society like ours, in a government of laws under a written Constitution, is a calling second to none. Melville Fuller had held no public office of any kind, unless you call being a member of a constitutional convention public office. He was fifty-five years old when he was appointed to the Supreme Court, and he had not only had no judicial experience, he had had, as I have said, no official experience of any kind. I think Fuller was the only man, with the exception of his immediate predecessor, who came to the chief justiceship so wholly without a record in official public life.

When you deal with a number as small as that of the chief justices of the United States, any inference from one or more cases is statistically not of much validity. I merely point out, parenthetically, that five chief justices came to the office without having had prior judicial experience. I do not want you to draw any inference from that fact which you cannot rationally defend. There is much to be said, and I have not time to say it now, on the general question of the relevance of prior judicial experience as a qualification for membership on the Supreme Court. Perhaps, parenthetically again, I can sum up my own views by saying that prior judicial experience should be neither an essential qualification nor, of course, a disqualification. I think that when the President of the United States comes to select someone to fill a vacancy on the Supreme Court, no single factor should be the starting point in his deliberation. He should not say, "I want a man who has had experience as a judge," or, "I want a man who hasn't had experience as a judge." I shall say more about this in a moment, but to me it is important that if you blot out the names of those who came to the Supreme Court without any prior judicial experience, you blot out, in my judgment, barring only two, the greatest names on its roster.

At all events, Fuller came to the Court as a man who had had wide experience at the bar, and, what is important, wide experience at the bar of the Supreme Court and with the kind of business that came before the Supreme Court in his day. He was a dapper little man. I remember vividly seeing him for the first time. I was a student at the Harvard Law School and he was president of the Harvard Alumni Association. He was introducing the speaker of the day, none other than William H. Taft, who had just returned from the Philippines to become secretary of war. Fuller had silvery locks, more silvery and more—what shall I say?—striking, because he was a little man, than the locks of the former senator from Texas, Tom Connally. He was an extremely cultivated man, which is important. He read the classics. He was a student of history. He had felicity of speech.

Fuller came to a Court that wondered what this little man was going to do. There were titans, giants on the bench. They were powerful men, both in experience and in force of conviction, and powerful in physique, as it happened. For myself, I think all justices of the Supreme Court should be big, powerful-looking men! Certainly those whom he met there, who welcomed him courteously but not hopefully, were as I have described them. (Believe it or not, there is ambition even in the breasts of men who sit on the Supreme Court of the United States. There is a good deal to be said for the proposal of Mr. Justice Roberts that no man should ever be appointed to the chief justiceship from the Court.) At any rate, Fuller met on that Court at least four or five men of great stature. The senior among them was Samuel F. Miller, who had been appointed by Lincoln and whose career, incidentally, is an exciting story of American life. Miller started out as a physician and practiced medicine for ten or twelve-odd years, until he became a lawyer and in very quick order a justice of the Supreme Court. He had great native ability, and was a strong man in every sense. Fuller, if they had had the expression in those days, might have been called an egghead. He was a blueblooded intellectual, and the contrast with Miller was great. Then there was Harlan, a six-foot-three, tobacco-chewing Kentuckian. You did not have to come from Kentucky to chew tobacco in those days. They did it in Massachusetts too. But Harlan was all Kentuckian. And there was a smallish man whom I regard as one of the keenest, profoundest intellects that ever sat on that bench, Joseph Bradley of New Jersey. And then were Matthews of Ohio and a six-foot-five- or six-inch giant from Massachusetts, Horace Gray. Those were the big, powerful, self-assured men over whom Melville Fuller came to preside.

They looked upon him, as I have indicated, with doubt and suspicion, but he soon conquered them. They soon felt that the man who presided over them justly presided over them. He had gentle firmness, courtesy, and charm. He also had lubricating humor. Justice Holmes was fond of telling a story. In his early days, he said, "I'm afraid my temper was a little short." (There could hardly have been two men more different than Mr. Justice Holmes, who wielded a rapier, and Mr. Justice Harlan, who wielded a battle-ax. A rapier and a battle-ax locked in combat are likely to beget difficulties for innocent bystanders.) Justice Harlan, who was oratorical while Justice Holmes was pithy, said something during one of the Court's conferences that seemed to Holmes not ultimate wisdom. Justice Holmes said he then did something that ordinarily isn't done in the conference room of the Supreme Court. Each man speaks in order and there are no interruptions, because if you had that you would soon have a Donnybrook Fair instead of orderly discussion. But Holmes afterward said, "I did lose my temper at something that Harlan said and sharply remarked, 'That won't wash. That won't wash.'" Tempers flared and something might have happened. But when Holmes said, "That won't wash," the silver-haired, gentle little chief justice said, "Well, I'm scrubbing away. I'm scrubbing away."

Whether you are in a conference room of the Supreme Court, or *en banc* in a court of appeals, or at faculty meetings, or in a law club, the same kind of thing can happen. When men get short of temper, humor is a great solvent. Fuller had that. He presided with great courtesy. He presided with quiet authority unlike Hughes's, of whom I shall speak shortly. He presided with great but gentle firmness. You couldn't but catch his own mood of courtesy. Advocates, too, sometimes lose their tempers, or, in the heat of argument, say things they should not. There was a subduing effect about Fuller. Soon these men, who looked at him out of the corner of their eyes, felt that they were in the presence of a chief whom they could greatly respect. I have the authority of Mr. Justice Holmes, who sat under four chief justices in Massachusetts before he came down to Washington, and under four (Fuller, White, Taft, Hughes) in Washington, that there never was a better presiding officer, or rather, and more important in some ways, a better moderator inside the conference chamber, than this quiet gentleman from Illinois.

Somehow or other the felicity of his pen, more of his tongue but also his pen—if you will read a speech he made on the occasion of the centennial of the founding of this country, reported in 132 United States Reports,—that charm which he had in occasional writings did not manifest itself, or he did not exert it, in his opinions. You cannot tell the quality or the importance of a man on the Supreme Court solely from his opinions. Mr. Justice Van Devanter, in passing, is a striking illustration of that. And so Fuller's opinions will give you nothing of his charming qualities. He is rather diffuse. He quotes too many cases. And generally he's not an opinion writer whom you read for literary enjoyment, though you can profitably read his nonjudicial things for that purpose.

Fuller was invited to leave the Supreme Court, not to become governor of New York, but because Grover Cleveland was very anxious to have him as his secretary of state. An important document in the history of the judiciary, and I think in the history of the law, is Fuller's letter to President Cleveland stating why a man shouldn't leave the chief justiceship, and, I should add, an associate justiceship, for any political office. He was, as I said, fifty-five years old when he came to the Court. He was chief justice for twenty-two years. The difference in functions between the chief justice and the other members of the Court, is, as Holmes said, mainly on the administrative side, and there never was a better administrator on the Court than Fuller.

I ought to add one thing that seems to me not without interest and not without pleasure to record. I said Fuller was appointed in 1888. That was, let me remind you, a presidential election year. Like every party out of power, the Republicans expected to be returned, as indeed they were. If mere partisanship had ruled, it would not have been difficult to await the result of the election and give the selection of a chief justice to the incoming administration. Instead, the Senate confirmed the Democratic choice of President Cleveland. This broad-minded action reflects honor on all the senators whose votes confirmed Fuller. Especial mention, however, should be made of Senator Shelby M. Cullom of Illinois, who knew Fuller and his qualifications as lawyer and man, and, transcending party considerations, pressed his confirmation. Now, that is a very gratifying thing to one who, like myself, is out of party politics and party attachments—that politicians did not play for position in relation to such a high office.

I must move on. Fuller died in 1910, and the appointment of his successor is a most interesting episode in American history, because Fuller died shortly after President Taft had named Governor Hughes of New York as an associate justice. As a matter of fact, Hughes had not even taken his place when, in the summer, shortly after he was named, Fuller died. President Taft was a great admirer, not unnaturally, of Hughes, who made the decisive campaign speech for Taft in 1908 at Youngstown, Ohio. In offering Governor Hughes the place on the Supreme Court, Taft, with that charming exuberance and forthrightness of his, indicated that Fuller couldn't live forever, and that, of course, he, Hughes, would be the natural choice of Taft for the chief justiceship. He indicated, as much as words can indicate, that he would name Hughes to be chief justice. Then, having doubtless reread the letter after he signed it, he scribbled under it a postscript, being fully aware of his delightful and generous indiscretion, "Of course, I do not make this as a firm promise," or words to that effect. (I'm not quoting accurately.) Governor Hughes, in accepting the position, told the president that of course he was as free as a bird as far as the chief justiceship was concerned.

Well, a vacancy in the chief justiceship did occur six

weeks after this exchange of letters, and everybody expected Hughes to be made chief justice. Hughes took his seat, and it must have been extremely embarrassing for the baby member of the Court to be the heir apparent to the vacant chief justiceship. Some of the older fellows must have disliked the idea. You know, the notion of a freshman runs all through life—younger brother, younger sister, freshman at college, freshman on the Supreme Court.

By that time—1910—the Court had completely changed. Of the men whom Fuller had found when he went there in 1888, only one survived. That was Harlan. There were very strong men on the Court in 1910. It would be a pathetic Court indeed if there weren't always at least some strong men on it. By 1910 there were some new strong men. When Hughes joined the Court he found there, in addition to Mr. Justice Harlan, that nice birdlike creature with a beard, Mr. Justice McKenna of California. Holmes by that time had been on for eight years. There was Mr. Justice White. There was Mr. Justice Day.

They did not like the idea of having this untried New York governor and politician become chief justice. They drew up a round robin to present to Taft, who had appointed some of them. They saw President Taft, I believe, and indicated that they did not like to have their junior member made chief justice. Mr. Justice Holmes, with his characteristic high honor, refused to join this kind of protest. He was perfectly ready to have Hughes become chief justice.

Taft appointed a member of the Court, a powerful member of the Court, Edward D. White of Louisiana. President Taft was glad to appoint—we are so much removed from 1910 in some ways—White as chief justice because White had been a Confederate. It was not until the 'eighties that a Confederate Southerner had again been put on the Supreme Court. That was Lucius Quintus Cincinnatus Lamar of Mississippi. But to make a Confederate, an ex-Confederate—are

Confederates ever "ex"?—chief justice was something that could contribute much, even then, so Taft thought, and I believe rightly, to the cohesion of our national life.

We shall never know the full story of what happened, but within twenty-four hours after the justices called on him there was a change in the mind of Taft, and it was then that White became chief justice. There is the most absurdly contradictory testimony of people who think they do know what happened. Within a half-hour after Taft had summoned Hughes, probably to tell him he was going to be chief justice, he canceled the request that Hughes come. During that time something happened.

Anyhow, White was made chief justice. At the Saturday conference following the sending of White's name to the Senate, Hughes, the junior member of the Court, made what I am told was one of the most gracious speeches of welcome to the new chief justice.

Now let me tell you about Edward D. White. He looked the way a justice of the Supreme Court should look, as I indicated a little while ago. He was tall and powerful. I think a jowl also helps a justice of the Supreme Court, and White had an impressive jowl. He had been a drummer boy in the Confederacy, and that had upon him a very important influence, not only in life, but as a judge—a very profound influence. It is a very interesting thing, but Edward D. White, the Confederate drummer boy, was much more nationalistic, if that phrase carries the meaning I should like it to carry, and was far more prone to find state action forbidden as an interference with federal power, than was Holmes, the Union soldier, who went to his death with three bullets in his body. White was so impressed with the danger of divisiveness and separatism, with the intensification of local interest to the disregard of the common national interest, that again and again and again he found that local action had exceeded the bounds of local authority, because it might weaken and endanger the bonds of national union. One of the most interesting things is the division between him and Holmes in specific instances, where White was, if one may use colloquial, inaccurate terms, for "centralization" and Holmes was for "states' rights."

White had "read" law. He did not have the advantage that you and I have had, of systematic training in the law in a university law school. He was educated by the Jesuits— another very important part of his life, because for him logic and logical analysis played a very important, sometimes an excessive role. Very early he was put on the Supreme Court of Louisiana, but he was there only two years because he was then legislated out of office, or rather the court to which he belonged was. So that he had had only two years of relatively unimportant judicial experience. During those two years he never had a case of the kind which most frequently came to the Supreme Court after he became a member of it. After his brief state judicial career, White practiced law and in 1891 was sent to the Senate of the United States, on the great issue of whether there should or shouldn't be a state lottery. That's a profound question, isn't it? Anyhow, it took him to the Senate of the United States, where he began to play an important part. He was an effective speaker, a man of cultivation, and much respected.

Then comes another one of those incidents which lead me to caution the young in this room not to fix their ambition on becoming the chief justice or even an associate justice of the Supreme Court of the United States. Mr. Justice Blatchford of New York died in 1893 and there were reasons why the natural thing was to pick a New Yorker for his place. This was in the second administration of Cleveland, after he had come back following Harrison's intervening presidency. But the New York politicians had got into an awful row with Cleveland, and the Democratic party in New York was split wide open. The leader of the anti-Cleveland forces, David B. Hill, was in the Senate of the United States. Mr. Cleveland,

who was himself a lawyer of very considerable parts and
knew the bar, first sent in the name of William B. Horn-
blower, a leading member of the New York bar. Senator Hill,
exercising a historic prerogative of senators, said, "I oppose
this nomination." (If a senator from the nominee's state is
opposed to him and speaks the traditional words, the nomination fails. This works on the theory of "you scratch my back
today and I'll scratch yours tomorrow.") So Mr. Horn-
blower's name fell by the wayside.

President Cleveland then sent in a second name, Wheeler
H. Peckham of New York, another one of the really top-
notch lawyers of his day. There was nothing against him
except that he was a Cleveland man, but that was enough for
David B. Hill. He again rose, swirled the toga about him,
and said that he was very sorry but that Mr. Peckham, an
otherwise estimable man, is "personally obnoxious." And so
Mr. Peckham's name was withdrawn. Cleveland was put to
it, and he did what presidents have done before and since.
He drew on that powerful force, the club feeling of the
Senate. And he said, "I'll fix you. I'll name a senator to the
Supreme Court." (They never reject senators for anything,
almost.) So he named Senator White of Louisiana, and within
fifteen minutes Senator White was confirmed.

That's how White came on the Supreme Court in 1894.
He sat for sixteen years as an associate, a very significant
member of the Court, until he was made chief justice at the
age of sixty-five. He had been a judge for sixteen years, but
it's important to remember again that when he was made a
judge he had only this rather unimportant, not very relevant,
not quite two years on the Louisiana Supreme Court. He
remained chief justice from 1910 to 1921.

An important thing in the work of a chief justice which
distinguishes him from other members of the Court is that
he is the presiding officer, and has guidance of the business
of the Court in his charge. It is not what he says in his opin-

ions that is more important than what his brethren say, but what he advises on the mechanics of doing the job—should we give a lawyer extra time, should we hear this case now or later, should we grant a rehearing if the Court is divided? These are things that pertain to the way that the business should be done, things that cannot properly be managed without knowledge of the nature of the business, or, since you deal with eight other human beings, without knowledge of the ways of the other justices.

It is thus very important that, number one, the chief justice should have had some familiarity with the business of the Court before he gets there, and, number two, that he start off on the right foot in his relations with his colleagues, whom he finds there. Of course, influence, in the sense of respect and deference, can be acquired in the course of time, but it makes a lot of difference if the start is a good one. White, when he came to be chief justice in 1910, dealt with men with whom he'd been a judge for periods varying in length from sixteen to a few years. But, as sometimes happens, there soon was a wholesale change in the Court. While a number of the associates remained—McKenna and Holmes and Day— a new lot came on in the other places. A very able lot they were too.

I ought to say something here about the differences in the nature of the business that has come to the Court in different periods. When Fuller assumed office in 1888, the Court dealt a great deal with problems arising from the vast industrialization which the Civil War had set into motion. It was also during Fuller's time that the war with Spain and the acquisition of territory led to new controversies. These events were reflected in the business of the Court—because the Court is a good mirror, of which historians for some reason have little availed themselves, of the struggles of dominant forces outside the Court. Sooner or later the conflicts in the economic and social world result in litigation before the Court. De Tocqueville, in 1832, when he wrote his great book, had the discernment to see what later writers have so often not seen, that by the very nature of our Constitution practically every political question eventually, with us, turns into a judicial question. The question may become somewhat mutilated in the process, but come before the Court it will.

One sometimes reads about the Supreme Court and wonders whether anyone ever studies history any longer. One would suppose that dissenting opinions were a recent discovery. In fact, I am sometimes told that they are an invention brought down by a Harvard professor. Well, the men on Fuller's Court divided drastically and fiercely on the issues of their time. In the Insular Cases, they wrote no fewer than two hundred pages of opinions, which were illuminatingly summarized by that great philosopher, Mr. Dooley, when he said that so far as he could make out, "the Supreme Court decided that the Constitoosh'n follows the flag on Mondays, Wednesdays, and Fridays."

Beginning about in the 'seventies, the states, not yet the Federal Government but the states, began to regulate business. And there came before the Court a series of questions as to the power of the states, in view of the Civil War Amendments. With the Interstate Commerce Act of 1887, we enter upon an era where the Federal Government intervenes. It is the era we are still in, in which I suppose the statistically predominant issues concern the relations between government and business, broadly speaking. During Fuller's period, on the whole, the outlook of the Court was very—what shall I say—inhospitable toward control of business. Restrictions upon the free activities of business came into Court, on the whole, under a serious handicap.

By the time White came to be chief justice the Federal Government had gone in for regulation more and more. Hughes was on the Court, with his great experience, as governor of New York, in regulating business. During White's tenure, Brandeis came on the Court, without any previous judicial experience, but with, I suppose, unparalleled experience in the domain of practical economics, with an understanding of the relations of business to society. Yet, though White came to the chief justiceship with full knowledge of the Court's business and with a strong hold on his colleagues, if anybody thought that merely because of that there would be unanimity of opinion and a want of differences, he was bound to be mistaken. Indeed, during White's tenure the divisions became more frequent and not fewer. But he was master of his job. There was something very impressive about him, both in appearance and otherwise. He was also a great personality. He was a master of speech, though sometimes too abundant speech. I should suppose, on the whole, his opinions are models of how not to write a legal opinion. He made three words grow, usually, where there was room for only one.

The Court became more and more divided in opinion during his period, not because of him, but because the issues became more contentious, the occasions for making broad decisions were fewer, and cases came more and more to be recognized, as Holmes early pointed out and for fifty years continued to point out, as presenting questions of degree.

White was chief justice for only ten years. When he died an astonishing thing happened, unique in the history of this country and not likely to recur, at least as far as one can look ahead—an ex-president of the United States became the chief justice of the United States. That was, of course, William H. Taft.

Now, his case may contradict what I said about not fixing your ambition on a particular job, because William H. Taft, from the time he came to manhood, wanted to become a member of the Supreme Court. His great ambition in life was to be a justice of the Supreme Court, and he finally not only attained it, but with, as it were, a dividend. He became chief justice of the United States. Yet, if I were you, I wouldn't draw too heavily on Taft for encouragement, let alone derive assurance from his case. Let me tell you why.

Taft was a brilliant student, as we all know, at Yale College. I think he would have continued to be even if he had gone to the Harvard Law School, as his son did after him. He went out to Cincinnati and had a quick success at the bar, vindicating the promise of his youth. At thirty-two he was solicitor general, having been on a lower court in Ohio before that. Shortly after the present system of Courts of Appeals, then called Circuit Courts of Appeals, was established in 1891, he became a circuit judge, and he was a notable judge, for eight years, from 1892 to 1900, when McKinley sent him to the Philippines as governor general.

While he was out there, vacancies occurred on the Supreme Court of the United States, and his then bosom friend, Theodore Roosevelt, who knew of his ambition, twice offered him a place on the Supreme Court. To the very great honor of his name it is to be recorded that Taft twice refused that which his personal ambition was most eager to have, because he thought he owed it to the Philippine people not to leave—what's the phrase?—"the plow in the furrow." So twice he put behind him the realization of his personal ambition, because duty commanded him otherwise.

Then he became secretary of war, and after that President of the United States. His heart must have twinged more than once as he had opportunity to put five men on the Supreme Court and fill places that he himself coveted. In 1913 Taft ceased to be President and was promoted to be a professor of law. Well, if any man ever put behind him the thought that he would ever be on the Court, it was William H. Taft, when he went up to New Haven to profess law. If you want to be foolish, if you want your life subject to the hazards of such fortuities as those which determined the fate of William H. Taft, then you can follow his example. Who could have foreseen that the course of events would be such that in 1921 Warren Gamaliel Harding would be President of the United States and would ask William H. Taft to be chief justice?

Taft became chief justice at the age of sixty-three, having been, as I have indicated, a notable judge, but having been out of the business of judging and out of touch with the Supreme Court, except for having filled five of its nine places, for twenty years. He himself said, and he was very happy to say, with that generosity of his which politicians would do well to, but do not often, imitate, that whatever he did as chief justice was made possible by his great reliance on him whom he called his "lord chancellor," Mr. Justice Van Devanter.

Mr. Justice Van Devanter is a man who plays an important role in the history of the Court, though you cannot find it adequately reflected in the opinions written by him because he wrote so few. But Van Devanter was a man of great experience. He'd been chief justice of Wyoming. He was then made a United States circuit judge and in 1910 he became a member of the Supreme Court. He had a very clear, lucid mind, the mind, should I say, of a great architect. He was a beautiful draftsman and an inventor of legal techniques who did much to bring about the reforms which were effectively accomplished by Taft as chief justice.

Taft's great place in judicial history, I think, will be as a law reformer. In the characteristic way of this country, various federal judges throughout the country were entirely autonomous, little independent sovereigns. Every judge had his own little principality. He was the boss within his district, and his district was his only concern. A judge was a judge where he was, and although he may have had very little business, he couldn't be used in regions where the docket was congested. This, as you know, was changed, and the change has been highly beneficial.

An even more important reform for which Taft was effectively responsible was the legislation authorizing the Supreme
Court to be master in its own household, which means that
the business which comes to the Supreme Court is the business
which the Supreme Court allows to come to it. Very few
cases can come up without getting its prior permission. So
that cases which never should take the time, energy, and
thought of the ultimate tribunal in the land are allowed to
rest, if they come from the federal courts, after those courts
have had two go's at them, or, if the cases come from the
state courts, after they have received the hierarchal adjudication provided by the state. No longer is it true, as it was
before this legislation, that a case would come to the Supreme
Court automatically after it had gone through, let us say, four
other courts, as though having an endless litigation were one
of the God-given rights of the American citizen.

So Chief Justice Taft has a place in history, in my judgment, next to Oliver Ellsworth, who originally devised the
judicial system. Chief Justice Taft adapted it to the needs
of a country that had grown from three million to a hundred
and twenty million.

Taft was, of course, very genial. He did not have to learn
to be genial. It is better to learn to be genial than not to be
genial at all, but Taft was instinctively genial, with great
warmth, and a capacity to inspire feelings of camaraderie
about him. When he came to the chief justiceship in 1921,
the papers had been full, as the papers are from time to time
nowadays, of talk about the great divisions on the Court.
Laymen are constantly troubled, even as are lawyers, especially when they lose a case, about divisions on the Court.
But why should anyone expect nine men, presumably there
because of their special capabilities, all to have the same
thoughts and views? One would suppose that nine men are
put there because you want variety of thought. No one ex-

pects such harmony and identity of views among physicists, let alone among professors of sociology or history. Why should they expect nine people to know how to apply in unison and in concord such delightfully vague phrases or concepts as "due process of law," phrases, as a great judge once said, of "calculated ambiguity"? To be sure, there can be no difference of opinion on the proposition that twelve is twelve; and it is clear, therefore, that a jury must have twelve members under the federal system. But when it comes to things like, when does a state encroach upon the right of Congress to regulate commerce, or what kind of limitations may you put upon people who want to speak at Hyde Park, or in Union Square, or on the Lawn of the University of Virginia, that's a different story.

When Taft became chief justice there had been this succession of great divisions on the Court—serious divisions on very serious matters. And every once in a while there were five-to-four decisions. Just as the newspapers do not print, "Mr. and Mrs. Jones have been happily married for fifteen years this day," but would print somewhere in the paper that Mr. and Mrs. Jones are getting a divorce, so the newspapers do not often publicize the cases in which the Court is unanimous. I can assure you that there are a great many such— most of them, in fact. What captures the headlines are the divisions: "The Supreme Court divides on minimum wages. The Supreme Court divides on child labor. The Supreme Court divides on this and that."

The appointment of Taft gave rise to the hope that all this would end. "He's such a charming man, don't you know?" I like to recall a newspaper editorial printed when Mr. Taft was appointed chief justice in June 1921. The present New York *Herald Tribune*, the then New York *Tribune*, commented, as did every paper in the country, on what a delightful man William H. Taft was, how charming, how everybody liked him, and now there would be no more five-to-four opinions. I thought the *Tribune* put it best: "Mr. Taft has such tact and good humor, and has so unconquerable a spirit of fair play, that he is greatly beloved of his fellow citizens. These gifts and this character may not be the first ones sought for in a chief justice, but even the most eminent judges are none the worse for having them. With Justice Taft as a moderator"—now listen to this—"it is probable that not a few asperities that mar the harmony of the celestial chamber, the consulting room, not a few of those asperities will be softened and that not quite so often in the future will the court divide five and four."

I really think that's very funny. The assumption of this serious editorial writer that Taft, C.J., would just smile and then Holmes would say, "Aye, aye, sir," or Justice Van Devanter would say, "For ten years I've been disagreeing with Holmes, but now that you've smiled at both of us, why we just love each other." I suggest a subject for a paper by one of you students. I have never done it, but my impression is strong that a count would show more five-to-four decisions during Taft's time than during White's time, or certainly just as many. Life was very pleasant with Taft as chief justice, but judicial conflicts existed because the problems before the Court evoked them. As for asperities during the period between '21 and '30, when Taft left—I think the conference was just as lively a place. I was not there, but the sparks even carried outside of the conference room to singe the pages of the United States Reports.

Of course Taft knew the men on the Court well, and he found there two whom he had appointed. That did not prevent those two from disagreeing with him, I can assure you. One of the strongest and most memorable of the dissenting opinions against Taft was written by a man whom he had appointed. What judge would be worth his salt if it made any difference to him that the President who appointed him, whether he was on or off the Court, disagreed with him?

What judge worth his salt would have his convictions influenced by whether the chief justice is a charming man and a delightful raconteur, or not? That isn't the nature of the enterprise.

In 1930 Taft became ill and retired. He always had the love and affection of his colleagues. He and Brandeis, when Taft was President, crossed swords very fiercely indeed; Brandeis was counsel in the famous Pinchot-Ballinger attack on the administration. But they became fast friends on the Court. One of the things that laymen, even lawyers, do not always understand is indicated by the question you hear so often: "Does a man become any different when he puts on a gown?" I say, "If he is any good, he does."

Taft was followed, of course, by Hughes. Now the last thing that Hughes ever expected to be after he left the Court in 1916 to run for the presidency (I have ventured to say in print that I believe this was the one act of his life which he regretted)—he later became secretary of state, then became a member of the World Court, and finally returned to the bar to, I suppose, as vast a practice as that of any man at the bar in our time, or at any time in the history of this country—the last thing Hughes expected to become was chief justice. He was, to Hoover's great surprise, subjected to severe attack when his name was sent in. He finally was confirmed, though it was a nip and tuck business. He took his seat at the center of the Court, with a mastery, I suspect, unparalleled in the history of the Court, a mastery that derived from his experience, as diversified, intense, and extensive, as any man ever brought to a seat on the Court, combined with a very powerful and acute mind that could mobilize these vast resources in the conduct of the business of the Court. There must be in this room lawyers who came before the Court when Chief Justice Hughes presided. To see him preside was like witnessing Toscanini lead an orchestra.

Aside from the power to assign the writing of opinions,

which is his by custom, and of which I shall speak, a chief
justice has no authority that any other member of the Court
has not. That really is an institution in which every man is
his own sovereign. The chief justice is *primus inter pares.*
Somebody has to preside at a sitting of nine people, and he
presides in court and at conference. But Chief Justice Hughes
radiated authority, not through any other quality than the
intrinsic moral power that was his. He was master of the
business. He could disembowel a brief and a record. He had
an extraordinary memory and vast experience in the conduct
of litigation, and of course he had been on the Court six years,
from 1910 to 1916. And he had intimate and warm relations
with some of the men he found on the Court. He was a great
admirer of that greatest intellect, in my judgment, who ever
sat on the Court, Mr. Justice Holmes. He was an old friend
at the bar of Mr. Justice Brandeis. He had been one year
in the cabinet with Stone. So he not only felt at home in the
courtroom, he felt at home with his colleagues.

I have often used a word which for me best expresses the
atmosphere that Hughes generated; it was taut. Everything
was taut. He infected and affected counsel that way. Everybody was better because of Hughes, the leader of the orchestra. That was true, too, of Cardozo, when he was chief judge
of the New York Court of Appeals. One is told that the
same men were somehow or other better when he was chief
judge than they were the next day after he had ceased to
be chief judge. That is a common experience in life. One
man is able to bring things out of you that are there, if they
are evoked, if they are sufficiently stimulated and directed.
Chief Justice Hughes had that very great quality.

Chief Justice Stone is the antithesis, in the fate that was
allotted to him, of Marshall and Taney and Fuller. If you're
chief justice for only five years, as Stone was, even though
you come to the chief justiceship after having been an associate, the opportunities to realize on the moral opportunities

that place gives you are necessarily very limited. Time plays
a very important part. Stone came to the head of the Court
in 1941. He had been an associate justice since 1925. Before
that he had been a professor of law and dean of a law school,
an extensive practitioner in New York, and then attorney
general of the United States. He was familiar with the business of the Court. He was a very different personality from
Hughes. Hughes was dynamic and efficient. That's a bad
word to apply to Hughes, because it implies regimentation.
It implies something disagreeable, at least to me. I don't like
a man to be too efficient. He's likely to be not human enough.
But that wasn't true of Hughes. He simply was effective—
not efficient, but effective. Stone was much more easygoing.
The conference was more leisurely. The atmosphere was less
taut, both in the courtroom and the conference room. It has
been said that there wasn't free and easy talk in Hughes's
day in the conference room. Nothing could be further from
the truth. There was less wasteful talk. There was less talk
that was repetitious, or indeed foolish. You just didn't talk
unless you were dead sure of your ground, because that gimlet
mind of his was there ahead of you.

Stone was an "easy boss," as it were. Boss is the worst word
to use with reference to a chief justice of the United States,
because that's precisely what he is not. Anybody who tried
it would not try it long. There is one function, however, that
the chief justice has by virtue of being chief justice, other
than being the administrator, presiding in open court, presiding at conference and there opening the discussion on each
case. That other function is, I believe, the most important of
all that pertains to the office of chief justice. I know not how
it is in the Supreme Court of Appeals of Virginia. The method
of designating the member of the court who writes the opinion for the court varies in the various state courts. In New
York, for instance, it goes by rotation. That's a practice very
common in this country. Even when it goes that way, a great

man can make a dent on the accidental system by which cases come to him. They used to say in New York, until they knew better, "Why is it that Cardozo always gets the interesting cases?" The answer was that no matter what case he got, he made it interesting; he didn't "get" it—it came to him in automatic order. I believe it is a fact, though it is so strange a fact that I shall not identify the state, but I am assured on dependable authority that in the Supreme Court of at least one of our states, and not the least populous of states, they shake dice to determine who should write an opinion. Having it go in order lacks, for my taste at least, that aleatory aspect that dice have.

From Marshall's time in the Supreme Court the chief justice has designated the member of the Court who writes the opinion of the Court. As most of you know, we hear argument five days a week and on Saturday there is a conference. After everybody has had his say, beginning with the chief justice and following in order of seniority—and everybody can say whatever he wants to say—there is a formal vote. In order that the junior should not be influenced, everybody having already expressed his view, the formal voting begins with the junior. (How careful we are not to coerce anybody!) After conference, in cases in which the chief justice is with the majority, as he is in most instances, he designates the member of the Court who is to write the opinion. If he is in the minority, then the next senior justice of those in the majority does the assigning. So that in most of the cases the chief justice decides who is to speak for the Court. As for dissents and concurrences—that's for each member to choose for himself.

You can see the important function that rests with the chief justice in determining who should be the spokesman of the Court in expressing the decision reached. The manner in which a case is stated, the grounds on which a decision is rested—one ground rather than another, or one ground rather

than two grounds—how much is said and how it is said, what
kind of phrasing will give least trouble in the future in a system of law in which as far as possible you are to decide the
concrete issue and not embarrass the future too much—all
these things matter a great deal. The deployment of his
judicial force by the chief justice is his single most influential
function. Some do it with ease. Some do it with great anguish. Some do it with great wisdom. Some have done it
with less than great wisdom.

No chief justice, I believe, equaled Chief Justice Hughes
in the skill and the wisdom and the disinterestedness with
which he made his assignments. Some cases are more interesting than others, and it is the prerogative of the chief justice
not only to be kindly and fair and generous in the distribution of cases, but also to appear to be so. The task calls for
qualities of tact, understanding, and skill in the effective
utilization of the particular qualities that are available. Should
one man become a specialist in a subject? Or is it important
not to place too much reliance on one man because he's a
great authority in the field? Should you pick the man who
will write the opinion in the narrowest possible way? Or
should you take the chance of putting a few seeds in the
earth for future flowering? Those are all very difficult, delicate, and responsible questions.

I must conclude this discursive narrative—this almost absurd
attempt, in a short talk, to give you some sense of five men
who have been at the head of a Court on which ultimately
rests the maintenance of the equilibrium between central authority and the constituent states, between the authority of
government, whether state or national, and the liberties of the
individual.

As I said earlier, when you deal with such few instances,
you do not have a statistical basis for generalization. If I
wanted to be a little playful, I might say I leave generalizations to political scientists who sometimes think that the

crude details are not worthy of high philosophical attention. I hope I have indicated enough, however, to disclose that in view of the functions of the Supreme Court what you want in a justice is not a specialist in this or that field, not necessarily a man who has had prior experience on the bench, not necessarily a man who has been broadened by high office, as was the case with Hughes, rather than broadened by the depth and range of his reading and his thinking, as in the case of Mr. Justice Holmes.

What is essential for the discharge of functions that are almost too much, I think, for any nine mortal men, but have to be discharged by nine fallible creatures, is that you get men who bring to their task, first and foremost, humility and an understanding of the range of the problems and of their own inadequacy in dealing with them, disinterestedness, and allegiance to nothing except the effort, amid tangled words and limited insights, to find the path through precedent, through policy, through history, to the best judgment that fallible creatures can reach in that most difficult of all tasks: the achievement of justice between man and man, between man and state, through reason called law.

Three

"The Administrative Side" of Chief Justice Hughes

(1949)

This article, discussing primarily the role of Chief Justice Hughes as presiding officer of the Supreme Court, appeared in the November 1949 issue of the *Harvard Law Review* (Vol. 63, p. 1).

IT IS OFTEN SAID of a contemporary figure destined for historical survival that it is too early to pass judgment on his work. The assumption is that the future will pass a definitive judgment. But there never is a definitive appraisal. Each generation places its own valuations; reputations grow and recede, only to grow again and recede. Even majestic figures— Shakespeare and Washington—have fluctuating recognition. No doubt the future attenuates merely personal bias, but it gives no assurance of freedom from partisanship. In any event, contemporary judgment may contribute the impact of vividness and immediacy, which only the most imaginative artist can later create. The limitations of contemporary judgment derive not so much from its closeness to the subject; they are due to the fragmentary materials on which judgment is based. Though history cannot be written solely out of documents, it cannot be written without relevant but as yet inaccessible documents.

This is peculiarly true of the appraisal of contributions made by members of the Supreme Court to the stream of thought which courses through its decisions. The Court's opinions often disclose merely the surface of the judicial process. The compromises that an opinion may embody, the collaborative effort that it may represent, the inarticulate considerations that may have influenced the grounds on which the case went off, the shifts in position that may precede final adjudication—these and like factors cannot, contemporaneously at all events, be brought to the surface.

It is true of opinions as of other compositions that those who are steeped in them, whose ears are sensitive to literary nuances, whose antennae record subtle silences, can gather from their contents meaning beyond the words. All this presupposes, of course, a grasp of the nature of the Supreme Court's functions—the scope and limits of its constitutional authority—and often, as well, familiarity with the record and briefs of a particular case whose opinion is under scrutiny. Even the most professionally equipped critic possessed of the faculties of a creative artist would be severely handicapped, however, in attempting a balanced estimate of the work of a chief justice of the United States if he were restricted to what is found in the United States Reports. And no fellow member of the Court may contemporaneously add to what those Reports tell.

But he may speak of the chief justice as head of the Court. Even of that not all can be told contemporaneously. The relations of a chief with his colleagues and with the officials of the Court affect the conduct of the Court's business. The influence of a tough-minded chief justice in encouraging, if not prodding, a temperamentally indecisive judge to make up his mind may have important consequences in the development of our law. But these are matters that call for exact knowledge that can only become available, if at all, when disclosure is justifiable. Such exact knowledge cannot be conveyed through the distorting and often falsifying medium of surmise and gossip.

For me the qualities of Charles Evans Hughes, as chief justice, are conveyed strikingly by Mr. Justice Holmes in speaking of Chief Justice Fuller:

> Of course the function of the Chief Justice differs from that of the other judges only on the administrative side, but on that I think he was extraordinary. He had the business of the Court at his fingers' ends, he was perfectly courageous, prompt, decided. He turned off the matters that daily called for action easily, swiftly, with the least possible friction, with inestimable good humor and with a humor that relieved any tension with a laugh.[1]

Chief Justice Hughes brought to this "administrative side" uncommon powers of concentration, wide relevant experience, a high sense of responsibility, complete absorption in the work of the Court, fidelity to its best traditions not as worship of the past but as a stimulus toward promoting the most fruitful administration of justice.

He knew that the manner of conducting the business of the Court affects the matter. This realization guided him in the watchful exercise of the power the Congress has vested in the Court to control its business. He tried to avoid a swollen docket which precludes the brooding process indispensable for wise adjudication. In Court and in conference he struck the pitch, as it were, for the orchestra. He guided discussion by opening up the lines for it to travel, focusing on essentials, evoking candid exchange on subtle and complex issues, and avoiding redundant talk. He never checked free debate, but the atmosphere which he created, the moral authority which he exerted, inhibited irrelevance, repetition, and fruitless discussion. He was a master of timing: he knew when discussion should be deferred and when brought to an issue. He also

---

[1] King, *Melville Weston Fuller*, (1950), pp. 334-35.

showed uncommon resourcefulness in drawing elements of
agreement out of differences and thereby narrowing, if not
always escaping, conflicts. He knew when a case was over;
he had no lingering afterthoughts born of a feeling of defeat,
and thereby avoided the fostering of cleavages. Intellectual
issues were dealt with by him as such. As a result, differences
in opinion did not arouse personal sensitiveness. Partly a disciplined mind, partly long experience at the bar, made him
treat a case that was over as over, whether victory or defeat
fell to his views. This capacity for detachment also reflected
his keen sense of humor, which it often pleased him to conceal; partly such detachment must be ascribed to great con-
servation of energy that saved him from crying over spilt
milk.

Perhaps no aspect of the "administrative side" that is vested
in the chief justice is more important than the duty to assign
the writing of the Court's opinion. In its discharge, Chief
Justice Hughes was like a general deploying his army. His
governing consideration was what was best for the Court as
to the particular case in the particular situation. That meant
disregard of self but not of the importance of the chief justiceship as a symbol. For there are occasions when an opinion
should carry the extra weight which pronouncement by the
chief justice gives. Selection of the Court's voice also calls
for resourcefulness, so that the Court should not be denied
the persuasiveness of a particular justice, though himself pro-
cedurally in dissent, in speaking for the Court on the merits.[2]
The grounds for assignment may not always be obvious to
the outsider. Indeed, they are not always so to the members
of the Court; the reasons normally remain within the breast
of the chief justice. But these involve, if the duty is wisely
discharged, perhaps the most delicate judgment demanded of
the chief justice.

[2] See Mr. Justice Cardozo's opinion in *Helvering* v. *Davis*, 301 U.S. 619,
639-640 (1937).

Chief Justice Hughes was an administrator of distinction: he brought things to pass effectively and without friction. But while he gave creative guidance to the Conference of Senior Circuit Judges and the Administrative Office of the United States Courts in making the federal judiciary more responsive to the tasks of a civilized legal system, he avoided the temptations of a strong executive. He realized fully that elaboration of administrative machinery is deadening to the judicial process, that the individual excellence of the judges, not paper efficiency, matters most.

The Supreme Court is a student's life and Chief Justice Hughes could tear the heart out of books because all his life he had been a student. He was also uncompromising with the Court's austere demands. He knew that these austerities promote dignity, that dignity makes for an atmosphere of respect, and that only in such an atmosphere can reason thrive. And without reason, law is merely a screen of words expressing will in the service of desire.

Four

The Impact of Charles Evans Hughes

(1951)

This review of Merlo J. Pusey's two-volume biography of Charles Evans Hughes appeared in the New York *Times* for November 18, 1951.

A REVIEWER OPENS with misgivings the Life of a contemporary public character with whom he worked intimately. Not that a current attempt to convey such a figure is undesirable, for though time may bring to light documents and disclosures not within reach of our uninhibited and indiscreet era, time also dims. About some aspects of a man, his contemporaries are the best witnesses. The true face even of a public man is his private face. That can be seen only off stage, in the manner in which he pursues his tasks, day by day, when only those in close association see and hear and feel what he is doing. But a dominant figure is bound to be controversial, and a contemporary biography too readily invites hagiography or debunking.

Let it be said at once that Merlo J. Pusey wholly escapes both temptations. Every biography reflects a viewpoint. The account and appraisal of another man's life are distilled in the alembic of the biographer's judgment. But it makes all the difference in the world whether the judgment is romantic, whether it imposes a preconceived view or passionate feeling upon objectively ascertainable materials, or whether judgment derives from those materials. During the years that Hughes frequently argued cases before him in the New York Court of Appeals, Judge Cardozo purposefully kept his mind in suspense for twenty-four hours after the conclusion of Hughes's argument. Cardozo said he did so after he came to realize the impact upon him of Hughes's personality. Pusey has felt that impact. No one who was actively associated with Hughes could fail to feel it, unless he were imperviously insignificant or self-consumed. The detached Balfour and the powerful Brandeis were equally impressed. Without reflecting this impact, Pusey could not fairly convey Hughes. But he is not subordinated by it in his search for the truth about Hughes's purposes and performance.

After finishing these eight hundred pages, at least one reader wishes that a pen as incisive as Walter Bagehot's or as tart as Lytton Strachey's could write a biographical essay in order to contribute to the understanding of a towering personality, even when economizing truth. But it is fortunate that Chief Justice Hughes entrusted his papers to so conscientious and responsible a digger into materials as Pusey for his authorized Life. The impact of Hughes has not only evoked in Pusey an admiring estimate of Hughes's great services to his country as well as of the power and charm of his personality; Hughes has also infected his biographer with his own judicial standards. Pusey faces the controversial aspects of Hughes—of his policies as well as of his personal conduct. It is unimportant how he strikes the balance. What matters is that he does not blink at what may fairly be brought against Hughes's position, and Pusey himself freely expresses criticism that is not mealy-mouthed.

The Life of Hughes has to be woven on the loom of a half-century of our political-judicial history. With a due sense of proportion, Pusey gives us Hughes in that context without losing him in it. Through Pusey's lucid and measured narrative, Hughes emerges as the clearheaded, impressive, self-disciplined, resourceful, witty, companionable, energizing, exacting, and considerate person that all who worked with him in the various roles of his long life will recognize through their own experience. And his lifelong romance with Mrs. Hughes should not go without mention.

Those of us who lived through the exciting days of the relentless but wholly fair investigator, through the Albany years with the moral and intellectual standards in government heightened not as precepts but in practice, through that day of dramatic leadership at the Washington Conference with its justifiable hopes of a disarming world, not the less significant because thereafter cruelly subverted, through the years of Hughes's occupancy of John Marshall's seat, will have the memories of those great days revivified by this account of them by Pusey. And the younger generation, whose participation in history comes through the printed page, should find in Pusey a reliable guide.

Major controversies, to which Hughes as Governor of New York and as Secretary of State gave rise, are bound to remain legacies for history. This is not the occasion, and I certainly am not the person, to indulge in the critical discussion of them or of their treatment by Pusey. Suffice it to say, as already indicated, Pusey does not flinch facing them and he strikes a fine note of temperateness for future disputants. History may alter Pusey's perspective or shift his emphasis, not merely because new documentation may come to the surface but also because from time to time historians reflect a change of mood or of interest in the past.

But one event in Hughes's life is bound to remain as much a matter of individual judgment, certainly within the legal profession, as it was a torturing issue for him—his resignation from the Supreme Court to accept the nomination for the presidency. Of one thing there cannot be a shadow of doubt

—that he did not lift a finger to secure the nomination and that he sorrowfully acted out of a sense of duty in a situation which was not of his making nor even of his encouragement. But the question will not down, futile as such doubts of retrospective wisdom are, whether at the end of his life he would not have preferred the rule of conduct he formulated in 1912, when he declined to be drafted, to the exception he made in 1916: "The highest service that I can render in this difficult situation is to do all in my power to have it firmly established that a Justice of the Supreme Court is not available for political candidacy. The Supreme Court must be kept out of politics."

On matters that lie in the domain of judgment, no book can have the last word. But a basic misconception concerning the manner of man Charles Evans Hughes was surely will not survive Pusey's Life. How the notion of Hughes as a cold, unfeeling, mental machine gained currency deserves a good chapter in any history of the dissemination of error. No doubt he was a man of terrific concentration and of the most disciplined intellectual habits. His work took possession of him—whether in his masterly examination of witnesses in the Insurance Investigation, or in his devastating campaign against Hearst, or in carrying to the people his policies as Governor, or in his various official appearances as Secretary of State, or in the Supreme Court, alike when arguing before it or presiding over it.

In short, he was seized by his task precisely as a poet by his inspiration. And since he had, as he once said of himself, "a positive genius for privacy," there was conveyed to the public, on the basis of his intense attention to public duties, this image of an unfeeling and humorless mere brain. His mode of life on the bench confirmed this caricature. He acted on the realization that aloofness is indispensable to the effective discharge of the Supreme Court's functions.

What a caricature! He was genial though not promiscuous,

full of fun and whimsy, a delightful tease and sparkling storyteller, a responsive listener and stimulating talker, drawing without show or pedantry on the culture of a man of wide interests and catholic reading. If he made others feel his moral superiority, they merely felt a fact. He was self-critical rather than self-righteous, extremely tolerant toward views he did not share and even deemed mischievous, impressed as he was, on reflecting a half-century's experience since leaving college, "first, that there was so much that we did not learn, and, second, that we learned so many things that were not so." When Hughes left the Court in 1916, Holmes, who was not drawn to the solemn and arid, wrote his friend Pollock: "I shall miss him consumedly, for he is not only a good fellow, experienced and wise, but funny, and with doubts that open vistas through the wall of a non-conformist conscience." (*Holmes-Pollock Letters*, (Howe ed., 1946), Vol. I, p. 237.)

But when Hughes put himself on paper the style is not the man. Except on rare occasions, he seemed consciously to exclude from his writing the qualities of his talk—apposite yarns, gay quotations, quiet irony, the wit of a tentative and skeptical outlook. The quality of his writing, particularly on the Court, is sober, rather lapidary, doubtless to conform to his notion of what an opinion should be, as a sonnet has its fourteen lines.

But the opinions of Supreme Court judges do not tell the tale of their significance. It is fair prophecy that it is as chief justice that Hughes will become an enduring figure. He was, in fact, the head of two courts, so different in its composition was the supreme bench in the two periods of the decade during which Hughes presided over it. However sharp the conflict on the issues that came before the Court, all who served with him recognized the extraordinary combination of qualities possessed by the chief justice—subordination of all else to the work of the Court, complete disinterestedness in its service, humor that saves differences from becoming discord, and the translation into daily practice of the precepts of tolerance and reason and bracing good will.

The nine men on the Court are coequals. Each in his work is a law unto himself, except for an overriding sense that he is the trustee of the most important traditions in our national system. The test of leadership in such a body is intrinsic authority. No one who served with him would gainsay that Chief Justice Hughes possessed it to a conspicuous degree. In open court he exerted this authority by the mastery and distinction with which he presided. He radiated this authority in the conference room. There was nothing meretricious or assertive about him. Chief Justice Hughes did not rely upon his position; he fulfilled it.

The legal system of every living society, even when embodied in a written constitution, must itself be alive. Such a constitution does not merely enshrine the past. It is designed to give full scope to the future. Of all the forms of a national community, a federal system is the most complicated. It demands the greatest flexibility and imagination to harmonize national and local interests. The Constitution of the United States is thus not a historic parchment in a glass case. It is a continuous process of delicate governmental adjustments. And its judicial application is not a mechanical exercise, but a profound task of statecraft exercised by judges set apart from the turbulence of politics.

The verdict of history will not be hurried. Nearly a century elapsed before we had an adequate account of the judicial labors of Chief Justice Marshall. But to anticipate history's verdict in some instances is neither folly nor arrogance. We can say with confidence that Chief Justice Hughes will join the enduring architects of the federal structure within which our nation lives and moves and has its being.

Barring only the narrow margin by which he missed the presidency (which he himself came to regard a stroke of fortune), Hughes's life is a story of triumph, remembering

Burke's reminder, as the Lord Chief Justice of England once reminded Hughes, that "calumny and abuse are essential parts of triumph."

What is the meaning of such a career as Hughes's in the life of the nation? Let me borrow the words of Judge Learned Hand to define it. "If any society is to prosper, it must be staffed with servants of such stuff; indeed, if any society is to endure, it must not be without them. Sure-footed time will tread out the lesser figures of our day; but, if our heritage does not perish, the work of this man and his example will remain a visible memorial of one who helped to keep alive and pass on that ordered freedom without which mankind must lapse into savagery, and repeat its slow and bitter ascent to even that level of mutual forbearance and good-will which it has now attained. We who knew him can do no better than to record our gratitude for a life to which we have owed so much." (*The Spirit of Liberty*, (Dilliard ed., 1952), p. 222.)

Five

Chief Justice Stone

(1946)

Mr. Justice Frankfurter wrote this biographical memoir of Chief Justice Stone for the *Year Book* of the American Philosophical Society (1946 vol., p. 334).

IT WAS CHARACTERISTIC of Harlan Stone's zest for life that he made no preparations for death. And the circumstances of his death were characteristic of his good fortune. There was no tapering off; rather was he interrupted in labor which engaged the whole of him and just after he had pronounced the principle which should be the polestar of the Supreme Court as he understood its place in our scheme. "It is not the function of this Court to disregard the will of Congress in the exercise of its constitutional power" (*Girouard* v. *United States,* 328 U.S. 61, 79)—such was the message he uttered from the seat of the chief justiceship at the very moment that death summoned him on April 22, 1946.

One may be preoccupied with law professionally in five different ways, as teacher, practitioner, administrator, judge, and philosopher. No one can pursue all these callings at the same time and the name does not readily occur of anyone who has done so in due succession if philosophy of law implies dwelling on the high plateau of original thought worthy of the company of thinkers like Holmes. But Stone followed all the other four callings and in each he achieved the acclaim of his professional compeers.

Little imagination is needed to clothe the bare facts of his life with the meaning and significance of his career. Harlan Fiske Stone, the second child of Frederick L. and Anne Sophia (Butler) Stone, was born on October 11, 1872, in Chesterfield, New Hampshire, one of those very small towns of New England with a shrinking population. He was of English stock, but, while professionally he was rooted in English legal traditions, in him, as in many a Yankee, a critical attitude of British policy could easily assert itself. During his childhood the Stone family moved to Amherst, Massachusetts, where the future chief justice attended the district school and Amherst High School. Harlan was destined by his father to become a scientific farmer and to that end entered the Massachusetts Agricultural College in 1889. The inscrutable fates evidently had purposes of their own. Harlan's student days at that college, and thereby his paternal predestination as a farmer, were quickly terminated by a row in which blows were said to have been exchanged between the sturdy freshman and a member of the faculty. Harlan went back to the ancestral farm until he entered Amherst the next fall. His college career gave promise of all that followed. Under a strong faculty and in rivalry with contemporaries who subsequently became notable in affairs as well as in the world of scholarship, Harlan was an outstanding man of his time at Amherst, attaining distinction both in the classroom and on the gridiron. On graduation in 1894, he followed a familiar American pattern by teaching for a year at the Newburyport, Massachusetts, High School. He taught science, for which he had a bent that happily stood him in good stead when as a judge he had to decide patent law cases. But science as a dominant strain emerged not in him but in his son, Marshall, a distinguished mathematician.

Harlan's drive was for law. He received this training at the

Columbia Law School from men of eminence as scholars and teachers. A year after he was graduated, he returned as a part-time lecturer while he quickly made his way at the bar. From 1905 to 1910, he devoted himself exclusively to practice with his firm, Satterlee, Canfield & Stone. In 1910 he accepted the call to head his law school. Throughout his deanship, he taught two of the basic courses in the training of lawyers, equity and trusts. These specialties were likewise reflected in his judicial work, for they are aspects of law bringing into play, perhaps more than others, ethical principles and their resourceful adaptation to changing circumstances. Only a man endowed with Stone's great vitality and his disciplined powers of concentration could have successfully led a great law school and at the same time met the demands of a large practice. Whether because the burden finally became too heavy even for him or the allurements of practice, particularly of advocacy, too great, he resigned from Columbia in 1923 to become a member of Sullivan & Cromwell.

Again the fates willed otherwise. Attorney General Harry M. Daugherty's malodorous administration of the Department of Justice had so shocked the public conscience that when he was finally retired that other Yankee, President Calvin Coolidge, saw clearly enough that the imperative need of the situation was an appointment that would at once restore public confidence in the integrity of the Department of Justice. And so, on April 7, 1924, President Coolidge appointed his Amherst college mate Harlan F. Stone. Thereby, the public disquietude was lifted. This restoration of confidence in the country's ministry of justice was Stone's dominant contribution as attorney general. He was there too short a time for much else. Within a year a vacancy on the Supreme Court fell in, through the retirement of Mr. Justice McKenna. On January 5, 1925, President Coolidge nominated Harlan Fiske Stone to fill the place left vacant, and he took his seat on the supreme bench on March 2, 1925. Because of professional as-

sociation between Stone and a son-in-law of the elder Morgan
there was opposition to his confirmation in the Senate, led by
Senator George W. Norris. This is worth noting because
of its sequel. When, upon the retirement of Chief Justice
Hughes in 1941, Mr. Justice Stone was nominated by President Roosevelt to be chief justice, he was promptly confirmed
and Senator Norris in the handsomest way recanted his opposition of 1925. This episode in the too uncommon chapter of
candor in American politics did credit alike to Senator Norris
and Mr. Justice Stone.

Stone's career divides into two major epochs: for twenty
years he was a teacher, for twenty years he was a judge. For
him these were not disparate callings. One was the logical
fruition of the other. His academic career deeply infused his
judicial work. As teacher he was concerned with the place of
law and lawyers in society. As a judge he made heavy drafts
upon the intellectual capital he had laid up in his own career
as an academician, and he continued to draw freely upon the
common property of scholarship.

As academician he helped to promote the movement of the
study of law, primarily not as occupational training but as a
branch of the social sciences. He recognized that a shift in
economic and social forces demanded a corresponding shift
in the training and the functions of the bar. The history and
the technique of law were related to its social purposes and
its study required to be pursued by application to working
hypotheses, constantly subjected to re-examination, of those
standards of accuracy and thoroughness which are the essentials of the scientific method. He was hospitable to new ideas,
responsive to critical reconsideration of methods of teaching
and student examination as well as of the validity of particular
institutions for contemporary needs, no matter what historical title deeds they might have. (See "The Public Influence of the Bar," November 1934, 48 *Harv. Law Rev.* 1,
and "The Common Law in the United States," November

1936, 50 *Harv. Law Rev.* 4, the two papers by which, perhaps, he would most want to be judged.) There are ample reflections in his opinions of his regard for learning as the path to understanding and as indispensable to wise adjudication. While recognizing necessary adaptations to changes in economic fact, he insisted, in his utterances, on the perdurance of the conditions essential for a free society, no matter how much direction or control comes increasingly from the center. Indeed, because of the almost inevitable extension and concentration of governmental authority, those conditions become more and not less necessary. He believed in freedom of utterance to the extent that he was ready to face the hazards of thought, even of murky or reckless thought.

His years on the Court, interestingly enough, made him feel more rather than less the importance of the law teacher in the circumstances of our time. Partly because of the influence of specialization and undue identification with interests of clients that are less than those of society, active practitioners have not the opportunity nor do they form the habit of seeing law as a historic process, or of helping to fashion it as a fair social instrument. The law teachers are set apart, as it were, for these services to law. Indeed, the life of a law teacher was probably the most congenial to him, if one is to judge from his memorial writings of colleagues in teaching. Almost invariably he speaks of "the durable satisfactions" of a law teacher's life.

His experience on the Court had an expanding influence on his mind, partly because of the intimacy that it gave him with Holmes and Brandeis, and, for too few years, with Cardozo, but partly no less because the nature of the issues that come before the supreme tribunal made him plow deeper into his own mind than the demands of his life in New York had permitted. It made him realize not merely how profoundly right Holmes was in insisting that we need more theory and not less, but that no judge is fit for his task, certainly on the highest court, unless he be truly cultivated. Stone had always had an interest in the arts. He had visited the best of the European museums and he took full advantage of the opportunities that Washington afforded. When as chief justice he became ex officio chairman of the Board of Trustees of the National Gallery of Art and chancellor of the Smithsonian Institution, and, as a distinguished son of Amherst, chairman of the Folger Shakespeare Library, he brought zeal to these offices and drew enrichment from them.

During his twenty years on the Court, Stone wrote either for the Court or in dissent some five hundred opinions. This constitutes a comprehensive body of views on the major legal issues of our time. What is no less important, perhaps even more important, such a body of opinions inevitably discloses the author's philosophy regarding a judge's function in our society, whether explicitly avowed or to be read between the lines. To these opinions, spread through sixty-one volumes of the Reports (268 U.S.-328 U.S.), the curious and the learned alike must be referred.

Stone was totally devoid of side, instinctively friendly alike with his colleagues, with his law clerks, and with the world at large. He was a great believer in dispatching promptly the business of the Court, knowing that justice unduly delayed is justice denied. He sought to maintain the standards set by his predecessors, particularly those of the chief justice whom he succeeded. It was his endeavor to dispose of the business of the Court with all deliberate speed, but only after the freest discussion by every justice preceding decision and with due regard for the deliberative process of opinion writing.

As is true in every calling, men vary greatly in the temperaments they bring to judging. Some decide without great inner turmoil and others suffer anguish in the process. Some are serene once the inner debate is concluded; with some the throes of conflict linger long and are easily revived. Some are painfully slow workers, trace and retrace their steps; others swiftly strike at the jugular of a case and are done. Stone's writing is deceptive. It does not give the impression of fluency. He was a quick writer. He was not, however, a quick decider. His was not the temperament that decided without much inner contest, or even rested securely after descending from the fence. A friendly wag of a colleague at Columbia once introduced him at a law school function as a person who turned neither to partiality on the one hand, nor to impartiality on the other.

He had his share in the "historic shift of emphasis in constitutional interpretation" which, he said, marked the magistracy of Chief Justice Hughes. But the shift had been made by the time he became chief justice. His work as such must be left for the judgment of the scholars of the future. Certainly it cannot now be attempted by one who served with him. Suffice it to say, he came to the great succession qualified by a national outlook, not the worse for having been rooted in New England, by an extraordinarily diversified professional experience, and with full appreciation of the demands that the business of the Court makes on legal learning.

He had a strong historic sense and naturally enough was concerned with his place in history. Chief justices of the United States are rarer than presidents. A chief justice cannot escape history.

Six

Mr. Justice Holmes

(1944)

This sketch of the life of Mr. Justice Holmes is reprinted from the *Dictionary of American Biography*, Supplement One (Vol. 21, p. 417).

OLIVER WENDELL HOLMES (March 8, 1841-March 6, 1935), jurist, was born at 8 Montgomery Place, now Bosworth Place, Boston, the son of Oliver Wendell Holmes, physician, poet, and essayist, and the grandson of Abiel Holmes, clergyman and historian. His mother was Amelia Lee Jackson, daughter of Charles Jackson, associate justice of the Supreme Judicial Court of Massachusetts. "All my three names," he once wrote, "designate families from which I am descended. A long pedigree of Olivers and Wendells may be found in the book called 'Memorials of the Dead—King's Chapel Burying Ground.' . . . Some of my ancestors have fought in the Revolution; among the great grandmothers of the family were Dorothy Quincy and Anne Bradstreet ('the tenth muse'); and so on. . . . Our family has been in the habit of receiving a college education and I came of course in my turn, as my grandfathers, fathers and uncles before me. I've always lived in Boston and went first to a woman's school there, then to Rev. T. R. Sullivan's, then to E. S. Dixwell's (Private Latin School) and then to College" (O. W. Holmes, Jr.'s, College Autobiography, quoted in F. C. Fiechter, "The Preparation of an American Aristocrat," *New England Quarterly*, March 1933).

Holmes was thus rooted in the Puritan tradition and his personal attachment to its meaning and environment went deep. "I love every brick and shingle of the old Massachusetts towns where once they worked and prayed," he said of his Puritan ancestors in one of his frequent references to them, "and I think it a noble and pious thing to do whatever we may by written word and moulded bronze and sculptured stone to keep our memories, our reverence and our love alive and to hand them on to new generations all too ready to forget" ("Ipswich—At the Unveiling of Memorial Tablets," July 31, 1902, *Speeches*, 1913, p. 92). After leaving Boston, he regularly returned to its nearby North Shore to enjoy each year its dunes and rocks and barberry bushes with refreshing devotion. But even as a college student he was a Bostonian apart. Very early his curiosities far transcended his emotional attachments. His own crowd in Boston, though fascinated, were quizzical about him for reasons that were implied in the remark of a leading lawyer who had been a boyhood friend: "I wish Wendell wouldn't play with his mind." From the time—before he was twenty—that he learned from Emerson the lesson of intellectual independence, his quest for understanding was hemmed in neither by geography nor by personal preferences. So whole-souled was his love of country that only fools could misunderstand when he said, "I do not pin my dreams for the future to my country or even to my race. . . . I think it not improbable that man, like the grub that prepares a chamber for the winged thing it never has seen but is to be—that man may have cosmic destinies that he does not understand" ("Law and the Court," *Collected Legal Papers*, 1920, p. 296). New Englander of New Englanders in his feelings all his life, Holmes disciplined himself against any kind of parochialism in his thinking. Because he so completely rid himself of it, he is a significant figure in the history of civilization and not merely a commanding American figure.

As a truth-seeking Puritan, then, he entered Harvard in the fall of 1857. But before he was graduated came the Civil War and Lincoln's call for men. In April 1861, Holmes, just turned twenty, joined the 4th Battalion of Infantry stationed at Fort Independence. On July 10—having in the meantime written and delivered his class poem and been graduated—he was commissioned second lieutenant and on Sept. 4 he started South with his beloved regiment, the 20th Massachusetts, part of the Army of the Potomac, to share, except when disabled, in its notable history (G. A. Bruce, *The Twentieth Regiment of Massachusetts Volunteer Infantry*, 1906). Three times he was put out of action and his war experiences are the stuff of heroic tales. Not unnaturally could his great friend Sir Frederick Pollock sixty years later chaffingly suggest to Holmes that he could reinforce his argument "as to the contra-natural selection of war by the example of a certain stray bullet whose deviation by a fraction of an inch would have deprived" the world of all that Holmes's lucky escape gave it (*Holmes-Pollock Letters*, II, 43). His own recital (*Who's Who in America*) gives Holmes's war record with austere completeness: "Served 3 yrs. with 20th Mass. Volunteers, lieutenant to lieutenant colonel; wounded in breast at Ball's Bluff, Oct. 21, 1861, in neck at Antietam, Sept. 17, 1862, in foot at Marye's Hill, Fredericksburg, May 3, 1863; a.-d.-c. on staff of Gen. H. G. Wright, Jan. 29, 1864, until mustered out July 17, 1864, with rank of captain."

On his return to Boston invalided from the front, his personal distinction and his war record irresistibly combined to make of him a military hero. Bishop William Lawrence gives the contemporary picture: "I saw him, a young officer, marching off to the front. . . . I watched his record, for we boys were alert to the heroes of those days, and as he was brought back wounded again and again . . . he was seen on the streets in Boston, a handsome invalid, to the great delectation of the girls of the city. He was a romantic hero, built for it" (Address of Bishop Lawrence at presentation of portrait of Mr. Justice Holmes, Mar. 20, 1930, *Harvard Alumni Bulletin*, Mar. 27, 1930). What he called a "flamboyant" piece (*Holmes-Pollock Letters*, II, 270) in *Harper's Weekly* of Nov. 9, 1861, and Dr. Holmes's famous but too stylized *Atlantic Monthly* (December 1862) account of the Antietam episode, "My Hunt after 'the Captain,'" extended young Holmes's martial reputation much beyond the confines of Boston. He himself harbored no romantic notions about war. He saw too much of it. Indeed, he shocked patriotic sentimentalists by speaking of war as an "organized bore," just as later he was to offend those whom he regarded as social sentimentalists by his insistence that war is merely a phase of that permanent struggle which is the law of life. "War, when you are at it, is horrible and dull. It is only when time has passed that you see that its message was divine. I hope it may be long before we are called again to sit at that master's feet. But some teacher of the kind we all need. In this snug, over-safe corner of the world we need it, that we may realize that our comfortable routine is no eternal necessity of things, but merely a little space of calm in the midst of the tempestuous untamed streaming of the world, and in order that we may be ready for danger. We need it in this time of individualist negations, with its literature of French and American humor, revolting at discipline, loving flesh-pots, and denying that anything is worthy of reverence,—in order that we may remember all that buffoons forget. We need it everywhere and at all times" ("The Soldier's Faith," a Memorial Day address, May 30, 1895, *Speeches*, pp. 62-63).

These are the convictions he took out of the Civil War. These were the convictions that dominated him for the long years to come—for the Civil War probably cut more deeply than any other influence in his life. If it did not generate it

certainly fixed his conception of man's destiny. "I care not
very much for the form if in some way he has learned that
he cannot set himself over against the universe as a rival god,
to criticize it, or to shake his fist at the skies, but that his
meaning is its meaning, his only worth is as a part of it, as a
humble instrument of the universal power" (*Collected Legal
Papers*, p. 166). "Life is a roar of bargain and battle, but in
the very heart of it there rises a mystic spiritual tone that
gives meaning to the whole" (*Speeches*, p. 97). "It is enough
for us that the universe has produced us and has within it, as
less than it, all that we believe and love. If we think of our
existence not as that of a little god outside, but as that of a
ganglion within, we have the infinite behind us. It gives us
our only but our adequate significance. . . . If our imagination is strong enough to accept the vision of ourselves as parts
inseverable from the rest, and to extend our final interest beyond the boundary of our skins, it justifies the sacrifice even
of our lives for ends outside of ourselves" (*Collected Legal
Papers*, p. 316).

This faith he expressed as a returning soldier and he repeated it, in enduring phrases endlessly varied, for seventy
years—in talk, in letters, in speeches, in opinions. But his "Soldier's Faith" was not merely an eloquent avowal of his philosophic beliefs regarding man's destiny, nor was it a gifted
man's expression, in emotionally charged phrases, of what
seemed to him "the key to intellectual salvation" as well as
"the key to happiness" (*Collected Legal Papers*, p. 166).
Holmes lived his faith. It would be difficult to conceive a life
more self-conscious of its directions and more loyal in action
to the faith which it espoused. His faith determined the very
few personal choices he was called upon to make after he left
the army; it was translated into concreteness in the multi-
farious cases that came before him for judgment for half a
century.

He left the army because his term was up. In later life he

said that if he had to do it again he would have stayed through the war. Instead, in the fall of 1864, he began the study of law. On graduating from the Harvard Law School in 1866, he made the first of his numerous visits to England. He had, of course, easy access to eminent Britishers but he won his way among them, even in his twenties, on his own intellectual distinction. Thus he met some of the great figures of the day—John Stuart Mill, Sir Henry Maine, Benjamin Jowett, the Master of Balliol—and in course of time formed friendships with Leslie Stephen, James Bryce, A. V. Dicey, Sir Frederick Pollock, and with gifted women like Mrs. J. R. Green, Mrs. W. K. Clifford, and Miss Beatrice Chamberlain. That a gay, handsome young man with a brilliant tongue— "that lanky talker of a Wendell Holmes" was the way an old servant in a Beacon Hill household described him—moved easily in English fashionable society is not surprising. Much more significant is the tender friendship that grew between him and an Irish parish priest, Canon Sheehan, whom he met on one of his English visits. Indeed, his last trip to England, in 1913, was made largely to see his friend, who was dying. Canon Sheehan, he wrote, "was a dear friend of mine—odd as it seems that a saint and a Catholic should take up with a heathen like me" (unpublished ms., May 19, 1917; see H. J. Heuser, *Canon Sheehan of Doneraile*, 1917). The most intimate of his English ties came to be with Sir Frederick Pollock. Their friendship was maintained by a steady exchange of letters over nearly sixty years. These, happily, were preserved, and their publication, thanks to the careful editing of Mark DeWolfe Howe, furnishes a cultural document of first importance for its era (*Holmes-Pollock Letters: The Correspondence of Mr. Justice Holmes and Sir Frederick Pollock, 1874-1932*, 2 vols., 1941).

England had a strong pull for Holmes. "I value everything that shows the quiet unmelodramatic power to stand and take it in your people," wrote Holmes to Pollock early in the First

World War (*supra*, I, 222). But he could be sharp in detecting any tendency toward condescension or insensitiveness. He was a proud American who had no sympathy with suggestions of inadequacy of the American environment for finer sensibilities. Thus he thought that "there was a touch of underbreeding" in Henry James's "recurrence to the problem of the social relations of Americans to the old world" (*ibid.*, II, 41).

After his fling in England, Holmes settled down to the serious business of law. He entered it with strong misgivings and not for years were they quieted. The magnetic disturbance was philosophy. But in 1886, to students whom his old anxieties might beset, he was able to say "no longer with any doubt—that a man may live greatly in the law as well as elsewhere; that there as well as elsewhere his thought may find its unity in an infinite perspective; that there as well as elsewhere he may wreak himself upon life, may drink the bitter cup of heroism, may wear his heart out after the unattainable" ("The Profession of the Law," *Speeches*, pp. 22-23). Toward the end, when he was past ninety, he put the wisdom of his choice more pungently: "I rather was shoved than went [into the law] when I hankered for philosophy. I am glad now, and even then I had a guess that perhaps one got more from philosophy on the quarter than dead astern" (unpublished letter, June 11, 1931).

In 1867 he was admitted to the bar and practiced his profession in Boston, first as an apprentice of Robert M. Morse, then in the office of Chandler, Shattuck & Thayer, and later with George O. Shattuck and William A. Munroe, as a member of the firm of Shattuck, Holmes & Munroe. With fierce assiduity he set himself to become master of his calling. "I should think Wendell worked too hard," wrote William James, in 1869, and the theme recurs in the correspondence of the James family. Holmes never made a fetish of long hours, however; indeed, he believed that what he called work—really creative labor—could not be pursued for more than four hours a day. But he worked with almost feverish intensity. For three years (1870-73), as editor of the *American Law Review*, he ranged the gamut of legal literature—reports, digests, casebooks, revisions of old texts, new treatises, lectures, and essays—and made his own the entire kingdom of law (see *American Law Review*, Vols. V-VII, and bibliography in *Harvard Law Review*, March 1931). During the same period he worked indefatigably to bring Kent's *Commentaries* "down through the quarter of a century which has elapsed" since Chancellor Kent's death, and thereby gave new and enduring significance to the most important survey of the earlier American law (see James Kent, *Commentaries on American Law*, 12th ed., 1873). Holmes thus soaked himself in the details of the law. When he began "the law presented itself as a ragbag of details. . . . It was not without anguish that one asked oneself whether the subject was worthy of the interest of an intelligent man" (*Collected Legal Papers*, p. 301). But his imaginative and philosophic faculties imparted life and meaning to dry details. Where others found only discrete instances he saw organic connection. Thus it was true of him, as he said of another, that his knowledge "was converted into the organic tissue of wisdom" (appreciation of John Chipman Gray reprinted in H. C. Shriver, *Oliver Wendell Holmes: His Book Notices and Uncollected Letters and Papers*, 1936, p. 135). At this time he also lectured on law at Harvard.

During all these years he was in active practice and getting desirable glimpses into actualities. In particular, what it meant to him to be associated with his senior partner, George Otis Shattuck, a leader among Massachusetts lawyers, is the theme of one of his memorable utterances (*Speeches*, pp. 70-74). His temperament being what it was, scholarly pursuits, though a sideline, doubtless enlisted his deepest interests. He would have welcomed appointment to the United States District

Court for the greater intellectual freedom it would have afforded him ("The place . . . would enable me to work in
the way I want to and so I should like it—although it would
cost me a severe pang to leave my partners," *Holmes-Pollock
Letters*, I, 10). But destiny had other plans for him.

The early writings of Holmes canvassed issues which, how-
soever formulated or disguised, are vital to a society devoted
to justice according to law. What are the sources of law and
what are its sanctions? What is appropriate lawmaking by
courts and what should be left to legislation? What are the
ingredients, conscious or unconscious, of adjudication? What
are the wise demands of precedent and when should the judicial process feel unbound by its past? Such were the inquiries
that guided Holmes's investigations at a time when law was
generally treated as a body of settled doctrines from which
answers to the new problems of a rapidly industrialized society were to be derived by a process of logical deduction.
But in rejecting a view of law which regarded it as a merely
logical unfolding Holmes had nothing in common with later
tendencies toward a retreat from reason. By disproving formal
logic as the organon of social wisdom he did not embrace
antirationalism. Quite the contrary. His faith was in reason
and in motives not confined to material or instinctive desires.
He refused to believe the theory "that the Constitution primarily represents the triumph of the money power over
democratic agrarianism & individualism. . . . I shall believe
until compelled to think otherwise that they [the leaders in
establishing the Union] wanted to make a nation and invested
(bet) on the belief that they would make one, not that they
wanted a powerful government because they had invested.
Belittling arguments always have a force of their own, but
you and I believe that high-mindedness is not impossible to
man" (*ibid.*, II, 222-23). Equally so, while fully aware of the
clash of interests in society and of law's mediating function,
Holmes had nothing in common with the crude notion ac-

cording to which law is merely the verbalization of prevailing force and appetites.

But at a time when judges boasted a want of philosophy, Holmes realized that decisions are functions of some juristic philosophy, and that awareness of the considerations that move beneath the surface of logical form is the prime requisite of a civilized system of law. In his analysis of judicial psychology, he was conscious of the role of the unconscious more than a generation before Freud began to influence modern psychology. Again, exploration of the meaning of law was attempted by Holmes half a century before C. K. Ogden and I. A. Richards wrote *The Meaning of Meaning* (1923).

These pioneer contributions, however, though they had organic unity, were made in seemingly disconnected and fugitive writings. An invitation to deliver a series of lectures at the Lowell Institute in Boston happily led him to systematize his ideas into "a connected treatise" and in 1881, before he had crossed forty—a goal he had fiercely set for himself—he published *The Common Law*. The book marks an epoch for law and learning. Together with half a dozen of his essays, *The Common Law* gave the most powerful direction to legal science. The way in which he conceived law and its judicial development was out of the current of the period. He reoriented legal inquiry. The book is a classic in the sense that its stock of ideas has been absorbed and become part of common juristic thought. A few of its opening sentences will give its drift. They represent the thought of today more truly than the temper of the time in which they were written. More than sixty years ago they placed law in a perspective which legal scholarship ever since has merely confirmed. "The life of the law has not been logic: it has been experience. The felt necessities of the time, the prevalent moral and political theories, intuitions of public policy, avowed or unconscious, even the prejudices which judges share with their

fellow-men, have had a good deal more to do than the syllogism in determining the rules by which men should be governed. The law embodies the story of a nation's development
through many centuries, and it cannot be dealt with as if it
contained only the axioms and corollaries of a book of mathe-
matics. In order to know what it is, we must know what it
has been, and what it tends to become. We must alternately
consult history and existing theories of legislation. But the
most difficult labor will be to understand the combination of
the two into new products at every stage. The substance of
the law at any given time pretty nearly corresponds, so far
as it goes, with what is then understood to be convenient; but
its form and machinery, and the degree to which it is able to
work out desired results, depend very much upon its past."

A work of such seminal scholarship as *The Common Law*
makes its way only slowly in affecting the mode of thought
of practitioners and judges; but it achieved prompt recognition from the learned world. Its immediate result was a call
to Holmes from the Harvard Law School. Largely through
the efforts of Louis D. Brandeis, as secretary of the then recently organized Harvard Law School Alumni Association, a
new chair was established for him, and in January 1882, he
became Weld Professor of Law, accepting the position with
the explicit understanding that he was free to accept a judge-
ship, should it come his way. On Dec. 5, 1882, Gov. John D.
Long appointed him to the Supreme Judicial Court of Massachusetts and on Jan. 3, 1883, Holmes took his seat as an associate justice on that bench. This, he used to say, was "a stroke
of lightning which changed all the course of my life." Why
did Holmes leave the chair for the bench? His aims were
never for external power—always his striving was only for
"the secret isolated joy of the thinker, who knows that, a
hundred years after he is dead and forgotten, men who
never heard of him will be moving to the measure of his
thought . . ." (*Speeches*, pp. 24-25). But the Civil War evi-

dently influenced him permanently against sheltered thinking. "To think under fire" was his test of most responsible
thought. "It is one thing to utter a happy phrase from a protected cloister; another to think under fire—to think for action upon which great interests depend" ("George Otis Shattuck," *Speeches,* p. 73).

While at the bar, on June 17, 1872, he married Fanny Bow-
ditch Dixwell, eldest daughter of his Latin school headmaster,
Epes Sargent Dixwell, and granddaughter of Nathaniel Bow-
ditch, the mathematician. Without some reference to her influence in the Justice's life no sufficiently discerning biography of him is possible. We get an early glimpse of her in
several letters from William James. "I have made the acquaintance of . . . Miss (Fanny) Dixwell of Cambridge, lately.
She is about as fine as they make 'em. That villain Wendell
Holmes has been keeping her all to himself at Cambridge for
the last eight years; but I hope I may enjoy her acquaintance
now. She is A1, if anyone ever was" (R. B. Perry, *The
Thought and Character of William James,* 1935, I, 228; see
also *The Letters of William James,* 1920, I, 76, II, 156). One
who knew both well for much of their lives, and respected
the reserves of both, wrote: "Her quick and vivid perception,
her keen wit and vigorous judgment, and the originality and
charm of her character cannot be forgotten by anyone who
knew her. It is impossible to think of Justice Holmes without
thinking of her also. Her effect on his life and career can
neither be omitted nor measured in any account of him"
(A. D. Hill, in *Harvard Graduates' Magazine,* March, 1931,
p. 268). She "was in many ways," according to another, "as
extraordinary a personality as the Justice himself." She died
on April 30, 1929, and to Pollock he wrote: "We have had
our share. For sixty years she made life poetry for me . . ."
(*Letters,* II, 243).

The stream of litigation that flowed through such an important tribunal as the Supreme Judicial Court of Massachu-

setts during the twenty years of his incumbency enabled
Holmes to fertilize the whole vast field of law. Although
questions came before him in the unpremeditated order of
litigation, his Massachusetts opinions—nearly 1,300—would, if
appropriately brought together, constitute the most comprehensive and philosophic body of American law for any period
of its history. Except for a synoptic table of his opinions
(*Harvard Law Review*, March 1931, pp. 799-819) and a small
selection from them (H. C. Shriver, *The Judicial Opinions
of Oliver Wendell Holmes*, 1940), they remain scattered in
fifty forbidding volumes of law reports. For him they had
the painful inadequacy of one whose aim was the unattainable. "I look into my book in which I keep a docket of the
decisions of the full court which fall to me to write, and find
about a thousand cases. A thousand cases, many of them upon
trifling or transitory matters, to represent nearly half a lifetime! A thousand cases, when one would have liked to study
to the bottom and to say his say on every question which the
law ever has presented, and then to go on and invent new
problems which should be the test of doctrine, and then to
generalize it all and write it in continuous, logical, philosophic
exposition, setting forth the whole corpus with its roots in
history and its justifications of expedience real or supposed!"
(*Collected Legal Papers*, p. 245).

Such standards were doubtless stimulating to a bar, but
were hardly calculated to leave it at ease in Zion. We have
a trustworthy view of him as he appeared to lawyers who
came before him in Massachusetts: "Nobody who sat on this
Court in my time had quite such a daunting personality,—to
a young lawyer at least. He was entirely courteous, but his
mind was so extraordinarily quick and incisive, he was such
an alert and sharply attentive listener, his questions went so
to the root of the case, that it was rather an ordeal to appear
before him. In arguing a case you felt that when your sentence was half done he had seen the end of it, and before the

argument was a third finished that he had seen the whole course of reasoning and was wondering whether it was sound" (unpublished remarks of United States Circuit Judge James M. Morton, Jr., at the exercises in memory of Mr. Justice Holmes before the Supreme Judicial Court of Massachusetts, Oct. 9, 1937). He hated long-windedness and recommended to the gentlemen of the bar the reading of French novels to cultivate the art of innuendo. He expressed himself, however, with sufficient explicitness in some labor cases to be deemed "dangerous" in important circles in Boston. Such was the direction of thought at the time that a dissenting opinion which has since established itself as a great landmark in legal analysis on both sides of the Atlantic (*Vegelahn* v. *Gunther*, 167 Mass. 92, 104) was seriously felt to be a bar to his judicial promotion. He had simply adhered to his detached view of the law and refused to translate fear of "socialism" "into doctrines that had no proper place in the Constitution or the common law" (*Collected Legal Papers*, p. 295).

He did become Chief Justice of Massachusetts, on Aug. 5, 1899; and the very opinions which disturbed the conservatism of Boston were in part the influences that led President Theodore Roosevelt to look in Holmes's direction when the resignation of Mr. Justice Horace Gray created a vacancy on the supreme bench. Gray was from Massachusetts, and it was natural to turn to Massachusetts for a successor. But the circumstances of Holmes's appointment illustrate what fortuitous elements determine Supreme Court choices. The near approach of the end of Justice Gray's service had been foreshadowed before President McKinley's assassination, and the nomination of Alfred Hemenway, a leading Boston lawyer and partner of McKinley's secretary of the navy, John D. Long, had been decided upon by McKinley. Before it could be made, Theodore Roosevelt had become president and "he did not feel himself bound by the informal arrangement which his predecessor had made with Mr. Hemenway" (un-

published remarks of Judge James M. Morton, Jr., *supra*).
Roosevelt hesitated not a little about appointing Holmes. A
letter to Senator Henry Cabot Lodge gives a full disclosure
of Roosevelt's mind on the subject (*Selections from the Correspondence of Theodore Roosevelt and Henry Cabot Lodge,*
1925, I, 517-19). Holmes himself, to a friend, wrote of the
curious doubt that troubled Roosevelt, as well as the circumstance that soon stirred his disappointment in Holmes:
". . . he was uneasy about appointing me because he thought
I didn't appreciate Marshall. I thought it rather comic. I have
no doubt that later he heartily repented over his choice when
I didn't do what he wanted in the Northern Securities Case
[*Northern Securities Co.* vs. *United States,* 193 U.S. 197].
. . . Long afterwards, at a dinner at the White House to
some labor leaders, I said to one of them who had been
spouting about the Judges: What you want is favor—not
justice. But when I am on my job I don't care a damn what
you want or what Mr. Roosevelt wants—and then repeated
my remarks to him. You may think that a trifle crude—but I
didn't like to say it behind his back and not to his face, and
the fact had justified it—I thought and think" (unpublished
letter, dated April 1, 1928).

Holmes took his seat on Dec. 8, 1902. He came to the Court
at a time when vigorous legislative activity reflected changing
social conceptions, which in turn were stimulated by vast
technological development. What was in the air is well epito-
mized by the observation that Theodore Roosevelt "was the
first President of the United States who openly proposed to
use the powers of political government for the purpose of
affecting the distribution of wealth in the interest of the
golden mean" (C. A. and Mary R. Beard, *The Rise of
American Civilization,* 1927, II, 597).

Though formally the product of ordinary lawsuits, constitutional law differs profoundly from ordinary law. Constitutional law is the body of doctrines by which the Supreme

Court marks the boundaries between national and state action and by means of which it mediates between citizen and government. The Court thus exercises functions that determine vital arrangements in the government of the American people. These adjustments are based, for the most part, on very broad provisions of the Constitution. Words like "liberty" and phrases like "due process of law" and "regulate Commerce . . . among the several States," furnish the text for judgment upon the validity of governmental action directed toward the infinite variety of social and economic facts. But these are words and phrases of "convenient vagueness." They unavoidably give wide judicial latitude in determining the undefined and ever-shifting boundaries between state and nation, between freedom and authority. Even as to these broad provisions of the Constitution distinctions must be observed. In a federated nation, especially one as vast in its territory and varied in its interests as the United States, the power must be somewhere to make the necessary accommodation between the central government and the states. "I do not think the United States would come to an end," said Mr. Justice Holmes, "if we lost our power to declare an Act of Congress void. I do think the Union would be imperiled if we could not make that declaration as to the laws of the several States. For one in my place sees how often a local policy prevails with those who are not trained to national views and how often action is taken that embodies what the Commerce Clause was meant to end" (*Collected Legal Papers*, pp. 295-296). The agency, moreover, must be one not subject to the vicissitudes and pressures under which the political branches of government rest. The Supreme Court is that ultimate arbiter.

Two major issues affecting the whole scheme of government have been the dominant concern of the Supreme Court throughout its history. The Court has had to decide in the most variegated situations from what lawmaking the states are excluded and what legislative domain Congress may enter. And as to both state and national authority it rests with the Court to determine under what circumstances society may intervene and when the individual is to be left unrestricted. But while the Supreme Court thus moves in the perilous sphere of government it does not itself carry the burdens of governing. The Court is merely the brake on other men's actions. Determination of policy—what taxes to impose, how to regulate business, when to restrict freedom—rests with legislatures and executives. The nature of the Court's task thus raises a crucial problem in our constitutional system in that its successful working calls for rare intellectual detachment and penetration, lest limitations in personal experience are transmuted into limitations of the Constitution.

His profound analysis of the sources of our law before he became a judge left in Holmes an abiding awareness of the limited validity of legal principles. He never forgot that circumstances had shaped the law in the past, and that the shaping of future law is primarily the business of legislatures. He was therefore keenly sensitive to the subtle forces that are involved in the process of reviewing the judgment of others not as to its wisdom but as to the reasonableness of their belief in its wisdom. As society becomes more and more complicated and individual experience correspondingly narrower, tolerance and humility in passing judgment on the experience and beliefs expressed by those entrusted with the duty of legislating emerge as the decisive factors in constitutional adjudication. No judge could be more aware than Holmes of these subtle aspects of the business of deciding constitutional cases. He read omnivorously to "multiply my scepticisms" (unpublished letter). His imagination and humility, rigorously cultivated, enabled him to transcend the narrowness of his immediate experience. Probably no man who ever sat on the Court was by temperament and discipline freer from emotional commitments compelling him to translate his own economic or social views into constitutional commands. He did not read merely his own mind to discover the powers that may be exercised by a great nation. His personal views often ran counter to legislation that came before him for judgment. He privately distrusted attempts at improving society by what he deemed futile if not mischievous economic tinkering. But that was not his business. It was not for him to prescribe for society or to deny it the right of experimentation within very wide limits. That was to be left for contest by the political forces in the state. The duty of the Court was to keep the ring free. He reached the democratic result by the philosophic route of scepticism—by his disbelief in ultimate answers to social questions. Thereby he exhibited the judicial function at its purest.

He gave such ample scope to legislative judgment on economic policy because he knew so well to what great extent social arrangements are conditioned by time and circumstances. He also knew that we have "few scientifically certain criteria of legislation, and as it often is difficult to mark the line where what is called the police power of the States is limited by the Constitution of the United States, judges should be slow to read into the latter a *nolumus mutare* as against the law-making power" (*Noble State Bank* v. *Haskell*, 219 U.S. 104, 110). But social development is an effective process of trial and error only if there is the fullest possible opportunity for the free play of the mind. He therefore attributed very different legal significance to those liberties which history has attested as the indispensable conditions of a free society from that which he attached to liberties which derived merely from shifting economic arrangements. Even freedom of speech, however, he did not erect into a dogma of absolute validity nor did he enforce it to doctrinaire limits.

For him the Constitution was not a literary document but an instrument of government. As such it was to be regarded not as an occasion for juggling with words but as a means

for ordering the life of a people. It had its roots in the past—
"historic continuity with the past," he reminded his hearers,
"is not a duty, it is only a necessity"—but it was also designed
for the unknown future. This conception of the Constitution
was the background against which he projected every inquiry
into the scope of a specific power or specific limitation. That
the Constitution is a framework of great governmental powers
to be exercised for great public ends was for him not a pale
intellectual concept. It dominated his process of constitutional
adjudication. His opinions, composed in harmony with his
dominating attitude toward the Constitution, recognized an
organism within which the dynamic life of a free society can
unfold and flourish. From his constitutional opinions there
emerges the conception of a nation adequate to its national
and international tasks, whose federated states, though subordinate to central authority for national purposes, have ample
power for their divers local needs. He was mindful of the
Union which he helped to preserve at Ball's Bluff, Antietam,
and Fredericksburg. He was equally alert to assure scope for
the states in matters peculiarly theirs because not within the
reach of Congress.

The nation was nearly deprived of one of its great men
because President Theodore Roosevelt resented that Holmes,
in his estimate of John Marshall, should have subordinated
the intellectual originality of the chief justice to his political
significance. It was to be expected, therefore, that on the Supreme Court he would be left unimpressed by what are called
great cases. What he cared about was transforming thought.
"My keenest interest is excited, not by what are called great
questions and great cases, but by little decisions which the
common run of selectors would pass by because they did not
deal with the Constitution or a telephone company, yet which
have in them the germ of some wider theory, and therefore
of some profound interstitial change in the very tissue of the
law" (*Collected Legal Papers*, p. 269). Judged by conven-

tional standards, therefore, his opinions not infrequently appeared to dispose rather cavalierly of controversies that were complicated in their facts and far-reaching in their immediate consequences. "This brief summary of the pleadings," he wrote of a litigation in which the record filled a five-foot shelf, "is enough to show the gravity and importance of the case. It concerns the expenditure of great sums and the welfare of millions of men. But cost and importance, while they add to the solemnity of our duty, do not increase the difficulty of decision except as they induce argument upon matters that with less mighty interests no one would venture to dispute" (*Sanitary District* v. *United States*, 266 U.S. 405, 425). With his vast learning he combined extraordinary rapidity of decision. His opinions were felicitous distillates of these faculties. His genius—put to service by rigorous self-discipline and deep learning—was to go for the essentials and express them with stinging brevity. He was impatient with laboring the obvious as a form of looseness, for looseness and stuffiness equally bored him. He genially suggested that judges need not be heavy to be weighty. ". . . our reports were dull because we had the notion that judicial dignity required solemn fluffy speech, as, when I grew up, everybody wore black frock coats and black cravats. . . ." (*Holmes-Pollock Letters*, II, 132).

In his opinions the thinker and the artist are superbly fused. In deciding cases, his aim was "to try to strike the jugular." His opinions appear effortless—birds of brilliant plumage pulled from the magician's sleeves. But his correspondence gives glimpses of the great effort that lay behind the seemingly easy achievement. "Of course in letters one simply lets oneself go without thinking of form but in my legal writing I do try to make it decent and I have come fully to agree with Flaubert. He speaks of writing French, but to write any language is enormously hard. To avoid vulgar errors and pitfalls ahead is a job. To arrange the thoughts so that one springs naturally from that which precedes it and to express them with a singing variety is the devil and all." And again: "The eternal effort of art, even the art of writing legal decisions, is to omit all but the essentials. The 'point of contact' is the formula, the place where the boy got his finger pinched; the rest of the machinery doesn't matter."

Whenever he disagreed with the majority of his brethren he was reluctant to express his dissenting views and did not often do so. In Massachusetts the number of his dissents is less than one per cent of all his opinions. On the Supreme Court of the United States the expression of dissenting views on constitutional issues has, from the beginning, been deemed almost obligatory. In Washington, therefore, they came from Justice Holmes's pen more frequently and sometimes were written with "cold Puritan passion." He gave a public hint of the forces that clashed in the Supreme Court in the decorous form of a mere lawsuit when he said "we are very quiet there, but it is the quiet of a storm centre . . ." (*Collected Legal Papers*, p. 292). In a letter to Pollock he gave more than a hint of the inevitable conflicts within the Court: "Today I am stirred about a case that I can't mention yet to which I have sent round a dissent that was prepared to be ready as soon as the opinion was circulated. I feel sure that the majority will very highly disapprove of my saying what I think, but as yet it seems to me my duty. No doubt I shall hear about it on Saturday at our conference and perhaps be persuaded to shut up, but I don't expect it" (*Letters*, II, 29). Some of his weightiest utterances are dissents, but they are dissents that have shaped history. (See *Adair* v. *United States*, 208 U.S. 161, 190; *Hammer* v. *Dagenhart*, 247 U.S. 251, 277; *Abrams* v. *United States*, 250 U.S. 616, 624; *Evans* v. *Gore*, 253 U.S. 245, 264; *Adkins* v. *Children's Hospital*, 261 U.S. 525, 567; *Tyson & Bro.* v. *Banton*, 273 U.S. 418, 445; *United States* v. *Schwimmer*, 279 U.S. 644, 653; *Baldwin* v. *Missouri*, 281 U.S. 586, 595.) Disproportionate significance has been attached to his dissents, however; they are merely a part of a much larger, organic whole.

After his retirement he played briefly with the suggestion that he put his ultimate thoughts on law between the covers of a small book, but all his life he had been driven by the lash of some duty undone and at last he reveled in the joy of having no unfinished business. Moreover, he felt strongly that he had had his say in the way in which he most cared to express his reflections—scattered in his more than two thousand opinions and in his lean but weighty collection of occasional writings. "I am being happily idle," he wrote to Pollock, "and persuading myself that 91 has outlived duty. I can imagine a book on the law, getting rid of all talk of duties and rights—beginning with the definition of law in the lawyer's sense as a statement of the circumstances in which the public force will be brought to bear upon a man through the Courts, and expounding rights as the hypostasis of a prophecy —in short, systematizing some of my old chestnuts. But I don't mean to do it . . ." (*Letters*, II, 307). He was no believer in systems. These, he felt, were heavy elaborations of a few insights—*aperçus*, to use his recurring word. Systems die; insights remain, he reiterated. Therefore, a few of his own *aperçus* will give the best clues to his philosophy of law and to his judicial technique in the most important field of his labors.

". . . the provisions of the Constitution are not mathematical formulas having their essence in their form; they are organic living institutions transplanted from English soil. Their significance is vital not formal; it is to be gathered not simply by taking the words and a dictionary, but by considering their origin and the line of their growth" (*Gompers v. United States*, 233 U.S. 604, 610).

". . . when we are dealing with words that also are a constituent act, like the Constitution of the United States, we must realize that they have called into life a being the devel-

opment of which could not have been foreseen completely
by the most gifted of its begetters. It was enough for them to
realize or to hope that they had created an organism; it has
taken a century and has cost their successors much sweat and
blood to prove that they created a nation. The case before us
must be considered in the light of our whole experience and
not merely in that of what was said a hundred years ago"
(*Missouri* v. *Holland*, 252 U.S. 416, 433).

"Great constitutional provisions must be administered with
caution. Some play must be allowed for the joints of the machine, and it must be remembered that legislatures are ultimate guardians of the liberties and welfare of the people in
quite as great a degree as the courts" (*Missouri, Kansas &
Texas Ry. Co.* v. *May*, 194 U.S. 267, 270).

"While the courts must exercise a judgment of their own,
it by no means is true that every law is void which may seem
to the judges who pass upon it excessive, unsuited to its
ostensible end, or based upon conceptions of morality with
which they disagree. Considerable latitude must be allowed
for differences of view as well as for possible peculiar conditions which this court can know but imperfectly, if at all.
Otherwise a constitution, instead of embodying only relatively fundamental rules of right, as generally understood by
all English-speaking communities, would become the partisan
of a particular set of ethical or economical opinions, which
by no means are held *semper ubique et ab omnibus*" (*Otis* v.
Parker, 187 U.S. 606, 608-09).

". . . I should not dream of asking where the line can be
drawn, since the great body of the law consists in drawing
such lines, yet when you realize that you are dealing with
a matter of degree you must realize that reasonable men may
differ widely as to the place where the line should fall"
(*Schlesinger* v. *Wisconsin*, 270 U.S. 230, 241).

It is futile to try to account for genius; and the term is not
inaptly used for one whom so qualified an appraiser as Mr.

Justice Cardozo deemed probably the greatest legal intellect in the history of the English-speaking judiciary. Holmes simply heeded his own deepest impulses. He was born to probe beyond the surface of things, to cut beneath the skin of formulas, however respectable. In his formative years he found most congenial the company of speculative minds like William James and Charles S. Peirce and Chauncey Wright. All his life his pastime was not courtroom gossip but "twisting the tail of the cosmos" (Perry, *The Thought and Character of William James*, I, 504-19). Although native bent was powerfully reinforced by his Civil War experience, the deeper ferment of his time also worked in him. He came to maturity when Darwin began to disturb ancient beliefs. If Genesis had to be "reinterpreted" no texts of the law, however authoritative, could claim sanctity. By whatever combination of native disposition and outside influences it came to pass, however, the result was that Holmes early rejected legal principles as absolutes. He looked beneath their decorous formulations and saw them for what they usually are—sententious expressions of overlapping or conflicting social policies. The vital judicial issue is apt, therefore, to be their accommodation. Decisions thus become essentially a matter of drawing lines. Again and again he adverted to that necessity, which he once summed up as follows: "I do not think we need trouble ourselves with the thought that my view depends upon differences of degree. The whole law does so as soon as it is civilized. . . . Negligence is all degree—that of the defendant here degree of the nicest sort; and between the variations according to distance that I suppose to exist and the simple universality of the rules in the Twelve Tables or the Leges Barbarorum, there lies the culture of two thousand years" (*LeRoy Fibre Co.* v. *Chicago, Milwaukee & St. Paul Ry.*, 232 U.S. 340, 354). Such a view of law of course implies the exercise of choice. But judicial judgment precludes the notion of capricious choice. It assumes judgment between defined claims, each of recognized validity and with a cultural pedigree of its own, but all of which necessarily cannot be completely satisfied. This process of adjustment is bound increasingly to fall to the legislature as interests and activities in society become more and more interdependent. The considerations which thus prompt legislation and the intricate, dubious materials out of which laws are written bring into sharp focus the duty of deference to legislative determinations demanded from the revisory process called adjudicative. In a thousand instances Holmes was loyal to that philosophy. Thereby he resolved into comprehending larger truths the conflicting claims of state and nation, of liberty and authority, of individual and society.

"It is right and proper that in the reading room of the Harvard Law School the portrait of Holmes should face in equal honor the portrait of Marshall" (A. D. Hill, *Harvard Graduates' Magazine, supra*, p. 284). There fell to Marshall, as Holmes took occasion to say, "perhaps the greatest place that ever was filled by a judge" (*Collected Legal Papers*, p. 270). That Marshall seized it, the role of the Supreme Court in American history bears witness. Holmes's claim to pre-eminence has a different basis. He is unsurpassed in the depth of his penetration into the nature of the judicial process and in the originality of its exposition. His conception of the Constitution cannot be severed from his conception of a judge's function in applying it; and his views of the judge's function derive from his intellectual presuppositions, that is, from his loyal adherence in judicial practice to his philosophic scepticism. His approach to judicial problems was inseparable from his consciously wrought notions of his relations to the universe. These abstractions appear far removed from the particular cases that came before him. But the clarity with which a specific controversy is seen, in the context of the larger intellectual issues beneath the formal surface of litigation, and the disinterestedness with which such analysis guides decision and opinion, are the ultimate determinants of American public law.

After a major operation in the summer of 1922, Holmes showed signs of age—he was then in his eighty-second year; but his marvelous physique gradually reasserted itself, though he strictly conserved his energy for his work. Some of his most powerful opinions were written in his ninth decade. Until near the end of his tenure he usually wrote more than his share of opinions. He was nearly eighty-nine when the illness and death of Chief Justice Taft cast upon Holmes for a considerable period the heavy burden of presiding in Court and the still more difficult task of guiding its deliberations at conferences. He did both, in the language of Mr. Justice Brandeis, "as to the manner born."

The machinery was running down, however, and on Jan. 12, 1932, he sent his resignation, in his own beautiful script, to the President—"the time has come and I bow to the inevitable." He continued his serene life, in Washington and in the summers at Beverly Farms, reading and being read to, enjoying the simple and familiar things of nature that had always refreshed him and the devoted attention of friends, especially the young. He had become a very old man but his faculties were never impaired. He had grown almost wistful in his gentleness. The fire of his exciting personality was dying down and on the morning of March 6, 1935, came the end.

With the sure response of the mass of men—given enough time—to goodness and gallantry of spirit, Holmes, the fundamentally solitary thinker, had become a pervasive and intimate national possession. His death elicited an outpouring of feeling throughout the country. But of all the moving things that were said he would probably have most liked the few words of his old friend and his closest colleague for fifteen years, Mr. Justice Brandeis, when the news was brought to him: "And so the great man is gone." On his ninety-fourth birthday—a raw March day with snow gently falling—he was buried with due military honors, in the Arlington National Cemetery, alongside his wife and near his companions, known and unknown, of the Army of the Potomac.

Without accompanying explanation, he left the bulk of his substantial estate to the nation, the largest unrestricted gift ever made to it. Congress established a Holmes Fund Memorial Commission, whose proposals, interrupted by the Second World War, await the consideration of Congress. In a message to that body recommending an appropriate use of the bequest, President Franklin Roosevelt thus interpreted Holmes's intention: "It is the gift of one who, in war and in peace, devoted his life to its [his country's] service. Clearly he thereby sought, with a generous emphasis, to mark the full measure of his faith in those principles of freedom which the country was founded to preserve." And the President expressed what he deemed to be the country's desire that Congress "translate this gift into a form that may serve as a permanent impulse for the maintenance of the deepest tradition that Mr. Justice Holmes embodied." That tradition, wrote President Roosevelt, "was a faith in the creative possibilities of the law. For him law was an instrument of just relations between man and man. With an insight into its history that no American scholar has surpassed; with a capacity to mold ancient principles to present needs, unique in range and remarkable in prophetic power; with a grasp of its significance as the basis upon which the purposes of men are shaped, Mr. Justice Holmes sought to make the jurisprudence of the United States fulfill the great ends our Nation was established to accomplish" (President's Message to Congress, April 25, 1935, *The Public Papers and Addresses of Franklin D. Roosevelt*, (1938), Vol. 4, p. 130).

Seven

Mr. Justice Brandeis

(1941)

Mr. Justice Frankfurter wrote this article for the December 1941 issue of the *Harvard Law Review* (Vol. 55, p. 181), which was dedicated to the memory of Mr. Justice Brandeis.

INSOFAR AS ultimate judgment of any man may be forecast by his contemporaries, that of Mr. Justice Brandeis has been pronounced by the one best qualified to judge. With characteristic pithiness, Mr. Justice Holmes summed up more than fifty years of knowledge in describing Mr. Justice Brandeis as "a really good man and a great judge." It is now left for history to annotate that summary. Every man who writes, in large measure writes his autobiography. Louis D. Brandeis was no exception. Despite his impersonal and almost ascetic style, he furnished a map of his mind in his occasional papers, in his testimony before legislative committees, and, above all, in his more than five hundred opinions. Placed in the context of American history for the half-century in which he played so large a part, his writings will enable imaginative historical scholarship to recreate for future generations the impress left on Mr. Justice Holmes through personal experience. Our present task is to fortify ourselves by his example, by his passionate dedication of great gifts to great purposes, by his

use of the versatile resources of law for the liberation and
enrichment of the potentialities of man.

The purposes of Mr. Justice Brandeis were no less than the
achievement of a gracious civilization—and by common con-
sent he did much to further its realization. Yet he did not
originate a new view of life, nor did he make his impact by
any single work of massive learning. He distrusted grandiose
schemes, tall talk, and easy ways. Painful thought, generously
bestowed upon the matter in hand seen in all its fullness, early
became a habit with him. It is the golden thread that runs
through all his work, first as an active practitioner, later as
a shining example of the lawyer as a public servant though
holding no public office, finally as a member of the Supreme
Court.

He was vividly aware that in the sociological domain large
abstractions often start as tentative summaries of limited experience, gradually find easy acceptance as proved generalizations, and finally harden into uncritical dogma. Thereby the
past unwarrantably obstructs the present and constricts the
future. He regarded generalities as traps for error, and
rhetoric as the enemy of wisdom. Problems that seemed simple to more shallow minds almost oppressed him with their
complexity. And so the instinct of the common law for the
concrete was congenial to a philosophy founded on experience. If a paleontologist can reconstruct a species from a
single vertebra, the legal historian will be able to lay bare
the mind of Mr. Justice Brandeis and its methods by an in-
tensive study of all that went into one of his distinctive
opinions.

But Mr. Justice Brandeis was the antithesis of a "case lawyer." To no one less than to him was a case a discrete phenomenon. It was an organism. It had antecedents and offspring. Looking beneath the surface of things he saw relationships that at first glance appear remote. To deal adequately
with the problems of the immediate case he had to deal with

its interlaced and peripheral problems. And so he brought to bear all the resources of a natively deep-plowing mind, enriched by wide experience, to conduct the intellectual campaign which he found presented in so many cases. This involved more than his familiar exploration of the technical and intricate facts in which formulated legal issues are enmeshed. Since law is the rational process for accommodating the conflicting interests of an inordinately complicated society, wise adjudication presupposes regard for the conditions and limits appropriate to the rational process. Mr. Justice Brandeis's conception of the function of the Court in the distribution of American governmental powers and his almost uniform regard for the proved canons of constitutional adjudication were but a special application of his whole philosophy of responsible thought.

Thought for him was the product of brooding, not the windfall of inspiration. He believed in taking pains, and the corollary of taking pains was taking time. And he spent no less time in the expression of thought than in its conception. Aim at excellence is often a paralyzing evasion of effort. In Mr. Justice Brandeis it was an expression of the aesthetic side of his nature, but even more it was a response to his desire for utmost effectiveness in communicating thought. The ultimately right word and the delicate use of punctuation were as carefully weighed as the idea of which they were the vehicles. He was rigorous in his standards of appreciation of others. Of himself, he was ruthlessly exacting. Even after the long incubating process of maturing an opinion—the wide range of investigation, the toilsome study within it, the slow, careful writing of findings and conclusions—it was routine for him to revise his draft opinion again and again, often more than a dozen times. In at least one instance there were fifty-three revisions.

A man so immersed in affairs as Louis D. Brandeis must have closed the door on many of his interests when he went on the bench. But one is tempted to believe that judicial office was most fitting for his nature. Man's true dignity meant to him self-discipline and self-direction. As a Justice, he had the utmost attainable intellectual and moral autonomy. Thereby, however, he became more of a judge of himself than of others. By that responsibility he wished to be judged, so far as he ever gave thought to himself. How completely he discharged that responsibility the contagious serenity of his presence attested. History will confirm him.

Eight

Mr. Justice Jackson

(1955)

Mr. Justice Frankfurter contributed these articles to the April 1955 issues of the *Harvard Law Review* and the *Columbia Law Review*, which were dedicated to the memory of Mr. Justice Jackson. The articles complement one another, and are reprinted here seriatim (*Harvard Law Review*, Vol. 68, p. 937; *Columbia Law Review*, Vol. 55, p. 435).

SUCH ARE THE PARADOXES of life that one with unique opportunities for understanding the operations of the judicial process in Mr. Justice Jackson is by that very fact barred from sharing with readers the adventure of pursuing insight. Not that Brother Jackson and I saw things with a common eye. How could we, if for no other reason than the great differences in our backgrounds. Apart from the influential dissimilarity between our professional training and experience, he was a child of the country before Ford came, while the big city marked me as its own. The first opinion written by Jackson, J., was in characteristically vigorous dissent from an opinion of mine. *Indianapolis* v. *Chase National Bank*, 314 U.S. 63 (1941). And in the last case in which he wrote, *United States* v. *Harriss*, 347 U.S. 612 (1954), we were on opposite sides. Our conflicting views in these two cases could readily be used as texts to expound differences of outlook on the larger issues of which the two cases were instances, of differences in evaluation of the clashing factors which had to be accommodated in the two situations. What is more immediately relevant, however, about these two cases at the beginning and at the end of his judicial career and others between them is their proof that what binds men in fellowship is not identity of views but harmony of aims.

That law in its comprehensive sense is at once the precondition and, perhaps, the greatest achievement of an enduring civilization since without it there is either strife or the enslavement of the spirit of man; that law so conceived expresses the enforcible insights of morality and the endeavors of justice; that law is not word jugglery or the manipulation of symbols; that precedents, while not foreclosing new truths or enlarged understanding, are not counters to be moved about for predetermined ends; that this significance and role of law must particularly be respected in a continental federal society like ours; that the Supreme Court as the ultimate voice of this law must always be humbly mindful of the fact that it is entrusted with power which is saved from misuse only by a self-searching disinterestedness almost beyond the lot of men—these were convictions which Justice Jackson passionately entertained. They were part of him. He scrupulously applied them, though he moved, like everyone else, within the outer limits of his temperament and understanding.

This estimate of his outlook and views is not the private gleaning of a fellow worker. To an unusual degree in the history of the Court, Justice Jackson wrote as he felt. It is my impression that the opinions of most Justices have conformed to what they conceived to be the appropriate form of an opinion. In the delicious classification that Mr. Justice Cardozo made of legal opinions, he emphasized literary style. But I think the style often reflects the writer's notion of the form in which an opinion should be cast or his desire to promote one purpose rather than another. A literary genius like

Holmes no doubt writes the way he must. But there have been men on the Court whose conception of the required austerity of a Supreme Court opinion rigorously held in check an otherwise lively pen. Again, it makes a difference whether an opinion writer consciously aims to be understood by the casual newspaper reader, or whether he has a strong sense of the educational function of an opinion within the profession, and more particularly among law teachers, or writes merely to dispose of the case.

While Justice Jackson and I never discussed the art of opinion writing, and so I speak only on the basis of impressions open to every reader of his opinions, I would put him in a different category. He belonged to what might be called the naturalistic school. He wrote as he talked, and he talked as he felt. The fact that his opinions were written talk made them as lively as the liveliness of his talk. Unlike what he praised in Brandeis, his style sometimes stole attention from the substance. He had "impish candor," to borrow one of his own phrases. Candor, indeed, was one of his deepest veins. Even an occasional explosion was a manifestation of his candor. There was nothing stuffy about him, and, therefore, nothing stuffy about his writing. To confess error was for him a show of strength, not of weakness. No man who ever sat on the Supreme Court, it seems to me, mirrored the man in him in his judicial work more completely than did Justice Jackson.

Of all the adjectives that have been used to characterize him for me the most apt are gifted and beguiling. He was ineluctably charming, but his charm was not a surface glitter. It compelled affection and was not marred by passing temper or irritation. Gifted in the case of Justice Jackson does not imply the talent only for brilliant flashes or evanescent displays. His gifts were solid. They were revealed in the Swiftian irony of his famous Alfalfa Club Speech on January 31, 1953, his arresting arguments before the Supreme Court, his im-

pressive opening and closing at Nuremberg. Mr. Justice
Brandeis said that Jackson should be solicitor general for life.
The function of an advocate is not to enlarge the intellectual
horizon. His task is to seduce, to seize the mind for a predetermined end, not to explore paths to truths. There can be
no doubt that Jackson was specially endowed as an advocate.
He appreciated a good phrase, even his own. But his aims
increasingly groped beyond that of mere advocacy. He
steadily cultivated his understanding in the service of these
aims; the advocate became the judge. Deeper insight made
him aware that the best of phrases may be less than the truth
and may even falsify it. He had the habit of truth-seeking and
faithfully served justice.

To "ADMINISTER JUSTICE . . . agreeably to the Constitution
and the laws of the United States" was the oath taken by
Robert H. Jackson when he took his seat on the supreme
bench. Regard for that oath confined the free play of his
personality as it had not been confined in his very active
professional life, either in his variegated private practice or
during the seven preceding years as lawyer for the Government. That oath was for him not the utterance of a mere
formula. It summarized the ingrained conviction that there
is such a thing as law and that judges are set apart to define
it. The duty of justices is not to express their personal will
and wisdom. Their undertaking is to try to triumph over the
bent of their own preferences and to transcend, through
habituated exercise of the imagination, the limits of their
direct experience. But since the designed or the inevitable
ambiguity of language makes the pronouncement of law not
a mechanical but a judgmatical process, ascertainment of
what the Constitution and the laws of the United States require partly depends on the personalities of the bench. The
notion that the text should yield the same meaning to every

conscientious member of the Supreme Court is the offspring either of ignorance or self-deception. Contrariwise, to apply Humpty-Dumpty's philosophy to the Constitution and the laws—"when I use a word, it means just what I choose it to mean, neither more nor less"—is to treat law as an ignoble game and to falsify the course of our history. Being fallible, justices have not always achieved their task of impersonalization. But neither are the United States Reports a record of systematic deception.

Inasmuch as the Constitution and statutes, as well as prior decisions, often render unavoidable variant interpretations, not infrequently of considerable range, the individuality of the justices inescapably enters into the judicial process of the Supreme Court. Not that men before coming on the Court normally have ready-made views regarding substantive issues that are in the air; besides, wholly new issues arise in the quick passage of time. Moreover, vital to the outcome of Supreme Court litigation is the attitude of justices toward problems of the Court's jurisdiction. This concerns not merely the technical aspects of the Court's power but, even more important, the effective regard entertained for those considerations that the Court has evolved for exercising its jurisdiction. Except in the rare instance of prior preoccupation with them, these are matters to which most members of the Court bring virgin minds. What becomes decisive to a justice's functioning on the Court in the large area within which his individuality moves is his general attitude toward law, the habits of mind that he has formed or is capable of unforming, his capacity for detachment, his temperament or training for putting his passion behind his judgment instead of in front of it. The attitudes and qualities which I am groping to characterize are ingredients of what compendiously might be called dominating humility.

Every man is the whole of his life, and to assess the driving forces within him, so far as relevant, which Mr. Justice Jack-

son brought to the Court, and the growth and change of the
man while he was on it, is for his biographers, particularly
those who will be writing about him in the perspective of
history. But a few strong elements in his composition were
manifest to his contemporaries. Time is not likely to displace
their significance.

He came from a rural background and in his essential feelings remained there. Spring Creek, Pennsylvania, where he
was born, was a community of fourteen hundred, and his
beloved Jamestown, New York, with all the extensive law
practice that it afforded him, had some forty thousand in-
habitants when he left it, in 1934, for his spectacular national
career. For him the rural background was not a backwash of
the great streams of American life. It generated, in his own
words, "a way of life much the same all over America." No
one can read his delicious review of Judge Arthur Gray
Powell's *I Can Go Home Again* (30 *A. B. A. Journal* 136)
without feeling that Mr. Justice Jackson's past left in him
not romantic nostalgia but an allegiance to qualities he never
ceased to deem essential. Self-reliance, good-humored tolerance, recognition of the other fellow's right to be and to
thrive even though you may not think he is as good as you
are, suspicion of authority as well as awareness of its need,
disdain of arrogance and self-righteousness, a preference for
truculent independence over prudent deference and conformity—these were the feelings that shaped his outlook on
life. He liked his kind without being sentimental about it;
he was gregarious but shy about intimacies.

I said in his essential feelings he remained in his rural background. But not in his mind. The depth and versatility of his
culture shamed many of us who have had what is called the
advantages of a higher education. He did not go beyond high
school, and he was one of the last, as he was by far one of
the very best, of office-trained lawyers. No matter how good
the Albany Law School may have been in his day, one year

at any law school affords a meager systematic legal training. He was a self-educated man and a self-taught lawyer. He had, of course, great native powers. His strength of character developed them into intellectual distinction. Happily he fell under the influence of one of those unsung, inspiring teachers who can profoundly affect a man's life. Miss Mary Willard spotted the voracious mental appetite of young Bob, fed it, and encouraged in him habits of wide and critical reading. This was not only reflected in his felicitous writing but bears on the breadth and depth of his understanding of issues that came before the Court.

His wide reading helped to counteract the powerful impact of the immediate and the concrete, natural enough in one so thoroughly immersed for so long in practice. Undue regard for the so-called practical leaves out of account the fact that a generalization based on it too often works injustice to the practical needs of the future. By keeping the pores of his intellectual interests open, Mr. Justice Jackson was alert against regarding his limited views, as any man's views are limited, as eternal verities and treating them as the commands of the Constitution. In addition to this unremitting effort to extend his understanding through wide and reflective reading, Nuremberg, I believe, had a profound influence on his endeavor to understand the human situation. An essentially good-natured, an even innocently unsophisticated, temperament was there made to realize how ultimately fragile the forces of reason are and how precious the safeguards of law so painstakingly built up in the course of the centuries.

His voice is stilled. His vitality persists. And not merely in the memory of his familiars. His speech breaks through the printed page. He was one of those rare men whose spoken word survives in type.

Nine

Mr. Justice Cardozo

(1955)

This biographical sketch of Mr. Justice Cardozo was written for the forthcoming Supplement Two (Vol. 22) of the *Dictionary of American Biography*.

BENJAMIN NATHAN CARDOZO was born in New York City, May 24, 1870, and after a heart attack and stroke, followed by a long illness, died at the home of his intimate friend Chief Judge Irving Lehman of the New York Court of Appeals, in Port Chester, New York, July 9, 1938. He was the younger son of Albert and Rebecca Nathan Cardozo, both of whom were descended from Sephardic Jews who had been connected with the Spanish and Portuguese Synagogue in New York from before the Revolution. Having been tutored by Horatio Alger, the popular author of stories for boys, he entered Columbia College from which he graduated at the age of nineteen and received his master's degree the following year, while attending the Columbia Law School. He did not stay for a degree in law and was admitted to the bar in 1891. For twenty-two years he modestly pursued what was essentially the calling of a barrister, that is, he was, in the main, counsel for other lawyers. As the practice of law is pursued in the United States, this was an unusual professional activity, even at the New York bar. Quite unknown to the general public, he rapidly gained the esteem of the bar and the bench of New York by his arguments and briefs, as counsel as well as referee, a functionary appointed by judges in specific cases, particularly those of a complicated commercial character, a field of law in which Cardozo especially excelled. His wide experience in arguing cases before the Court of Appeals (the highest in the hierarchy of New York courts) led him to write his first book, *Jurisdiction of the Court of Appeals of the State of New York*, published in 1903.

President Taft offered him a place on the United States District Court for the Southern District of New York. He had two sisters to support, and he felt compelled to decline it because of the then too meager salary. In 1913, as a result of one of those occasionally successful anti-Tammany movements in New York City, Cardozo was lifted out of his wholly private life by nomination and subsequent election as a justice of the Supreme Court of New York. This is the court that carries the heavy burden of litigation in New York. He was, however, destined to have little experience as a trial judge. Within six weeks, on the request of the Court of Appeals, the judges of which had for long held him in high esteem, Governor Glynn designated him to serve temporarily as an associate judge of that Court. In January 1917 he was appointed a regular member by Governor Whitman to fill out a vacancy, and in the autumn was elected for a term of fourteen years on the joint nomination of both the major parties. In 1927, he was elected without opposition chief judge.

As he had been a lawyers' lawyer, so Cardozo became a judges' judge. For eighteen years his legal mastery, conveyed with great felicity, gave unusual distinction to the New York Reports. Joined as his learning was with an uncommonly charming personality, Cardozo exerted such intrinsic influence upon his court as to make it the second most distinguished judicial tribunal in the land. His philosophic temper of mind was nourished on wide reading. Naturally enough, this needed an outlet for freer expression than legal opinions permit. In four volumes, slender in size but full of insight, he set forth his views upon the relations of law to life: *The Nature of the Judicial Process* (1921); *The Growth of the Law* (1924); *The Paradoxes of Legal Science* (1928); *Law and Literature* (1931). Their common theme is the task that confronts the judge, but a candid scrutiny of what confronts the judge must face what confronts the law. By deftly spelling out much that was implicit in the early writings of Holmes and luminously analyzing what others gropingly felt, *The Nature of the Judicial Process* has established itself as a little classic. The essay form chosen by Cardozo was the fit instrument for a thinker whose concern was to lay bare the contending claims that seek the mediation of law and to give some indication how this process of mediation in fact operates. An essay is adaptable to the tentative and suggestive, incomplete or even contradictory. It is thus an appropriate vehicle for conveying the zest and complexities and intractabilities of life.

The New York Court of Appeals, with its wide range of predominantly common-law litigation, was a natural field for Judge Cardozo. Barring only Mr. Justice Holmes, who was a seminal thinker in the law as well as vastly learned, no judge in his time was more deeply versed in the history of the common law or more resourceful in applying the living principles by which it has unfolded; and his mastery of the common law was matched by his love of it. His evolutionary adaptation of common-law principles to situations to which our industrial civilization gave rise influenced adjudication of courts throughout the English-speaking world. For example, in *MacPherson* v. *Buick Motor Co.*, 217 N.Y. 382, Judge Cardozo's opinion convincingly established the right of redress against the manufacturer of a person injured by a latent defect in a car purchased at retail, for the reason that the defect might have been discovered had the manufacturer exercised appropriate care. The specific instance gave rise to a radiating principle which was so convincingly vindicated that it eventually commended itself to the House of Lords, *McAllister* v. *Stevenson*, [1932] A.C. 562, and has now become an established part of the law of torts.

Not only was the stuff of the litigation before the Court of Appeals of New York congenial to his professional interest, he was wholly happy in his personal associations. It was therefore a severe wrench for him to be taken from Albany to Washington. Probably no man ever took a seat on the supreme bench so reluctantly. This he did in 1932, when President Hoover, upon the resignation of Mr. Justice Holmes, named him as Holmes's successor. (285 U.S. iii.) While his nomination was universally acclaimed, from the point of view of "practical politics" serious obstacles emerged against it before he was named. There was the geographic objection: two New Yorkers, Chief Justice Hughes and Mr. Justice Stone, were already on the Court, and it would make for imbalance for one state, particularly New York, to have a third of the membership of the Court. When this objection was made, Senator William E. Borah of Idaho, one of the Republican leaders and chairman of the powerful Committee on Foreign Relations, told President Hoover that Cardozo belonged as much to Idaho as to New York. As Professor Chafee put it, "President Hoover ignored geography and made history." (*Harper's Magazine*, June 1932, p. 34.) When the sectarian difficulty was whispered, in that there was already one Jew, Brandeis, on the Court, Senator Borah said to the President (who was himself singularly free from this bias), "The way to deal with anti-Semitism is not to yield to it," adding, "Just as John Adams is best remembered for his appointment of John Marshall to the Supreme Court, so you, Mr. President, have the opportunity of being best remembered for putting Cardozo there." Disregarding all irrelevancies, the President named Cardozo because he was Cardozo.

Fate granted him less than six full terms on the supreme bench. With rare exceptions, the great reputations on that Court have been partly a function of time. It is some measure of Cardozo's qualities that in so short a time he left so enduring a mark on the constitutional history of the United States. With astonishing rapidity he made the adjustment from preoccupation with the comparatively restricted problems of private litigation to the most exacting demands of judicial statesmanship. Immense learning, deep culture, critical detachment, intellectual courage, and unswerving disinterestedness reinforced imagination and native humility, and gave him in rare measure the qualities which are the special requisites for the work of the Court to whose keeping is entrusted no small share of the destiny of the nation.

It bespeaks much for the responsiveness of the mass of mankind to sheer goodness that so shy and sensitive a man, so withdrawn a nature as Cardozo, should have communicated his exquisite qualities on so wide a scale. The feeling of respect bordering on reverence which Cardozo aroused was strikingly manifested in relation to a poignant episode in his life. His father was one of the so-called Tweed judges—William M. Tweed, the Tammany Hall boss and corrupt ruler of New York—and resigned under a cloud when Tweed was deposed. By tacit agreement the press kept quiet about this incident when Cardozo ran for high judicial office in New York and on the occasion of his nomination to the Supreme Court. He did not have the common touch, but he was tender and compassionate. Great courtesy, accentuated by the slight stoop of the cloistered scholar, a face, according to Holmes, "beautiful with intellect and character" (*Holmes-Laski Letters*, II, p. 837), a fine head with silken white hair, combined to give him a striking personal appearance. Though he was most at ease with a few familiars talking law, he charmed whenever he ventured forth, on rare occasions, into the social life of Washington. He never married, but he had chivalric feelings about women. When he dedicated one of his books to the "sacred memory" of his sister Ellen, he described precisely what he felt. In his writing generally, he was given somewhat to the heightened language of rhetoric and a tendency toward figurative language dangerous to judicial speech. While pedestrian critics complain that Holmes was unduly incisive, Cardozo may fairly be charged with being elegantly diffuse. His style was Corinthian, not Doric.

Greatness implies uniquity. It is idle, therefore, to compare Mr. Justice Cardozo with other towering figures among American judges. That Cardozo belongs among our great judges—not more, surely, than a dozen—is not in dispute. Indeed, his achievement in Washington merely confirmed and amplified the distinction he made manifest in Albany. He was translated to the Supreme Court, despite all the considerations of narrow expediency against his selection, precisely because of his unique qualifications. Chief Judge Cardozo was the one man, in the general opinion of bench and bar, fit to succeed Mr. Justice Holmes.

With an accent of reverence, Cardozo always spoke of Holmes as "the Master." Both served the same mistress—the law—with complete devotion. Neither St. Francis nor Thomas More led a more dedicated life than these two men, so different in antecedents and temperament, who applied their great endowments to resolving by law the conflicts between man and man and between liberty and authority—law compounded of wisdom from the past and insight into the future. Cardozo spoke for all great judges when he wrote that the judge must be "historian and prophet all in one." For law is "not only as the past has shaped it in judgments already rendered, but as the future ought to shape it in cases yet to come." The common law, which was Cardozo's preoccupation during his long tenure on the New York Court of Appeals, is a process of constant rejuvenation to meet the demands of a society that is not stagnant. Such readjustments require a proper balance between retaining and changing. Under the influence of his master, Cardozo was second only to Holmes in making of the judicial process a blend of continuity and creativeness.

Like Holmes, Cardozo carried his philosophic outlook on law into the more spacious and more treacherous field of constitutional law. That he should have attained pre-eminence after so short a tenure on the supreme bench (where one does not get one's bearing, so Chief Justice Hughes said, for at least three years), is only partly due to the unusual flow of litigation of far-reaching import during his few years on the Court. Mr. Justice Cardozo did not derive distinction from the distorting significance of so-called "great cases." Some cases are born great and a judge shares the great occasion. Other cases achieve distinction through the creative power of the judge, especially when insight is conveyed with felicity. Cardozo imparted intellectual significance to cases great or small, whether of inflamed public interest or of recondite technicality.

To select representative samples of Cardozo's judicial prowess and of his art in manifesting it is an ungracious task. The range and richness of his seven-score Supreme Court opinions could be demonstrated equally well by others than those here named. Of the six here chosen, three are in private litigation, three in public, three are opinions of the Court, three are dissents. They are: *Reed* v. *Allen*, 286 U.S. 191, 201 (dissent), because of its resourcefulness in making the law of remedies an instrument of justice; *Stewart Dry Goods Co.* v. *Lewis*, 294 U.S. 550, 566 (dissent), because of its illuminating analysis of problems of taxation; *McCandless* v. *Furlaud*, 296 U.S. 140, because it proves the law of corporate trusteeship can master the skill of individual chicanery; *Ashton* v. *Cameron County District*, 298 U.S. 513, 532 (dissent), because it demonstrates, with a persuasiveness that eventually carried the day, that the distribution of power between the nation and the states does not mean the impotence of both; the *Social Security Cases,* 301 U.S. 548, and 301 U.S. 619, because of the proof that the Constitution does not preclude the federal system from meeting exigent and pervasive human needs; *Palko* v. *Connecticut,* 302 U.S. 319, because of its penetrating exposition of the task confronting the Court in the enforcement of the due process clause of the Fourteenth Amendment.

Courage is especially shining when exercised by a markedly gentle nature. This lawyers' lawyer, this man of the cloister, as he faced the application of the Constitution to a rapidly changing world, at times dared to free the future from the tyranny of slogans and outmoded formulas when some of his brethren, who came from the world of affairs, imprisoned themselves in the ephemeral past. The few short years on the Supreme Court of this gentle and withdrawn spirit coincided —such is the sardonic play of Fate—with one of the most tempestuous periods in the Court's history, the years of its invalidation of much of the New Deal legislation and the consequent proposal by President Roosevelt for reconstruction of the Court, the so-called "Court packing plan." But so dominant was his serene temper that he transcended the heated controversies in which the labors of the Court were enmeshed. Mr. Justice Cardozo's opinions during those troubled years have already come to reflect, not the friction and passion of their day, but the abiding spirit of the Constitution.

Ten

Mr. Justice Roberts

(1955)

This article was written for the December 1955 number of the *University of Pennsylvania Law Review* (Vol. 104, p. 311), which was dedicated to the memory of Mr. Justice Roberts.

THE DICTUM THAT HISTORY cannot be written without documents is less than a half-truth if it implies that it can be written from them. Especially is this so in making an assessment of individual contributions to the collective results of the work of an institution like the Supreme Court, whose labors, by the very nature of its functions, are done behind closed doors and, on the whole, without leaving to history the documentation leading up to what is ultimately recorded in the United States Reports. To be sure, the opinions of the different justices tell things about them—about some, more; about some, less. As is true of all literary compositions, to a critic saturated in them, qualities of the writer emerge from the writing. However, even in the case of an opinion by a justice with the most distinctive style, what is said and what is left unsaid present to students of the Court a fascinating challenge of untangling individual influences in a collective judgment.

To discover the man behind the opinion and to estimate the influence he may have exerted in the Court's labors, in the case of Mr. Justice Roberts, is an essentially hopeless task. Before I came on the Court I had been a close student of its opinions. But not until I became a colleague, and even then only after some time, did I come to realize how little the opinions of Roberts, J., revealed the man and therefore the qualities that he brought to the work of the Court. In his case it can fairly be said the style—his judicial style—was not the man.

The *esprit* of Roberts's private communications leaves little doubt that when he came to writing his opinions he restrained the lively and imaginative phases of his temperament. I speak without knowledge, but he had evidently reflected much on the feel and flavor of a judicial opinion as an appropriate expression of the judicial judgment. The fires of his strong feelings were banked by powerful self-discipline, and only on the rarest occasion does a spark flare up from the printed page. The sober and declaratory character of his opinions was, I believe, a form consciously chosen to carry out the judicial function as he saw it. We are told that Judge Augustus N. Hand, in disposing of a case that excited much popular agitation, set himself to writing an opinion in which nothing was "quotable." The reasons behind this attitude doubtless guided Justice Roberts in fashioning his judicial style. Moreover, his was, on the whole, a hidden rather than an obvious nature—hidden, that is, from the public view. His loyalties were deep, as was his devotion to his convictions. Both were phases of an uncompromising honesty. They constituted the most guarded qualities of his personality, and he would not vulgarize them by public manifestation.

In not revealing, indeed in suppressing, the richer and deeper qualities of his mind and character, the Roberts opinions reflect his own underestimation of his work. Partly, he was a very modest man, partly his judicial self-depreciation expressed his sense of awe to be a member of the bench charged with functions, in the language of Chief Justice

Hughes, "of the gravest consequence to our people and to the future of our institutions." Above all, the standards for his self-appraisal were, characteristically, judges of the greatest distinction in the Court's history. On leaving the bench, he wrote: "I have no illusions about my judicial career. But one can only do what one can. Who am I to revile the good God that he did not make me a Marshall, a Taney, a Bradley, a Holmes, a Brandeis or a Cardozo."

Roberts was unjust to himself. He contributed more during his fifteen years on the Court than he himself could appraise. His extensive, diversified experience at the bar and his informed common sense brought wisdom to the disposition of the considerable body of litigation, outside the passions of popular controversy, that still comes before the Court. Again, his qualities of character—humility engendered by consciousness of limitations, respect for the views of others whereby one's own instinctive reactions are examined anew, subordination of solo performances to institutional interests, courtesy in personal relations that derives from respect for the conscientious labor of others and is not merely a show of formal manners—are indispensable qualities for the work of any court, but pre-eminently for that of the Supreme Court. Probably no justice in the Court's history attached more significance to these qualities than Mr. Justice Brandeis. It tells more than pages of argumentation that Brandeis held Roberts in especial esteem as a member of the Court.

It is one of the most ludicrous illustrations of the power of lazy repetition of uncritical talk that a judge with the character of Roberts should have attributed to him a change of judicial views out of deference to political considerations. One is more saddened than shocked that a high-minded and thoughtful United States senator should assume it to be an established fact that it was by reason of "the famous switch of Mr. Justice Roberts" that legislation was constitutionally sustained after President Roosevelt's proposal for reconstructing the Court and because of it. The charge specifically relates to the fact that while Roberts was of the majority in *Morehead* v. *New York ex rel. Tipaldo,* 298 U.S. 587, decided June 1, 1936, in reaffirming *Adkins* v. *Children's Hospital,* 261 U.S. 525, and thereby invalidating the New York Minimum Wage Law, he was again with the majority in *West Coast Hotel Co.* v. *Parrish,* 300 U.S. 379, decided on March 29, 1937, overruling the *Adkins* case and sustaining minimum wage legislation. Intellectual responsibility should, one would suppose, save a thoughtful man from the familiar trap of *post hoc ergo propter hoc.* Even those whose business it is to study the work of the Supreme Court have lent themselves to a charge which is refuted on the face of the Court records. It is refuted, that is, if consideration is given not only to opinions but to appropriate deductions drawn from data pertaining to the time when petitions for certiorari are granted, when cases are argued, when dispositions are, in normal course, made at conference, and when decisions are withheld because of absences and divisions on the Court.

It is time that this false charge against Roberts be dissipated by a recording of the indisputable facts. Disclosure of Court happenings not made public by the Court itself, in its opinions and orders, presents a ticklish problem. The secrecy that envelops the Court's work is not due to love of secrecy or want of responsible regard for the claims of a democratic society to know how it is governed. That the Supreme Court should not be amenable to the forces of publicity to which the Executive and the Congress are subjected is essential to the effective functioning of the Court. But the passage of time may enervate the reasons for this restriction, particularly if disclosure rests not on tittle-tattle or self-serving declarations. The more so is justification for thus lifting the veil of secrecy valid if thereby the conduct of a Justice whose intellectual morality has been impugned is vindicated.

The truth about the so-called "switch" of Roberts in connection with the *Minimum Wage* cases is that when the *Tipaldo* case was before the Court in the spring of 1936, he was prepared to overrule the *Adkins* decision. Since a majority could not be had for overruling it, he silently agreed with the Court in finding the New York statute under attack in the *Tipaldo* case not distinguishable from the statute which had been declared unconstitutional in the *Adkins* case. That such was his position an alert reader could find in the interstices of the United States Reports. It took not a little persuasion—so indifferent was Roberts to misrepresentation—to induce him to set forth what can be extracted from the Reports.[1] Here it is:

A petition for certiorari was filed in *Morehead* v. *Tipaldo*, 298 U.S. 587, on March 16, 1936. When the petition came to be acted upon, the Chief Justice spoke in favor of a grant, but several others spoke against it on the ground that the case was ruled by *Adkins* vs. *Children's Hospital*, 261 U.S. 525. Justices Brandeis, Cardozo and Stone were in favor of a grant. They, with the Chief Justice, made up four votes for a grant.

When my turn came to speak I said I saw no reason to grant the writ unless the Court were prepared to re-examine and overrule the *Adkins* case. To this remark there was no response around the table, and the case was marked granted.

Both in the petition for certiorari, in the brief on the merits, and in oral argument, counsel for the State of New York took the position that it was unnecessary to overrule the *Adkins* case in order to sustain the position of the State of New York. It was urged that further data and experience and additional facts distinguished the case at bar from the *Adkins* case. The argument seemed to me to be disingenuous and born of timidity. I could find nothing in the record to substantiate the alleged distinction. At conference I so stated, and stated further that I was for taking

[1] Mr. Justice Roberts gave me this memorandum on November 9, 1945, after he had resigned from the bench. He left the occasion for using it to my discretion. For reasons indicated in the text, the present seems to me an appropriate time for making it public.

the State of New York at its word. The State had not asked that the *Adkins* case be overruled but that it be distinguished. I said I was unwilling to put a decision on any such ground. The vote was five to four for affirmance, and the case was assigned to Justice Butler.

I stated to him that I would concur in any opinion which was based on the fact that the State had not asked us to re-examine or overrule *Adkins* and that, as we found no material difference in the facts of the two cases, we should therefore follow the *Adkins* case. The case was originally so written by Justice Butler, but after a dissent had been circulated he added matter to his opinion, seeking to sustain the *Adkins* case in principle. My proper course would have been to concur specially on the narrow ground I had taken. I did not do so. But at conference in the Court I said that I did not propose to review and re-examine the *Adkins* case until a case should come to the Court requiring that this should be done.

August 17, 1936, an appeal was filed in *West Coast Hotels* [*sic*] *Company* vs. *Parrish*, 300 U.S. 379. The Court as usual met to consider applications in the week of Monday, October 5, 1936, and concluded its work by Saturday, October 10. During the conferences the jurisdictional statement in the *Parrish* case was considered and the question arose whether the appeal should be dismissed [2] on the authority of *Adkins* and *Morehead*. Four of those who had voted in the majority in the *Morehead* case voted to dismiss the appeal in the *Parrish* case. I stated that I would vote for the notation of probable jurisdiction. I am not sure that I gave my reason, but it was that in the appeal in the *Parrish* case the authority of *Adkins* was definitely assailed and the Court was asked to reconsider and overrule it. Thus, for the first time, I was confronted with the necessity of facing the soundness of the *Adkins* case. Those who were in the majority in the *Morehead* case expressed some surprise at my vote, and I heard one of the brethren ask another, "What is the matter with Roberts?"

Justice Stone was taken ill about October 14. The case was argued December 16 and 17, 1936, in the absence of Justice Stone,

[2] Evidently he meant "should be reversed summarily," since the Washington Supreme Court had sustained the statute.

who at that time was lying in a comatose condition at his home. It came on for consideration at the conference on December 19. I voted for an affirmance. There were three other such votes, those of the Chief Justice, Justice Brandeis, and Justice Cardozo. The other four voted for a reversal.

If a decision had then been announced, the case would have been affirmed by a divided Court. It was thought that this would be an unfortunate outcome, as everyone on the Court knew Justice Stone's views. The case was, therefore, laid over for further consideration when Justice Stone should be able to participate. Justice Stone was convalescent during January and returned to the sessions of the Court on February 1, 1937. I believe that the *Parrish* case was taken up at the conference on February 6, 1937, and Justice Stone then voted for affirmance. This made it possible to assign the case for an opinion, which was done. The decision affirming the lower court was announced March 29, 1937.

These facts make it evident that no action taken by the President in the interim had any causal relation to my action in the *Parrish* case.

More needs to be said for Roberts than he cared to say for himself. As a matter of history it is regrettable that Roberts's unconcern for his own record led him to abstain from stating his position. The occasions are not infrequent when the disfavor of separate opinions, on the part of the bar and to the extent that it prevails within the Court, should not be heeded. Such a situation was certainly presented when special circumstances made Roberts agree with a result but basically disagree with the opinion which announced it.

The crucial factor in the whole episode was the absence of Mr. Justice Stone from the bench, on account of illness, from October 14, 1936, to February 1, 1937, 299 U.S. iii.

In *Chamberlain* v. *Andrews,* and its allied cases, decided November 23, 1936, the judgments of the New York Court of Appeals sustaining the New York Unemployment Insurance law were "affirmed by an equally divided Court." 299 U.S. 515. The constitutional outlook represented by these cases would reflect the attitude of a justice toward the issues involved in the *Adkins* case. It can hardly be doubted that Van Devanter, McReynolds, Sutherland, and Butler, JJ., were the four justices for reversal in *Chamberlain* v. *Andrews, supra.* There can be equally no doubt that Hughes, C.J., and Brandeis and Cardozo, JJ., were for affirmance. Since Stone, J., was absent, it must have been Roberts who joined Hughes, Brandeis, and Cardozo. The appellants petitioned for a rehearing before the full bench, but since the position of Stone, as disclosed by his views in the *Tipaldo* case, would not have changed the result, *i.e.*, affirmance, the judgments were allowed to stand and the petition for rehearing was denied. Moreover, in preceding terms, Roberts had abundantly established that he did not have the narrow, restrictive attitude in the application of the broad, undefined provisions of the Constitution which led to decisions that provoked the acute controversies in 1936 and 1937.

Indeed, years before the 1936 election, in the 1933 term he was the author of the opinion in *Nebbia* v. *New York*, 291 U.S. 502, which evoked substantially the same opposing constitutional philosophy from Van Devanter, McReynolds, Sutherland, and Butler, JJ., as their dissent expressed in *West Coast Hotel Co. v. Parrish, supra.* The result in the *Nebbia* case was significant enough. But for candor and courage, the opinion in which Roberts justified it was surely one of the most important contributions in years in what is perhaps the most far-reaching field of constitutional adjudication. It was an effective blow for liberation from empty tags and meretricious assumptions. In effect, Roberts wrote the epitaph on the misconception, which had gained respect from repetition, that legislative price-fixing as such was at least presumptively unconstitutional. In his opinion in *Parrish*, the Chief Justice naturally relied heavily on Roberts's opinion in *Nebbia,* for the reasoning of *Nebbia* had undermined the foundations of *Adkins.*

Few speculations are more treacherous than diagnosis of motives or genetic explanations of the position taken by judges in Supreme Court decisions. Seldom can attribution have been wider of the mark than to find in Roberts's views in this or that case a reflection of economic predilection. He was, to be sure, as all men are, a child of his antecedents. But his antecedents united with his temperament to make him a forthright, democratic, perhaps even somewhat innocently trusting, generous, humane creature. Long before it became popular to regard every so-called civil liberties question as constitutionally self-answering, Roberts gave powerful utterance to his sensitiveness for those procedural safeguards which are protective of human rights in a civilized society, even when invoked by the least appealing of characters. See his opinions in *Sorrells* v. *United States*, 287 U.S. 435, 453, and *Snyder* v. *Massachusetts*, 291 U.S. 97, 123.

Owen J. Roberts contributed his good and honest share to that coral-reef fabric which is law. He was content to let history ascertain, if it would, what his share was. But only one who had the good fortune to work for years beside him, day by day, is enabled to say that no man ever served on the Supreme Court with more scrupulous regard for its moral demands than Mr. Justice Roberts.

Eleven

Judge Learned Hand

(1947)

On the occasion of Judge Learned Hand's seventy-fifth birthday the *Harvard Law Review* dedicated its February 1947 issue to him. Mr. Justice Frankfurter contributed this article (Vol. 60, p. 325).

ONE OF THE MARKS of a fine civilization is the esteem it accords to excellence. That Holmes, Brandeis, and Cardozo have become part of our national tradition is one of the more encouraging aspects of contemporary America. For these are men who labored far from the madding crowd. They have stirred deep response not because they aimed at popularity but in part, certainly, because they were indifferent to it. Pervasive recognition of excellence in such an undramatic and austere calling as that of a judge is at best a slow process. Happily it has come to Judge Hand at the full tide of his powers.

Learned Hand is heading straight for the glory and the dangers of a legend. The glory needs no gilding. The dangers may be lessened by exposure. Legends too readily enlist laziness of thought and weaken the influence that comes from critical appreciation. It is important for American law and letters that Judge Hand remain a mentor and not become a memory. It is important that he continue to enter not merely anthologies but the minds of men. In time, hundreds of his

specific rulings will cease to have interest for the most avid
legal archaeologist. Even now not one of his opinions has the
formal authority which derives not from intrinsic ascendancy
but from accident of place. Yet, so long as we shall continue
to conceive of law not as the disguised manifestation of mere
will but as the effort of reason to discover justice, the body
of his opinions will be an enduring source of truth-seeking
and illumination. His insights, the morality of the mind which
respects those insights, the beauty with which they are expressed, make them so. And this is true even when he deals
with issues which to meager perceptions appear meager. I
must leave to others a detailed exposition and estimate of
Judge Hand's contributions. But I would not willingly forego
the opportunity afforded by the happy occasion of his seventy-
fifth birthday to express a word of gratitude for one at whose
feet I sat almost from the time that I came to the bar and
at whose feet I still sit.

In sponsoring Learned Hand's appointment to the District
Court, Attorney General Wickersham showed a keen scent
for intellectual powers and a realization of their need particularly on the federal bench. Learned Hand would hardly
have appeared as an inevitable choice had there been deference
to the usual considerations guiding the selection of federal
judges. While the discerning were at once excited by Mr.
Wickersham's bold recommendation of Hand to President
Taft, it took the pedestrian members of the profession some
time to make their adjustment to this new planet in the judicial sky. Nor has he become wholly comfortable for the
conventional-minded in the law. He has never been under the
delusion that law is a collection of nicely wrapped-up formulas, ready to be applied to the ticklish and tangled controversies that come before courts. He is aware as few judges
have been that, whatever may appear on the smooth surface
in earlier opinions, law must deal mainly with probabilities,
not certitudes. Particularly is this a demand upon law in an

epoch of vast physical and social changes. But Judge Hand is no less mindful of the fact that law is the framework of order within which the conflicts and contingencies of life must be subdued, if a society is not to court chaos or be ruled by tyranny. And chaos is the usual precursor of tyranny.

When considerations of such magnitude influence if they do not underlie the accommodations that determine important adjudications, it is not surprising that on occasion we find in Learned Hand, as in Holmes, a certain vagueness of formulation and a penumbral scope to decisions. This is a manifestation of clarity of thought. It is the kind of clarity which, in Professor Whitehead's phrase, "leaves the darkness unobscured." Analysis of a difficult problem may still be incomplete or its solution as yet unattained. The search for truth at a given time may require even of a judge avowed agnosticism or inexplicitness of statement. I believe it was Artemus Ward who said "it is better not to know so many things than to know so many things that ain't so." Learned Hand knows what he does not know; and he knows the importance of not obstructing deeper analysis tomorrow by the illusory certainty of obsolete or premature generalization. When he rejects, he has taken in what he rejects, which is different from rejecting without understanding. In short, he does not meet difficulties by evading them. Intricate problems do not appear simple to him, nor does he make them appear simple to others by verbal legerdemain. He does not have the treacherous strength that draws on jaunty confidence in one's power to solve problems. He has that rarer strength which comes from readiness to grapple fearlessly with issues defying sleazy answers.

The law no doubt is "the calling of thinkers." But it is necessary to add, as Learned Hand did long ago, that "the good judge is an artist, perhaps most like a *chef*. Into the composition of his dishes he adds so much of this or that element as will blend the whole into a compound, delectable

or at any rate tolerable to the palates of his guests." Like a
good chef he makes the best dish when he uses the best materials. At any rate he avoids stale and underripe materials,
and certainly noxious ingredients. Figures of speech in the
realm of thought are notoriously dangerous. One had best
say in plain English that a calling which so deeply involves
the well-being of society and is so dependent on the scientific
spirit of truth-seeking, but which has few of the aids of scientific verification, calls for men of the highest professional
and moral qualities. Disinterestedness and discernment are the
prime requisites. As the adjusters of conflicts, judges should
be as free as the lot of man permits, from allegiance to any
cause or class less than the whole of society. He must be
capable of transcending the limitations of his own experience
and not confuse the familiar with the necessary. These are
not cries for utopia. They are conditions that have been met
often enough to prove that society has available the gifts, if
it will only use them.

The understanding and disinterestedness of a judge largely
derive from that by which his imagination is fed. Not a little
of Holmes is explained by a list of his reading as recorded in
the famous "black book." Learned Hand has indicated the
equipment to be possessed by a judge passing on questions of
constitutional law. Other questions are no less demanding.
"I venture to believe that it is as important to a judge called
upon to pass on a question of constitutional law, to have at
least a bowing acquaintance with Acton and Maitland, with
Thucydides, Gibbon and Carlyle, with Homer, Dante, Shakespeare and Milton, with Machiavelli, Montaigne and Rabelais,
with Plato, Bacon, Hume and Kant, as with the books which
have been specifically written on the subject. For in such
matters everything turns upon the spirit in which he ap-
proaches the questions before him. The words he must construe are empty vessels into which he can pour nearly anything he will. Men do not gather figs of thistles, nor supple

institutions from judges whose outlook is limited by parish or class. They must be aware that there are before them more than verbal problems; more than final solutions cast in generalizations of universal applicability. They must be aware of the changing social tensions in every society which makes it an organism; which demand new schemata of adaptation; which will disrupt it, if rigidly confined." (*The Spirit of Liberty*, (Dilliard ed., 1952), p. 81.) Learned Hand has made these exactions for others. He himself satisfies them. They are the best commentary on his judicial labors.

The dullards who talk about phrase-making in a judge like Learned Hand miss the happy conjunction of thought and its expression in enduring language. When form and substance are dissevered, it is not because they are intrinsically discrete but because artistic fusion has not been attained. Hand's language is at once rich and colloquial, imparting power and rhythm to his writing. Occasional flashes of sardonic humor and dissolving wit irradiate it. He vindicates Holmes's admonition to judges that in order to be weighty they need not be heavy. After years of close association, Judge Julian Mack, a connoisseur of excellence, once remarked that he never knew a man whose writings so conveyed the life of his talk as did Hand's. Those who have heard his talk will never forget it. The other day I happened on a passage by Pepys which gives some inkling of its qualities. He was speaking of Lord Clarendon. Centuries separate Lord Clarendon and Judge Hand, and their temperaments even more. But what Pepys wrote of Clarendon singularly fits Hand: "I am mad in love with my Lord Chancellor, for he do comprehend and speak out well, and with the greatest easiness and authority that ever I saw man in my life . . . his manner and freedom of doing it, as if he played with it, and was informing only all the rest of the company, was mighty pretty."

Of course Learned Hand's work has limitations. To call them the defects of his qualities is to employ a lazy phrase.

They are the imperfections which are the lot of man's finitude. Holmes coupled Learned Hand with Cardozo as the
two judges whom he wished to see on the supreme bench.
That Hand was never chosen must surely serve those, if any
there be, who seek to be chosen and those who are there, as
a temptation to reflection on the caprices of fortune. For
Learned Hand belongs to that very select company of judges
in whom one does not find greatness in order to justify merely
personal preference.

III

DIRECTIONS OF AMERICAN DEMOCRACY

———————

One

The Bold Experiment of Freedom

(1949)

The circumstances in which this address was delivered were most appropriate to its theme. On October 23, 1949, at Aaronsburg, Pennsylvania, ceremonies were held in celebration of the one-hundred-and-fiftieth anniversary of the gift by Aaron Levy, a Jew of Revolutionary days who founded the town, of the land on which was built the Salem Evangelical Lutheran Church. Mr. Justice Frankfurter gave the principal address (later printed in the Winter 1950 number of the *Menorah Journal*, Vol. 38, p. 1).

BY ITS FOUNDERS this nation was committed to democracy, in which we all profess our faith. Even its enemies pay democracy the tribute of appropriating its name. For democracy is the only form of social arrangement that fully respects the richness of human society and, by respecting it, helps to unfold it. Democracy is thus the only adequate response to the deepest human needs and justified as such by the long course of history. All the devices of political machinery—parties and platforms and votes—are merely instruments for enabling men to live together under conditions that bring forth the maximum gifts of each for the fullest enjoyment of all. Democracy furnishes the political framework within which reason can thrive most generously and imaginatively on the widest scale—least hampered, that is, by the accident of personal antecedents and most regardful of the intrinsic qualities in men.

Not only the experience to which history testifies but nature herself vindicates democracy. For nature plants gifts and graces where least expected, and under circumstances that defy all the little artifices of man. To meet nature's disregard of distinctions that are not intrinsic, but merely man-made, we need political and economic institutions that allow these mysterious natural bounties their fullest outlet.

Thus we Americans are enlisted in a common enterprise—whatever our antecedents, whatever the creed we may avow or reject—the bold experiment of freedom. It is bold because it cannot be realized without the most difficult and persistent collaborative effort. It demands the continuous exercise of reason, and self-discipline of the highest order. This is so because it places ultimate faith for attaining the common good in the responsibility of the individual.

We are thus engaged in the most difficult of all arts—the art of living together in a free society. It is comfortable, even if slothful, to live without responsibility. Responsibility is exacting and painful. Democracy involves hardship—the hardship of the unceasing responsibility of every citizen. Where the entire people do not take a continuous and considered part in public life, there can be no democracy in any meaningful sense of the term. Democracy is always a beckoning goal, not a safe harbor. For freedom is an unremitting endeavor, never a final achievement. That is why no office in the land is more important than that of being a citizen.

And we can say with all humility that the United States has a special destiny because its moral cohesion derives from a unique circumstance. No other nation has been composed of such heterogeneous elements. We represent a confluence of peoples whose bond of union is their common intrinsic human qualities. From its very beginning this country has bestowed upon those born under other skies the great boon of participation in its fellowship, with a single exception that created a moral lesion in the nation, requiring the healing forces of a civil war and its aftermath.

The saga of our republic is the story of the most significant racial and religious admixture in history. The fifty-six signers of the Declaration of Independence were men of varying religious outlook and eighteen of them of non-English stock. It cannot be too often recalled that when the Continental Congress chose John Adams, Franklin, and Jefferson as a committee to devise the national emblem, they recommended a seal containing the national emblems of England, Scotland, Ireland, France, Germany, and Holland, as representing "the countries from which these States have been peopled."

The event that the Commonwealth of Pennsylvania is so worthily commemorating today makes the reminder especially pertinent. Our cultural history—the sciences and the arts—reflects the genius and labors of men and women who came to these shores from all corners of the world. If a single faith can be said to unite a great people, surely the ideal which holds us together beyond any other is our belief in the worth of the individual, whatever his race or religion. In this faith America was founded; to this faith have her poets and seers and statesmen and the unknown millions, generation after generation, devoted their lives.

The opportunity which America has afforded implies the deepest obligations. What have those who have come here, beckoned by America's hospitality, made of this opportunity? Franklin Roosevelt gave the final answer. What he said on the occasion of the fiftieth anniversary of the Statue of Liberty was true of the stream of immigrants that came here, like Aaron Levy, before the Revolution; it is no less true of those who made their discovery of America more recently:

I like to think of the men and women who, with the break of dawn off Sandy Hook, have strained their eyes to the west for a first glimpse of the New World.

·   ·   ·   ·   ·   ·   ·

They came to us speaking many tongues—but a single language, the universal language of human aspiration.

How well their hopes were justified is proved by the record of what they achieved. They not only found freedom in the New World, but by their effort and devotion they made the New World's freedom safer, richer, more far-reaching, more capable of growth. *The Public Papers and Addresses of Franklin D. Roosevelt*, (1938), Vol. 5, p. 542.

I shall not call the roll of the foreign-born and those who have been treated like aliens who, since this nation was founded, have performed distinguished service on the field of battle, in legislative halls, in executive offices, on our judiciary. For the ultimate heroes are always the unknown—the unnumbered, obscure people who have brought and today bring the dreams of America nearer to living truths.

This is our heritage. In confidence that their successors will maintain it the founders built this nation. That heritage is always endangered by inertia and complacency, by timidity and reluctance to keep abreast of the needs of a progressive society. This is a graver challenge than any from without. With active devotion to the ideals we profess it would be unworthy of our whole past to fear challenge by any rival system.

The upheavals of the war let loose forces from which hardly a corner of the world is immune. Over vast areas the very foundations of society have been shaken. Great events are in process, and great events must be met by greatly daring. The ultimate task of the statesmanship of today is to translate edifying precepts about the dignity of man into their progressive fulfillment. Here in Aaronsburg, at the very birth of the republic, a handful of men, of whom Aaron Levy was only one, well realizing that faith without works is sterile, proved by deed their belief in the common humanity. Thereby they stored this very spot with electric example.

Thus it has fallen to the honor of this tiny village to charge the conscience of this nation and to invigorate its endeavors.

You and I are heirs of a noble past. But . . . *what's past is prologue; what to come, in yours and my discharge.*

Two

Regionalism in America

(1951)

A symposium on American regionalism was held at the University of Wisconsin in April 1949. The papers delivered there were published in 1951 in a volume entitled *Regionalism in America*, edited by Merrill Jensen and printed by the University of Wisconsin Press. Mr. Justice Frankfurter wrote this foreword.

FOR A NONSPECIALIST to praise the work of scholars implies a bit of impertinence. My justification for venturing to greet this collection of essays is that the supreme bench affords unparalleled opportunities for realizing that the contributors to this volume have cast illumination from their different angles upon our basic internal problem. For the concern underlying all these essays is how a country that is a continent can be governed by organs that fairly represent its disciplined will and at the same time adequately evoke the diverse civilized potentialities of its people.

With the exception of regionalism in architecture and in painting, all the phases of regionalism treated by these scholars as intellectual issues have made themselves felt in adjudications before the Supreme Court. To be sure, the social, economic, and cultural influences and needs comprised by regionalism usually do not appear in litigation with candid impact. But they are there, if at times only in the interstices of legal records. Through these too often dreary proceedings there emerge precisely those considerations of homogeneous diversities within the nation that do not correspond to the division between the Union and the forty-eight states. There are organic developments other than the nation and its constituent states that press for expression through various forms: through national legislation recognizing regional differences, through the constitutional device of compact among different combinations of states to meet different needs, through various informal arrangements among states, through legal uniformities of one sort or another, and through all the multiform recognitions of need for institutionalizing the harmonies and common interests and feelings within different regions.

The prescience of the founders of this country happily did not preclude the devising of these regional arrangements. They did not make the whole life of the people flow exclusively through national or through state organs. The vast and variegated resources of a nation lying between the Atlantic and the Pacific—above all, the rich resources within the people themselves—were not denied opportunities for resourcefulness in making a unity out of diversities apart from the union of the states.

Not the least important lesson of these essays is that regionalism is not just another name for the political device of decentralization. It is not a delegation of authority from above. Regionalism is a recognition of the intractable diversities among men, diversities partly shaped by nature but no less derived from the different reactions of men to nature. And since man takes increasing liberties with nature, regionalism is not a fixed concept. No region, whether natural or cultural, is stable. At bottom, the problems of American regionalism are the problems of American civilization: the continuous process of bringing to fruition the best of which American men and women are capable.

It is because such is the concern of this book and because illuminating scholarship has been spent on it that I hope for it the wide attention its importance deserves.

Three

The Permanence of Jefferson

(1943)

A meeting was held at the Library of Congress in Washington, D. C., on April 13, 1943, to celebrate the bicentennial anniversary of the birth of Thomas Jefferson. Mr. Justice Frankfurter made the principal speech.

AFTER DEBATING the appropriate way to observe the centenary of George Washington, the Congress of the United States finally decided to celebrate it by the offering of a prayer. I am not sure that that is not the wisest mode of commemorating, at appropriate times, the great names in our political calendar. For we come to patriotic shrines and celebrate the permanent leaders of a nation not to vaunt new ideas but to draw strength from the past. Lincoln's Gettysburg Address endures not as the enunciation of novelties but as a perfect expression of new devotion to an ancient faith.

All history, we are told, is contemporary history. This is certainly true today. And not merely because we see everything through the prism of the world's anguish. Strength to endure comes from confidence, and confidence is rooted in faith. But faith is not self-generated. It is moral energy stored up in the past. And so, when an obvious challenge to the foundations of our society finally became an indisputable threat to our very existence, even the most complacent or blindest could not continue to float unthinkingly on the stream of history. All of us, the most alert as well as the most indifferent, were brought up sharply to consider the meaning of our national life, whether it has a meaning, and indeed to consider the meaning of life itself. Fate showered Thomas Jefferson with many gifts but none greater than the gift of good fortune. That the two-hundredth anniversary of his birth should fall now makes him also an uncommon favorite of history. One can imagine the spirit of Thomas Jefferson on his beloved hilltop brooding over the circumstances of our times and their relation to the hopes and aspirations he entertained for mankind. And as he surveys the past and pierces what is yet to come with an insight not vouchsafed to mortals, he could not, had he free choice, fix upon a better day than this for our reconsideration of the meaning of his life.

To be at all alive in the consciousness of his people, a statesman must at least have been responsible for some decisive event in a nation's life. There are a few who are identified with an epoch. Rarest of all are those whose personal significance, surviving long after their particular policies have lost their meaning and been forgotten, far transcends the benefits, however precious, of particular acts. Jefferson's administration as governor of Virginia and his foreign policy during the Napoleonic Wars have long been the dry bones of controversy among specialists, and I shall leave to future historians the diminishing interest in the importance of these events. Jefferson, to be sure, drew the title deeds of American liberty, and by triumphing over his own constitutional theories determined the course of empires. But history cast him for a role of even more unique achievement. Neither the incandescent phrases of the Declaration of Independence, nor the winning of the West through the Louisiana Purchase, would have made Jefferson a national tradition.

He is one of those extraordinary figures in politics whose thoughts permeated the life of his time, enlightened the impulses of popular feeling, and established a tradition which has so incorporated itself into the sentiments of our people as to constitute one of the binding forces of a sprawling continent to which appeal is made in times of crisis. Jefferson shares with Lincoln—for Washington is a man apart—the power of fortifying and replenishing the moral resources of our nation by renewal in action of that democratic faith which their lives represent and to which, as they believed, our nation was dedicated. In explaining why he wanted to transplant to this country, Du Pont de Nemours wrote to Jefferson, "Liberty does not exist only in the laws, which are always more or less badly executed, but chiefly in the constant habits of the nation." This was the essence of Jefferson's social philosophy and the devotion of his life. It is the permanence of his meaning—to establish sentiments of freedom as the enduring habits of a people. Constitutions and laws can confirm and further such sentiments; they cannot create them.

Until lately, belittling explanations of great events have been too readily embraced as proof of the skeptical temper. This attitude has not spared the American Revolution. I put to one side the fact that the union of thirteen states by agreement was in itself a very great accomplishment which should serve as a source of sober hope, though not of guarantee, for associated action among peoples pursuing common purposes. To reject a luridly romantic view of the separation of the colonies from Great Britain does not require that we should squander the hallowed great national patrimony of the essential significance of that Revolution. The colonies had the seeds of a great nation. That nation was terminating the relics of feudalism and founding its life upon ultimate principles of faith in human nature. These days we do well to recall the perspective in which even so hypercritical a historian as Lord Acton placed the choice of the colonies in making their hazardous leap for liberty:

The suffering that would be caused by submission was immeasurably less than the suffering that must follow resistance, and it was more uncertain and remote. The utilitarian argument was loud in favour of obedience and loyalty. But if interest was on one side, there was a manifest principle on the other—a principle so sacred and so clear as imperatively to demand the sacrifice of men's lives, of their families and their fortune. They resolved to give up everything, not to escape from actual oppression, but to honour a precept of unwritten law. That was the transatlantic discovery in the theory of political duty, the light that came over the ocean. It represented liberty not as a comparative release from tyranny, but as a thing so divine that the existence of society must be staked to prevent even the least constructive infraction of its sovereign right.

The Declaration of Independence was thus the formulation of a momentous event in history. It was no less the generator of the process of liberty everywhere. The significance of the Declaration does not lie in the ideas which it expressed but in their realization and their continuing ferment. Every great man is at once heir and ancestor. Jefferson was not the originator of the aspirations of which he is the enduring symbol. Originality was not even his aim. When that crusty old Puritan, John Adams, wrote that "there is not an idea" in the Declaration "but what had been hackneyed in Congress for two years before" (Letter to Timothy Pickering, August 6, 1822, reprinted in *The Works of John Adams*, (C. F. Adams ed., 1850), Vol. II, p. 514), Jefferson put the matter in its proper light: "This was the object of the Declaration of Independence. Not to find out new principles, or new arguments, never before thought of, not merely to say things which have never been said before; but to place before mankind the common sense of the subject, in terms so plain and firm as to command their assent, and to justify ourselves in the independent stand we are compelled to take. Neither aiming at originality of principle or sentiment, nor yet copied

from any particular and previous writing, it was intended to
be an expression of the American mind, and to give to that
expression the proper tone and spirit called for by the occasion." (Letter to Henry Lee, May 8, 1825, reprinted in *The
Writings of Thomas Jefferson*, (Memorial ed., 1904), p. 118.)

Novelty of ideas is not the special function of a statesman.
It is his calling to further in practice a better vision of society,
to promote social arrangements more conformable to reason
and justice. Jefferson's seminal achievement was to institu-
tionalize familiar eighteenth-century ideas. He made abstract
notions about freedom a dominating faith and thereby the
dynamic element in the strivings of men. Jefferson thus shaped
the direction and defined the purpose of America. There may
be indifference and deviations, and there have been both, but
the standard for national self-respect was set. Lincoln summarized it all from the deep sincerity of his heart, when
called upon unexpectedly at Independence Hall on his way
to Washington.

. . . all the political sentiments I entertain have been drawn,
so far as I have been able to draw them, from the sentiments
which originated in and were given to the world from this hall.
I have never had a feeling, politically, that did not spring from
the sentiments embodied in the Declaration of Independence. I
have often pondered over the dangers which were incurred by
the men who assembled here and framed and adopted that Declaration. I have pondered over the toils that were endured by the
officers and soldiers of the army who achieved that independence.
I have often inquired of myself what great principle or idea it
was that kept this Confederacy so long together. It was not the
mere matter of separation of the colonies from the motherland,
but that sentiment in the Declaration of Independence which
gave liberty not alone to the people of this country, but hope
to all the world, for all future time. It was that which gave
promise that in due time the weights would be lifted from the
shoulders of all men, and that all should have an equal chance.
This is the sentiment embodied in the Declaration of Independ-

ence. . . . But I have said nothing but what I am willing to live by, and, if it be the pleasure of Almighty God, to die by. (*Works of Abraham Lincoln,* (Nicolay and Hay ed., 1894), Vol. 6, pp. 157-58.)

Let it be conceded, then, that Jefferson was not an original thinker who created a new society, but one who, deeply sharing popular opinions, feelings, and interests, gave them expression. He gave them expression, however, not merely in enduring language. There are creators of ideas and creative translators of ideas into the habits and institutions of society. At their highest the two functions are perhaps never combined in a single person. Jefferson was a statesman who was a philosopher, not a philosopher who became a statesman. The creative impulse in him could not rest with the understanding and enunciation of noble ideas. For him they could not remain images in the sky. They had to be made roads toward realization. Jefferson understood, none better, that only concerted action can translate political ideals from words into life. He had that rarest of political talents, the capacity to organize a political party for the realization of his ideals.

The democratic forces of 1789 were scattered, divided, nebulous in thought, and ill-equipped for action. Jefferson gave this budding democracy the power of political cohesion and the momentum of effective utterance. He made America conscious of a purpose and a special destiny. The quality of a society is determined by the hopes and enthusiasms that animate it. Jefferson infused the rising democracy with his hopes and filled it with his enthusiasm. And so, even the fastidious and unsympathetic Henry Adams, reporting on the democracy fashioned by Jefferson, is infected with the self-confident spirit, however at times crudely manifested, of a people whose mission was the free unfolding of the human spirit:

European travellers who passed through America noticed that everywhere, in the White House at Washington and in log-cabins beyond the Alleghanies, except for a few Federalists, every

American, from Jefferson and Gallatin down to the poorest squatter, seemed to nourish an idea that he was doing what he could to overthrow the tyranny which the past had fastened on the human mind. Nothing was easier than to laugh at the ludicrous expressions of this simple-minded conviction, or to cry out against its coarseness, or grow angry with its prejudices; to see its nobler side, to feel the beatings of a heart underneath the sordid surface of a gross humanity, was not so easy. (*History of the United States*, (1890), Vol. I, p. 175.)

But we stultify the significance of the heritage that is Jefferson if we treat him as a book of precepts for the solution of specific problems which he never could have contemplated, rather than as a source of energy in grappling with problems of our generation with the same faith and unflagging courage with which he met those of his time. Jefferson's preoccupation was to strike artificial fetters from men, to give their talents the fullest opportunities for development in a society radically different from our own. He was concerned with the abolition of unnecessary social restraints and could hardly foresee that this is not at all identical with the creation of social controls made necessary by very different circumstances. To treat remarks of Jefferson addressed to the particular aspects in which problems of human freedom presented themselves to him as though they were political encyclicals, as justifications for resisting the pressure for freedom in the intricate new context of society in our day, is to reduce the sweep of Jefferson's spirit to our own littleness.

That such use should be made of Jefferson merely proves the malleability of abstract doctrine. What matters is the uses to which we put principles and that in turn depends on the sympathies which dominate. The difference between Jefferson and Hamilton is the vital lesson for us. As inheritors of great events, we need not be imprisoned by them. And so today only gratuitous partisanship fails to recognize the indispensable share that the genius of Hamilton contributed in starting the nation on its career. But Hamilton is not a national tradition because he was bounded by fears and distrust. Jefferson, partly because he was sanguine by temperament but also because conviction and reflection confirmed it, passionately and persistently followed his insight that the permanence of the American scheme could rest on nothing less than the whole American democracy. But he was no simple-minded believer in the popular will. The popular will can steer a proper course only when sufficiently enlightened to know what is the proper course to steer. No one was more conscious than he that democracy is not remotely an automatic device for a good society. Democracy, he well knew, is dependent on knowledge and wisdom beyond all other forms of government. The grandeur of the aims of democracy is matched by the difficulties of their achievement. For democracy is the reign of reason and justice on the most extensive scale. And the difficulties have appallingly multiplied since Jefferson's day. Not only has our industrial civilization, which he so feared even in its incipiency, thrown up an intricate range of new problems, but the misuse and manipulation of modern devices, chain newspapers, cheap magazines, popular polls, the movies, and the radio, have enormously enlarged opportunities for arousing passions, confusing judgment, and regimenting opinion. And now we also know how slender a reed is reason—how recent its emergence in men, how deep the countervailing instincts and passions, how treacherous the whole rational process.

Jefferson had faith but it was not founded on naïveté. He would not gainsay Santayana's observation that "If a noble and civilized democracy is to subsist, the common citizen must be something of a saint and something of a hero. We see therefore how justly flattering and profound, and at the same time how ominous was Montesquieu's saying that the principle of democracy is virtue." Jefferson would not gainsay this, but neither would he shrink, any more than he did one hundred and fifty years ago, from the exhilarating adventure of a free people determining its own destiny.

Four

The Paths Must Be Kept Open

(1941)

Mr. Justice Frankfurter contributed this essay to *Our Bill of Rights: What It Means to Me* (p. 59), a volume published in 1941 by the Bill of Rights Sesqui-Centennial Committee, of which Mr. Herbert Bayard Swope was national chairman.

THE THIRTEEN COLONIES justified their claim to a place among the nations of the world by insisting on "the pursuit of happiness" as "an inalienable right." Two thousand years before Jefferson expressed the underlying faith of our American society, Pericles, who was not a stranger to Jefferson's spirit, revealed "the secret of happiness to be freedom." To "secure the Blessings of Liberty to ourselves and our Posterity" the thirteen states formed the Union. The Constitution is thus an instrument of government under which the pursuit of happiness through freedom may be realized. The Bill of Rights, as an organic part of our scheme of government, was not intended as a blueprint of Utopia. Written into the Constitution to guard against the recurrence of well-defined historic grievances, the Bill of Rights was the product not of rhetoric but of experience. The early American statesmen were alive to abuses of arbitrary power which have their seeds in the nature of man and may thrive under any form of government. And so they summarized their experience and made explicit the conditions of freedom—a rational and disinterested procedure when men are accused of crime, prohibition of "unreasonable searches and seizures," freedom of thought and of conscience, and the amplest opportunity for expressing both.

It misconceives, however, the inner significance of the Bill of Rights to think of it as constituting merely technical provisions of a legal code. An independent, learned, courageous, and imaginative judiciary is indispensable to a free society, and especially to a federated democracy. But one does not minimize the role of courts in acknowledging that, for the ultimate protection of the liberties of the people, it is not sufficient to rely on the specialized and very limited function of the judiciary. Litigation is, as it were, the pathological aspect of society. Health comes from the thoughts and feelings permeating its atmosphere and guiding its everyday actions. The real import of the Bill of Rights is the conception of man's dignity and destiny which underlies it, and which can effectively be vindicated only if it controls public feeling and inspires all measures of government.

Lincoln magnificently illustrates that Nature herself is democratic. The arrangements of society should not thwart her purposes. Tolerance for dissident views is not an exercise in benignity but a form of practical wisdom. Truth is an eternal chase. The history of man's endeavor to achieve truth shows the displacement of yesterday's dogma by today's skepticism. And today's folly may prove itself tomorrow's wisdom. The paths to the City of God must be kept open.

The spirit of man and the means for achieving its glories can never be captured and confined by words and formulas. But the framers of the Bill of Rights put into enduring language the conditions essential for the "Blessings of Liberty" to themselves and their posterity. By celebrating their wisdom in this formulation we invigorate our own strength to maintain that liberty. The founders of the republic knew, as did Pericles, that if the secret of happiness was freedom "the secret of freedom was a brave heart." Let us be worthy of their example.

Five

The Conduct of Our Foreign Relations

(1949)

This article, written primarily in tribute to Mr. Dean G. Acheson, who had been appointed Secretary of State earlier in the year, appeared in the *Groton School Quarterly* for April 1949.

FOR MOST OF THE PERIOD between the founding of this nation and the Jackson era, the Department of State was headed by the most distinguished public men of the day. More than the long arm of coincidence must account for the fact that Jefferson, Madison, Monroe, and John Quincy Adams guided our foreign relations. The fierce currents loosed by the French Revolution and the Napoleonic Wars inevitably affected the fate of the fledgling republic. It required understanding of these forces, of their sources and their directions, to guide the frail bark of the new Union into safe waters. In short, the conduct of our foreign relations in the early decades demanded statesmen steeped in history, with imaginative power to draw its lessons.

In those days Europe was the concern of the United States so that the destiny of the new nation might not become entangled in European quarrels. A hundred years later found the United States the inheritor of European culture for its fructification on a virgin continent. Man's prying into the mysteries of nature had so changed the environment in which

the great experiment in democracy was being pursued that
the "best hope" to which this country was dedicated lost the
shelter of two oceans. The United States was no longer
merely in this world but inextricably of it. Monroe and John
Quincy Adams took an extraordinarily bold stroke in relation
to nations much more powerful than this country because the
safety of our own destiny required it. A century later the
United States became an active participant in a world struggle out of loyalty to the same causes that made it necessary
in the earliest days of the republic to be free from European
entanglements.

Such has been our history, since the hopes of our destiny
are based on the progressive unfolding of what is implied by
the phrase Western civilization—those achievements of the
mind and spirit known as Hebraism and Hellenism, fortified
and furthered by all that the law of Rome and the Renaissance
and the Reformation brought to them. What we are seeking
to preserve in order to improve is

> The fair sum of six thousand years'
> Traditions of civility.

Nothing less is at stake. They are the issues that underlie the
items appearing in the daily press as the business of the State
Department.

The greatness of these issues requires capacity appropriate
for dealing with them. Expert knowledge, suppleness in argument, and felicity of speech are inadequate. They call for
character self-disciplined by training and habit, a mind steeped
in historic knowledge but aware that history never quite re-
peats itself, a confidence born of humility, and a consciousness
of the human limitations due to the inherent conflict between
the forces of good and evil in all men. Above all they call
for an understanding of the difference between greatness and
bigness and for a will that acts on that difference in the exercise of power.

That such is the needed equipment for a Secretary of State today Dean Acheson would, I have little doubt, admit. That no one the President could have chosen to succeed General Marshall has these qualifications in greater measure than Secretary Acheson, I am not alone in believing.

This is not the place to trace the influences of Groton and Yale and the Harvard Law School in the shaping of him, and it would be presumptuous for me to attempt it. But at a moment when candor may disregard his modesty, one can say of Dean Acheson what Maynard Keynes said of another: "He was sceptical of most things except those which chiefly matter, that is, affection and reason." By these habits of character he will be guided in exercising the country's responsibility for the peace and well-being of the world—love of country, which means passion for the heritage and trust of Western civilization, and the employment of reason on behalf of that civilization.

Six

The Big City Press and Democracy

(1953)

This article was written for the Seventy-fifth Anniversary Supplement of the St. Louis *Post-Dispatch*, December 13, 1953.

As LINCOLN HAS BECOME the moral symbol of this nation, so the verdict of time has agreed on Jefferson as the philosopher of our democratic faith. When the Union was in the process of being founded, Jefferson expressed with the emphasis of hyperbole the relation of the press to our society. In a letter to Edward Carrington, January 16, 1787, he wrote: "The basis of our governments being the opinion of the people, the very first object should be to keep that right; and were it left to me to decide whether we should have a government without newspapers, or newspapers without a government, I should not hesitate a moment to prefer the latter." (*The Papers of Thomas Jefferson*, (Boyd ed., 1955), XI, p. 49.) This philosophy regarding the function and place of the press in our constitutional system has made as lasting an impress as any concept in our national life.

The seventy-fifth anniversary of the St. Louis *Post-Dispatch*, therefore, has a significance that far transcends an important birthday of a particular enterprise. From the moment on that memorable day when the *Dispatch* was knocked down to Joseph Pulitzer on the steps of the St. Louis Court

House for $2,500, to what may be called Pulitzer's testament to American journalism—his exposition of the purposes of a school of journalism—Mr. Pulitzer saw eye to eye with Jefferson regarding the inextricable relationship between the country and its press. And the *Post-Dispatch* has remained as loyal to the purpose of its founder as can fairly be expected of any fallible human institution.

The increasing impact of government on the lives of men has put more and more responsibility on the press. As Jefferson so early pointed out, democracy implies the active participation in its affairs by the mass of citizens. This presupposes adequate information as the basis of responsible judgment. Since the press is the chief agency for instructing the public on the issues of the day, and since in our day the world is every man's parish, an informed opinion requires the greatest practicable accuracy and adequacy in the presentation of news.

Yet the conditions under which the newspapers now operate are making it more and more difficult for them to discharge their responsibility for accurate and adequate news presentation. There is an increasing tendency toward monopolistic or, at least, concentrated control of the press. The manipulation of opinion by means of propaganda as news has become a so-called science. And the nationwide utilization of syndicated "Washington columns," often with factitious implications of inside information, works against the clash of opinions and diversity of views indispensable for critical inquiry.

The need for the widest possible dissemination of information derived from a multiplicity of sources is greater today than ever before because the range of concern of the individual citizen is wider than ever before, is indeed worldwide. But the springs supplying information to the American public have been diminishing. Not the volume of matter offered to readers, but the sources of the reading matter are shrinking, and the competition making for verification of fact and diversity of interpretation is narrowing.

This steady shrinkage of diffused newspaper ownership raises far-reaching questions as to the meaning of the "freedom" of a free press. And the fact that the shrinkage is not the product of evil design but is largely attributable to economic and technological influences does not lessen the implications. Moreover, concentration of press ownership is a world-wide trend, which attests the complexity of the problem and the obduracy of its solution.

Without a free press there can be no free society. That is axiomatic. However, freedom of the press is not an end in itself but a means to the end of a free society. The scope and nature of the constitutional guarantee of the freedom of the press are to be viewed and applied in that light.

Even more important than the legal implications of a constitutionally guaranteed freedom of the press are the moral and professional responsibilities of the press for that freedom. A free press is vital to a democratic society because its freedom gives it power. But the very nature of a democratic society implies responsibility on all who exercise power; that is precisely what differentiates a democracy from an autocracy. No institution in a democracy, either governmental or private, can have absolute power. In plain English, freedom of the press is not a freedom from responsibility for its exercise. Nor can professional responsibility fairly be avoided by disputation about constitutional rights. Only recently we have had a striking instance of editors finding an escape in constitutional talk from their own professional and moral responsibility.

The delicate issues that arise in making a wise accommodation between various freedoms and their attendant responsibilities in a democratic society are well illustrated in the relation of the press to the administration of justice. If a free press is vital to a democratic society, no less so is an independent judiciary. Neither has primacy over the other, and both are indispensable to a free society. The freedom of the press in itself presupposes an independent judiciary through which that freedom can be vindicated, as it often has been. And one of the potent means of assuring judges their independence is a free press.

It is frequently necessary to reconcile these two indispensable elements of a free society, for they do not always pull in the same direction. A judiciary is not independent unless courts of justice are enabled to administer law free from external pressure, whether exerted through the blandishments of reward or the menace of disfavor.

The judiciary cannot function properly if what the press does is calculated to disturb the judicial judgment in its duty and its capacity to act solely on the basis of what is before the court. Especially in the administration of the criminal law, independent courts are a prerequisite of a free society. The safety of society and the security of the innocent alike depend upon impartial and wise criminal justice.

Criticism, therefore, must not feel cramped, not less so criticism of the administration of criminal justice. Weak characters ought not to be judges, and the scope of free utterance allowed the press for society's sake may assume that they are not. No judge fit to be on the bench is likely to be influenced consciously except by what he sees and hears in court and by what is judicially appropriate for his deliberations. (Extraneous influences from newspaper publications upon jurors obviously raise a different question.) However, we are better aware than were our forebears of the powerful influence exerted by the unconscious, and the treacherous nature of the rational process. While the ramparts of reason have been found to be more fragile than the Age of Enlightenment had so romantically and comfortably believed, the means for arousing passion and confusing judgment have been powerfully reinforced today. Since judges, however professionally disciplined, are human, the delicate task of administering justice ought not to be diverted from its true course by inaccurate or irresponsible or judicially inadmissible print.

Of course, trials must be public (subject to exceptions not now relevant) and the public should have alert interest in trials. The public's legitimate interest precludes, however, distortion of what goes on inside the courtroom, and dissemination of matters that do not come before the court at all, or other trafficking with truth intended to influence the proceedings or inevitably calculated to disturb the delicate balance of the scales of justice. Every experienced lawyer and judge knows that the atmosphere in the courtroom is subtly susceptible to influence from without.

Too often cases are tried in newspapers before they are tried in court, and thereby the assurance of a fair trial is enormously decreased. The characters, as presented in the newspaper trial, often differ from the real persons who appear later in the court trial, and the latter usually suffer from this unfair distortion.

The press does have the right, which is its professional function, to criticize and to advocate. The whole gamut of public affairs is the domain of fearless and critical comment, and not least the administration of justice. The steady growth in the intervention of government, no matter what party is in power, enlarges the range of the functions of the press as chronicler and critic, though its responsibilities are not contracted.

The public functions which belong to the press and the legal immunities which it enjoys put it under an honorable obligation to exercise its functions and to rely on those immunities only with the fullest sense of responsibility. Without such a lively sense of responsibility a free press may readily become a powerful instrument of injustice.

At the core of any appraisal of the functioning of the press is the stubborn fact that, although newspapers discharge civic functions and for this reason may be deemed public under-takings, they are private ventures operated for commercial profit. The public does not pay for the enlightenment which it is furnished and which is indispensable for its participation in public affairs. Because of habit or training, comparatively few individuals today are ready to pay more than a trifling sum for their daily paper.

The deficit is recouped through advertising, and the axis upon which the volume of advertising turns is circulation. To live, a newspaper must under present conditions reach the largest possible number of readers at the smallest possible cost. Thus, for one thing, even under the improved conditions of employment in more recent years, high-salaried specialists with devotion to professional standards not sub-ordinated to dependence on their employment are relatively few in the news departments of papers.

Moreover, the modern daily is in the grip of mechanical and social forces. Time is a powerful factor. Particularly is this true of afternoon papers with their multiple editions. The compulsion of speed affects judgment of what is significant as well as the accuracy and adequacy with which the significant is conveyed. The drive of appealing to the public throughout the day by means of successive editions throws the emphasis upon what feeds curiosity. This element of speed, this evanescent timeliness, is partly the slave of the press and partly its master. No doubt the public "wants" an exciting stream of news, but, no doubt also, the press continues feverishly to stimulate that "want." Mechanical inventions have had their share in the process. Partly they have spurred newspapers to their present-day methods; partly the inventions have been stimulated by newspaper enterprise.

In the past, newspaper competition within cities has been a powerful factor in all this stimulation. The withering competition among newspapers has been replaced by the fact, or the fear, of the radio and television. It is not for me even to adumbrate the new problems raised by the dissemination of news by radio and television and the new problems involved in the concentrated ownership of press, radio, and television. One thing surely is clear, that the radio and television have introduced with powerful impact new forms of the old struggle for the capture of the public's mind and feelings.

The arts exercised in this struggle, the interests excited or neglected, are bound to have vital reflexes upon that amorphous but controlling factor in the conduct of our affairs and the quality of our civilization called public opinion.

It is in the light of these tendencies, these profound functions, and their more or less inevitable distortions, that we must consider the truism that our government and the country's well-being ultimately rest on public opinion. The influence exerted by the public, whether directly through the ballot box or in manifestations between elections, is dependent upon what the ordinary mass of people think and feel about matters. And what they think and feel is more or less what is in the air—not over the air but in the air. The chief source of the views people entertain, what predominantly influences those who read, is not what is said on the editorial pages but what is rubbed off, as it were, from the news columns.

News columns are not only accepted as affording a true narrative of events; through headlines, spacing, repetition, and characterization they subtly infuse the reader's mind and largely influence his standards for judgment. It is the news columns that heavily determine the thinking habits of the reading public. It is they that shape an attitude of lazy credulity receptive to fear and prejudice rather than one of critical open-mindedness.

The unconscious, and therefore, uncritical, absorption of print is much more powerful than any skeptical alertness which most readers bring to print. To an extent far beyond the public's own realization, public opinion is shaped by the kind, the volume, and the quality of news columns. It depends on the quality of the news column, day after day, whether the public's judgment is confused instead of enlightened, whether its feelings are debilitated or steadied, its reason deflected or enlisted. Everything, therefore, depends on what news is presented and how the news is presented.

C. P. Scott sententiously summarized the relative functions of the news column and the editorial page. "Opinion is free; facts are sacred." For a half a century Scott was loyal to this dictum in *The Manchester Guardian*, and the momentum of tradition which he generated has been maintained by his successors. But his simple-seeming formula covers intricacies. "Facts" are not like Rotarians that identify themselves by badges. The ascertainment of facts, the sifting of the relevant from the irrelevant or confusing, the balanced statement of the relevant, call for a disciplined profession, for the will, capacity, and opportunity for disinterested communication.

In 1951 Prime Minister Nehru, who has spent many years of reflection on the nature and destiny of man, dealt with the abuses of the press in a debate in the Indian Parliament. Yet the only light he could bring to bear was that "ultimately this problem as any other problem depends upon the quality of human beings and the community at large. If in India the quality is good, it is well with us. If it is not, then it is not well with us, whatever constitutional guarantees we might have or not have." This will hardly satisfy those who want quick, easy, almost mechanical solutions for subtle, wide-flung, deeply-rooted problems. Yet Mr. Nehru's unspecific wisdom is almost an echo of Mr. Justice Holmes's solution for the great problems which his prescience foreshadowed some forty years ago. Distrusting panaceas, he said, "the answer to most of our problems is for us to grow more civilized." There's the rub. Neither a man nor a society grows more civilized by a single leap or overnight.

IV

IN MEMORIAM

———————

One

Harry Shulman

(1955)

Harry Shulman (1903-1955) was, at the time of his death, dean of the Yale University Law School, where he had taught since 1930. A former student of Professor Frankfurter at the Harvard Law School, Dean Shulman became an outstanding arbitrator of labor disputes, principally as umpire under the contract between the Ford Motor Company and the United Auto Workers. He collaborated with Professor Frankfurter on *Cases on Federal Jurisdiction and Procedure,* published in 1937. This memorial is reprinted from the May 1955 issue of the *Yale Law Journal* (Vol. 64, p. 799).

ACCORDING TO A philosophic observer of the human situation, character is an achievement. It presupposes struggle, a triumph over baser elements in man's nature. Harry Shulman exposes the emptiness of this paradox. Just as the gifts of genius, whether as thinker or artist, are innate, not to be attained by the utmost effort, so, in rare instances, superior moral qualities are born, not made. Harry Shulman was one of these rare creatures.

So fine was the texture of the man, outwardly so simple and intrinsically so unpretentious, that only after a time did one become aware of the beauty and strength of his character. All who knew him will respond to this sense of him. But how can one convey it to those who did not know him? His special savor had to be experienced. There was a distinctiveness about it—a blend of the homespun and the subtle—that eludes recapture, certainly by me. The only authentic intimation of what manner of man he was is to give a bit of Harry Shulman himself.

It is especially appropriate to give to the Yale community an unbosoming of himself in the candor of intimate friendship. When he decided to remain at Yale and to decline a call from his own law school, a call appealing to him on many scores, this is what he wrote:

Yale University
School of Law
New Haven, Connecticut

10/2/45

Dear F. F.:

About two weeks ago I finally made my choice on the Harvard-Yale matter. I yielded to the emotional and sentimental forces and determined to stay at Yale.

But, as you said to me at Lyme, in the last analysis the decision depends on something inside. That is what happened here. I doubt whether I can articulate the feelings that led to the choice. Maybe it was only inertia—or that laziness which I could not conceal from you. Both the Dean and the President urged me strongly to stay and stated their belief that my leaving would be a very serious blow to Yale—particularly at this critical time. You know I don't take myself that seriously. But I could not bring myself to let them feel that I let them down—or the several members of the faculty who genuinely wanted me to stay. I did not want to be cited as proof of the argument that has been made here against the appointment of "Harvard men," "They'll go back to Harvard at the first opportunity anyway." (Not that this and other untenable arguments won't be made anyway!) And I wanted to kill the report which I began to hear that I harbored some form of grudge or ill-will or feeling of hurt as a result of the Deanship business of more than five years ago. (Actually, I was and am very happy that I was not asked to be Dean; and I feel that I gained rather than lost in that incident.) These factors would probably not be enough were I unhappy at Yale, or were the School to interfere with my work. But neither is true. Such unpleasantness as exists is not basic and is not invulnerable to a moderate sense of humor. All in all, I felt that, after 15 years here, Yale was entitled to the loyalty which I felt and which I believed would be breached if I left.

All my good wishes for the new Term; and our best to Marion.

Harry

P.S. I have written very freely—for you and Marion alone!

"I don't take myself that seriously." ". . . not invulnerable to a moderate sense of humor." How relaxed, how unrestrained in making a decisive choice! How easy he made appear a hard decision! But everything about him was modulated—his voice, his temper, his thoughts, his actions. In speaking of the "laziness" which he "could not conceal" from me, he referred to a teasing remark of mine, during our year together at Cambridge, about the seeming effortlessness with which he did such excellent work. There was no waste motion, no false stroke, and so I said to him one day: "Harry, I cannot make up my mind whether you are intellectually economical because you are lazy or whether you can afford to be lazy because you are intellectually economical." Admiration of his intellectual powers by all who had basis for judgment—Mr. Justice Brandeis, Professor Bohlen, and his eminent advisors on the *Restatement of Torts*, the seasoned critics who listened to his Holmes Lecture, delivered when the end was near—was excelled only by an uncommon want of self-recognition. Indeed, one of his most vivid qualities was his complete humility. This superb disinterestedness, in the service of his keen analytical faculties and his genial common sense, explains why both the Ford Company and the union deemed him indispensable to the success of the Ford–Auto Workers collective agreement. Only perversity could withstand the firm benignity of his spirit, harnessed to the shrewd resourcefulness of his mind. Controversies and bitterness were bound to dissolve in his presence.

One always returns to his moral qualities. But his morality never turned rancid. His righteousness was never tinctured with self-righteousness. Simple, abounding goodness saved him from it. He too was tried. Like everyone who mixes with men and has to manage them, he encountered the foolish and the obstreperous. But he treated them with intelligent neglect. For his judgment was enlightened by an understanding heart and his strength was fortified by a prophylactic humor.

What Harry Shulman has meant to legal education, what he will continue to mean in the lives of generations of his former students, the insights that he added for the unraveling of legal problems, and the guiding lines he has left for others to pursue in the peaceful evolution of industry—the various aspects of his fruitful life must receive the accounting of others. Mine is the poor effort of an aching heart to give some intimation of the man that was Harry Shulman. Would I could do so in more enduring words.

Two

Thomas Reed Powell

(1956)

Thomas Reed Powell (1880-1955) had a place of pre-eminence among modern teachers of American constitutional law. His colleagues on the faculty of the Harvard Law School, where he taught for almost a quarter of a century (from 1925 to 1949), have written of him: "His special role was to serve as a kind of intellectual conscience to the Supreme Court. . . . He knew as well as anyone, and earlier than most . . . , that the law of the Constitution is the law of the Justices. Unlike lesser followers of the gleam, however, his knowledge did not stop at this point; he was aware of the compulsions of history and logic and a viable federal system, and in his writings and teachings he addressed himself vigorously to these." (*Harvard Law School Bulletin*, October 1955, p. 7.) This memorial of Professor Powell appeared in the March 1956 issue of the *Harvard Law Review* (Vol. 69, p. 797).

ONE CANNOT COMMAND his illuminating wit and his analytic trenchancy in trying to convey T. R. Powell's significance as law teacher and writer. But to speak of him without rigorous honesty would disrespect his character. As warm praise as any I ever received from him, in the course of our long friendship, was commendation for disregard of *de mortuis*, for not indulging in the style of mortuary perfection in what I wrote of an academic colleague whose solid virtues could easily withstand candid recognition of his limitations. "Can you not praise the dead man sufficiently unless you tell lies

257

about him?" is a sentiment that expressed his intellectual integrity. His judgment was never subservient to his affection.

The influence of a teacher who does not dole out inert ideas but fertilizes the mind is at once enduring and most elusive. Just as the result of his endeavor is incommensurable, so the art of creative teaching is largely incommunicable. It is somewhat akin to the triumph of great acting. To convey what a great teacher did and how he did it needs the critical gifts of a William Hazlitt reporting on Mr. Kean's and Mrs. Siddons' performances. For want of such, the description of T.R.P. in the classroom, by one of his best-beloved and wisest students, is deeply revealing. Speaking of "the period which most challenged the [Harvard Law] School's existence," he wrote, "it was T.R.P. who knew how to be vexatious and nasty and snide and, consequently somehow, stimulating." This sequence of adjectives reaches T.R.P.'s goal and achievement: stimulating! For fifty years Tom Powell (in recent years he preferred "Reed," but to his oldest friends he remained "Tom") jolted law students into thinking about the nature of the problems of constitutional law, instead of allowing them to go to sleep on the smooth formulas that disposed of problems by evading them.

While he aroused the minds of his students, he less often satisfied them. He compelled thought, but he did not deem it a teacher's function to seed his views in the student's mind, or to seed any views. He himself was wont to say, half proudly and half self-disparagingly, that he emptied the minds of his students but did not furnish them. However, he stirred to inquiry minds of men, otherwise slothful or conforming, who were sent out by the thousands, from Columbia and Harvard and other law schools at which he intermittently taught, to be lawyers and legislators and administrators and teachers. The currents of influence which these men in turn generated were, no doubt, enormous. And his was an influence not merely in the realm of law, far-reaching as that realm is in a *Rechtsstaat* like ours. The intellectual tradition was not strong with us even before "intellectual" became a term of contumely. For T.R.P., law infused culture, and culture was part of law. When it is not, law becomes an obstruction to culture.

He powerfully vindicated the claims of law as a university study. For he approached problems enmeshed in bias and partisanship with as close to scientific indifference as is humanly possible. This was the deepest, if indeed not the only, article of his juristic faith. The admixture that is every man was also Powell. He had his preferences and biases, his allegiances and aversions. Indeed, because his partialities were as strong as they were, his professional triumphs over them are more shining.

The sum of his writings, his hundreds of essays and book reviews, are the responses of an academic student of the law to contemporaneous and usually exigent problems of public law. They constitute, essentially, a critique of other men's answers to those problems and, mostly, the answers that judges gave to them. Theirs was the responsibility of decision. His was the responsibility of a disinterested critic, scrutinizing not only the results reached but the path of reason by which they professed to be reached. An academic critic has not a court's duty to decide; he is without need of accommodations, the pressures appropriate for agreement within a tribunal. An academician's grappling of legal problems, particularly the problems of constitutional law that were the main concern of T.R.P., demands, to the utmost attainable degree, judgment free from private preferences and stripped of social or economic or logical bias. The task is admeasurement of judicial conclusions according to intrinsic coherence, to harmony with professed criteria, to consistency with invoked precedents and regard for relevant but unmentioned and unrejected precedents. These are at least some of the factors by which judicial opinions call for testing. It can hardly be denied that

T. R. Powell applied these valid tests to the decisions of the Supreme Court and their opinions more systematically, more searchingly, and more illuminatingly than any other critic of the Court's work during the last half-century. His Socratic temperament was singularly well fitted for the most fruitful period of T.R.P.'s scrutiny of the Supreme Court's adjudications. He was a master in exposing question-begging, however subtle, in laying bare presuppositions unavowed and embedded in premises out of which, and not by a process of compelling reason, conclusions were drawn and legislation invalidated.

In his writings, as in the classroom, his spear, sheathed in velvety English, knew no brother. But his spear was, after all, tongue or pen. Bruising it was, not poisonous. The occasional wounding wisecrack and swift ferocity of utterance revealed the wisecracker and the wounder only to those who knew not the essentially tender and affectionate creature that he was. There was not a little of Dr. Johnson in him, and how he would have felt at home in the Johnson circle or with Charles James Fox at Brooks's. His was a convivial and sentimental nature which made him delightful company. He was that rare combination in our day of a club man with a passion for rigorous thinking and candid exposure of those interests and partialities where thinking ceased and feeling ruled. If Mark Hopkins at one end of the log and a student at the other afforded an education, some of the best seminars in our time consisted of a student or a colleague in an easy chair and T. R. Powell drinking copious draughts of beer out of his favorite pewter mug to the accompaniment of stories of his beloved Vermont, unrivaled ribald limericks, shrewd comments on colleagues, wise saws, penetrating analysis of the latest Supreme Court decisions, unsparing but unpitying self-analysis. On those occasions, not even his slashing tongue would quite betray his more generous and affectionate nature.

Three

Eugene Wambaugh

(1940)

Eugene Wambaugh (1856-1940) was a member of the Harvard Law School faculty for thirty-three years, and was widely respected as an authority on constitutional and international law. Felix Frankfurter was a student in his classes at the Law School and subsequently became his colleague on the faculty. This tribute to Mr. Wambaugh was written for the November 1940 issue of the *Harvard Law Review* (Vol. 54, p. 7).

SOMEONE SAID OF Lord Acton that he was the author of great books that were never written. Eugene Wambaugh stirs a like wistful appreciation. In range and depth and precision of scholarship he was not unequal to his illustrious associates on the faculty of the Harvard Law School—Ames and Gray and Thayer, to speak only of the dead. And if to give a sample of one's best is true success, Professor Wambaugh attained it in his edition of Littleton's *Tenures*. To be sure, his Littleton is only a miniature beside the sweep of Maitland's *Domesday Book*. To couple them, however, is not to compare great with small. Both are rare products of elegant scholarship—creations of an extraordinary historic imagination which revivifies ancient and departed institutions and manifestations of learning as a living stream of culture.

Wambaugh could summon the tough and supple powers of English speech. His prose often had the cadence of poetry.

I need only recall the austere perfection of his inscription on
the memorial tablet for the Harvard Law School students
who fell in the First World War. And none of us who heard
him bid Godspeed to John Bassett Moore, the first American
on the World Court, is likely to forget the grace and eleva-
tion of his eloquence in expressing the hopes represented by
the Hague Tribunal. Why a scholar who wrote so well wrote
so little has long puzzled his friends. Perhaps the question
lays bare a phase of his unique personality. There was in him
a strain of genial perversity. Just as he often baffled literal-
minded students by indulging in a brilliant detour to avoid
direct answer to a specific question, so his puckish nature
may have found secret pleasure in frustrating the plain command of the Fates that he fulfill the scholar's office by publication.

Whatever the reason, the most enduring impact of Wambaugh was not through print but through person. He was a
teacher in the oral tradition. Moreover, his strong impulse
to play an intellectual blindman's buff had ampler scope with
a small, informal group than in a large assembly. The Socrates
in him showed perhaps at his best after he became *Emeritus*.
In his famous weekly teas he proved for fifteen happy years
that the essence of teaching is joint adventure in understanding. Wambaugh had exquisite powers of analysis and he
explored problems with implacable thoroughness. But the
mechanical limitations of classroom and courses curbed the
radiations of his mind. With him the best things were not
the product of studious preparation. They came as moments
of ignition in discursive talk. On the whole, he did not make
himself felt by building up from day to day an architectural
edifice of learning. His was the faculty to convey insight by
a shrewd and even mordant phrase, by a quizzical paradox or
extravagant understatement.

He knew truth to be a shy bird and so shrank from dogmatism. His own nature, too, was shy and used whimsy as

a protection for his tenderness. But no teacher could invest hopes in students more deeply or give them a more devoted friendship. One of those fortunate accidents of which friendships are born brought Professor Wambaugh and me together early in my law-student days. In the course of thirty-five years the forms of our association changed and opportunities for intimacy greatly varied. But to the very end our relation retained essentially the same quality of bantering companionship between teacher and pupil. I saw him, happily, very shortly before the end, and we talked about everything and else beside. As I started to leave—and he must have felt that never would there be talk between us again—he raised himself in his bed and, shaking his familiar forefinger, said: "Sonny, you're a very fortunate man. As you well know, abiding work on the Supreme Court almost necessarily requires long years of service. You are very lucky to have been put on the Court at an age that entitles you to look forward to long years of service." Then a pause and the glint in his eye which foreshadowed a snapper—"In other words, Sonny, you have a great opportunity"—longer pause—"for weal or woe."

In this last episode Professor Wambaugh crowded the quality of a lifetime's friendship. Where he cared, praise from him took the form not of approval but of spur. Since finitude is the lot of man, judgment remains open until life is done. And this lesson of his long brooding upon life and law he has put into words that the Greek epigrammatists would not have disowned:

> Let not the judgment that is just
> Be judged too soon,
> But be reserved, if judge one must,
> Till noon,
> Or yet till evening, that the way
> Repentant may lie open all the day.

Four

Joseph H. Beale

(1943)

Joseph Henry Beale (1861-1943) was one of the great teachers at the Harvard Law School. He wrote numerous treatises on legal subjects, particularly in the field of conflict of laws. Felix Frankfurter was one of his students, and later served with him on the faculty. This appreciation of Mr. Beale is reprinted from the March 1943 number of the *Harvard Law Review* (Vol. 56, p. 701).

IN THE RICHNESS and range of his intellectual interests, if not in his temperament, Joseph Henry Beale was an eighteenth-century figure. Certainly no modern comes to mind of whom it could be more truly said that he took all law for his province. He broke through the confines of even generous specialization within the comprehensive legal curriculum not because he was a spawner of systems or a pedantic pursuer of learning. Driven by zest for life and ardor for law's share in it, he went from one subject to another quite unrelated as judged by ordinary considerations of systematic scholarship. And so it requires the competence of a good-sized law faculty to do justice to the influence which Professor Beale exerted upon law through his writings, his legislative proposals, and, above all, his teaching.

But generations of law students can bring their own competent testimony of mind and heart to the significance of his teaching. When we recall that it has fallen to the lot of no other American law teacher, barring only his legal twin, Professor Williston, to train such a succession of lawyers for nearly half a century, we have some measure of the uses to which Professor Beale put his remarkable gifts. And when we consider further the share these lawyers have had in shaping the history of a country in which the sway of the law is as pervasive as in America, we begin to see in proper perspective the impress upon his times, as well as its perdurance, of this modest scholar.

So vivid and provocative a personality as that of Professor Beale scratched different temperaments differently, and differently at different periods of his teaching. But if the chief function of a teacher be that of a midwife, then surely he was hugely successful in bringing minds to life. When my generation arrived at Austin Hall, we entered into a glorious inheritance. The heavy sea of controversy which Langdell's innovations had stirred was wholly calmed, and under the beloved leadership of Dean Ames the Harvard Law School was sailing on placid waters with a pride that stimulated new achievement. Fortunately, also, it was the time before the School had become a leviathan—when greatness unembarrassed by bigness was the exclusive ambition of the School. This meant that the faculty was small enough to permit insistence on fastidious standards of excellence, and that students had opportunity to know all the professors and most of them on terms of intellectual intimacy. Two of the great were already gone from the School. Langdell could still be seen—a venerable old figure tapping his way along the streets of Cambridge. And that James Bradley Thayer was no more when my class entered the School has been a lifelong bereavement for at least one member of that class. The atmosphere of Austin Hall in those days was charged with vitality, and not merely by contrast with the inadequacies, for most of us, of our undergraduate days. The discussions, both in and outside the classroom, stirred in us the feeling that we were all engaged in an exciting enterprise. And no classroom was more electric than that in which Joey Beale was at the desk.

Normally it was teaching by combat and a free-for-all. Quarter was neither given nor asked. Often, minds good but slow or timid were laid by the heel and not always by the serene judgment of reason. Verbal fencing and specious dialectic were not wholly eschewed in what was as much an effort to sharpen wits as it was to discover legal truths. A colleague once remarked that Professor Beale was the theologian of the law, so skillful was he in evolving doctrines and so resourceful in defending them. But he appeared more dogmatist than he was. At least his dogmas were contemporaneous and not immutable, for, unlike Luther, he could also do otherwise. For him teaching law was an attempt to bring rational order out of the welter of cases, leaving practice and adjudication to make the necessary inroads upon mere rational harmony. But although he used no uncouth jargon he knew that the future grows out of the past and not merely out of itself.

Those days in the School illustrate that in a faculty of predominantly great teachers, issues touching the formal contents of a curriculum recede into appropriately subordinate importance. In my time we were not taught legal ethics except atmospherically, in that Dean Ames's course on trusts was suffused with the most exquisite standards for right conduct. Likewise, we had no formal course in jurisprudence. Roscoe Pound had not yet come, and John Chipman Gray had stopped giving the lectures which later, like vintage Burgundy, were given to the world in his wise and delicious little volume *The Nature and Sources of the Law*. But every really good course in law is a course in jurisprudence. For us this was peculiarly true of Professor Beale's course on the conflict of laws. The nature of the subject and the bent of Professor Beale's mind made the course an exhilarating inquiry into the presuppositions of one's legal thinking. It challenged all the smooth words of the legal vocabulary like "right" and "remedy" and "jurisdiction" and the whole tribe of them that deceptively summarize too-variant situations and more often than not put analysis to sleep. Long before phrase-mongers talked about "fundamental legal conceptions" and the word "semantics" was revealed to the multitude, Professor Beale imparted to thousands of students an awareness of these problems and spurred in them the critical desire to think things and not words. Culture, someone has said, is the deposit of things forgotten. Dogmas which Professor Beale expounded may long since have evaporated from our memory, as from time to time they were recanted by him. But he imparted ferment—the most precious quality of a teacher—which supplies exhilarating energy even when we are not aware of its source and continues gratefully in memory even when it can no longer be translated into action.

The leaves are falling as they have fallen in season and sometimes out of season, but the great oak of the Harvard Law School stands—its deep roots nourished by noble tradition and high purpose.

Five

Edward H. Warren

(1945)

Edward Henry Warren (1873-1945) was known to two generations of students at the Harvard Law School as "The Bull." Felix Frankfurter was a student in his classes, and afterward his faculty colleague. The qualities of "The Bull" are vivified by an anecdote told by another former student, Mr. Joseph N. Welch of the Boston bar: "On one occasion a student made a curiously inept response to a question from Professor Warren. 'The Bull' roared at him, 'You will never make a lawyer. You might just as well pack up your books now and leave the school.' The student rose, gathered his notebooks, and started to leave, pausing only to say in full voice, 'I accept your suggestion, Sir, but I do not propose to leave without giving myself the pleasure of telling you to go plumb straight to Hell.' 'Sit down, Sir, sit down,' said 'The Bull.' 'Your response makes it clear that my judgment was too hasty.' "[1]

Mr. Justice Frankfurter wrote this tribute to Mr. Warren for the October 1945 issue of the *Harvard Law Review* (Vol. 58, p. 1128).

PROBABLY THE MOST SALIENT quality of Edward H. Warren was an almost truculent honesty. The author of *Spartan Education* would despise the notion, to use his own pungent language, that he should be dealt with by the flabby standards of *de mortuis nil nisi bonum*.

Professor Warren began his law teaching while I was a student at the Harvard Law School. In his first year (1904-

[1] *Harvard Law Review*, Vol. 58, p. 1136.

1905), dissatisfaction with his teaching became so pronounced that some of the ablest students, manifesting that critical spirit which the School has so wisely fostered, complained to Dean Ames of Warren's inadequacy. By the time I joined the faculty, eight years later, he held the distinguished Story Professorship, was a potent voice in the councils of the School, and one of the most influential of its teachers. So far as I am familiar with the history of the Harvard Law School, no other member of its faculty ever made such strides in prestige and authority from such a beginning as did Warren. For more than a quarter of a century he left a deep mark upon thousands of students—that ultimate touchstone of a teacher's life

Excellence in the learned professions usually begins at the end of a long and toilsome journey. Only the rare, inborn artist at teaching, like Professor Williston, captures the mind and enlists the devotion of students at the very outset. But E. H. Warren got off to such a bad start because his defects and limitations were as vivid as his qualities, and the defects of his temperament and the limits of his powers were prominent before his powers attained their fruitful scope. Like many generous and warmhearted men, he had a temper. While he never learned to suffer fools gladly, time subdued his irascibility. More important, however, is the fact that it took time before the School put his special talents to their best use.

The reputation of courses at the Harvard Law School is transmitted from generation to generation. Anyone who took over Dean Ames's famous course in Equity II, as Warren did with the second-year class in my time, would have started with a serious handicap. But Warren's mind was temperamentally unsuited for the problems that are the concern of equity. His craving was for definiteness and certitude. The balancing of imponderables, the accommodation of variables, basing judgment on more or less, were uncongenial to him. He floundered in penumbral regions. With the third-year class, in his course on corporations, he had a less stormy time. His professional experience at the New York bar gave him a certain authority in elucidating problems of corporate law, and for their narrowly practical aspects he had a natural flair. But even with these advantages he was far from satisfying to the keener minds among third-year men.

The fact is that Warren survived his turbulent novitiate largely because of his engaging forthrightness. Fastidious truthtelling is noteworthy even among teachers. I do not of course mean avoidance only of falsity. The foible of omniscience is an occupational hazard of teaching, and face saving is not an oriental specialty. Warren was wholly devoid of these refined deviations from truth. In those early days it was not uncommon for Warren to begin his hour with "Gentlemen, yesterday I said so and so. I was wrong—dead wrong." But his regard for truth went much beyond blunt confession of error. Candid disclosure of ignorance was habitual with him, and he took scrupulous care not to appear to have more knowledge than he had. The honesty of his mind was more significant than its dogmatic temper. His dogmatism was due to the limits of his imagination. But he never withheld revision of judgment, or denied himself deeper understanding because of petty pride of opinion.

Not until he taught Property to first-year law students did these sterling qualities of character, united to his great gifts of exposition, enable him to make his important contribution to law teaching. Warren regarded first-year men as raw recruits to be trained to rigorous thinking. It can hardly be denied that, on the whole, the products of our colleges, certainly until the great depression, had not been disciplined by rigorous and systematic intellectual effort, and came to the professional schools with the easygoing habits of men for whom the colleges were too much in the nature of junior country clubs. Warren was a believer in stern discipline and intense application because he was himself a thorough workman and knew that durable results only come from driving effort.

The law of property was a medium for training these raw recruits best suited to Warren's mental temperament. It is the least fluid branch of the law, most resistant to change, readily susceptible of dogmatic formulation. Nobody saw more clearly than Warren what came within the range of his vision. Nobody could put what he saw more vividly. And he demanded explicitness and exactitude from his students. Warren did not enlarge the horizon of his students. He did not impart outlook. But he inculcated mental habits without which mirages are mistaken for horizons, and rhetoric for outlook. Thousands of lawyers throughout the country owe to Warren this indispensable training for hardy thinking.

His was not an ascetic nature. He was a warm friend and a frank enemy, whose bristles concealed much tenderness. If at times he seemed unduly severe, he was severest with himself. One sometimes felt that he was reared too much on the romantic notion that the Puritan tradition outlawed happiness. One who knew him well is tempted to say, "Rest, rest, perturbed spirit."

Six

Harold J. Laski

(1950)

Harold Joseph Laski (1893-1950), the distinguished English political scientist and historian, came to America in 1916 when he was called to teach at Harvard. He soon formed a close friendship, which lasted until his death, with Felix Frankfurter. This memorial was written for the Michaelmas 1950 issue of the *Clare Market Review* (Vol. 46, p. 51), which is published by the Students' Union of the London School of Economics.

To "CARRY COALS TO Newcastle" is no longer a derisive term for the superfluous. But to attempt to elucidate Harold Laski to the students of the London School of Economics, to estimate his significance and to lay bare how much has gone out of the world by his premature death strikes me as almost impertinence. Those who only yesterday had the fires of their minds and souls lit by Harold Laski and their wills fortified for the great adventure of living in this era so fraught with good or ill for mankind know best what manner of man Professor Laski was and need least to have their sense of his significance illumined. Were I tempted to do so, my occupations would deny me the necessary time, even within the fields concerning which I have competence to speak. But I would not forgo the opportunity extended to me to join the student body of the London School of Economics in grateful recognition of what he has abidingly left with us through the good fortune of having known him.

If I said what I felt about him you would understand, but to those who had not known him, it would seem extravagant. The reach of his interests, the range of his intellect, the flow of his sympathy, all combined in one person, touched the incredible. And that leaves out of reckoning the amplitude of his learning and his uncanny talents as a bibliophile. All of these qualities and more were fused in him, to make him indisputably one of the great teachers of our time.

To call him a great teacher is not to give one more proof of the American tendency to overstate. Not to recognize him as such is not to know what a great teacher is, and not to have felt the impact of Harold Laski as a teacher. So versatile and vivid, so provocative and passionate a nature as Harold Laski's is bound to engender differences of opinion, even violent differences, about him. Judgment about a contemporaneous figure is formed largely at the point of contact with him. Those who knew only the Laski of the hustings naturally were influenced by their own biases regarding his biases. Those who encountered him in the sharp give-and-take of debate were apt to judge him by what to a born debater like Laski was merely the thrust of debate. Those for whom the basis for judgment was his quickly, even casually tossed-off journalistic writing, thought of him according to the standards of daily journalism. Above all, those who encountered him merely as he broke lances for those political causes which seemed to him to forward his dream of a better life for all mankind, however inadequately, naturally judged him merely as a partisan promoter of partisan political ends. All these manifestations of Laski were not merely segments of him, but in my view surface segments.

For in his central activity, as a teacher, Laski was the antithesis of a propagandist and a partisan. It is not because he taught in what Mr. Justice Holmes called "the grand man-

ner," whereby he made a recondite figure of the thirteenth
century come to life, and come to life by showing his organic
relation to the apparently disparate problems of today. He
met the test of Socrates for a great teacher, that of a midwife
for the minds and spirits of his students. He was no more
eager to stimulate the thinking of a student who shared his
general direction of opinion than he was to bring to life a
piece of scholastic thinking by a devout Catholic. A distinguished physiologist, familiar with universities on both sides
of the ocean, gave public expression of gratitude to Laski as
"one of the most remarkable teachers who have ever graced
the academic scene in Great Britain or in North America."
Substantially the same has been said by men and women in
the widest diversity of callings—economists, lawyers, sur-
geons, college presidents, businessmen, politicians. But Professor John F. Fulton's expression of gratitude gains significance because he found Laski "one of the most constructively
stimulating personalities with whom I have ever had contact"
although they were "poles apart in political thought."

He cared passionately about the young because he was
endowed so to care. But insofar as conscious purpose directed
his natural endowment he cared about the young because he
wished for them an environment in which their powers could
come to the fullest possible fruition. His war experience in
London only confirmed his deep faith in the possibilities of
the gifts implanted in man. He gave all that he had to his
conviction that the possibilities of a good and gracious society
were not intended for the few, but were attainable on the
widest scale. They were attainable only, however, if the opportunities for attainment were not artificially restricted and
if the ends sought by man were worthy of his dignity. It is
absurd to sum up any man's dominant faith in a few words,
even words that have thundered down the ages. But if action
on a maxim be the best proof of knowledge, then it may be
said that Laski knew "the secret of happiness to be freedom

and the secret of freedom a brave heart." One of the striking characteristics of Harold Laski was his indifference to self. He was little concerned with himself. His energy was absorbed by his sympathies, his affections, his devotions. Had he given thought to himself, he would have been entitled to say, if any man is: "Lay a sword on my coffin; I too was a brave soldier in the war of mankind's liberation."

Seven

Holmes and Laski

(1953)

Mr. Justice Frankfurter wrote this foreword to the *Holmes-Laski Letters: The Correspondence of Mr. Justice Holmes and Harold J. Laski, 1916-1935,* edited by Mark De Wolfe Howe, published by the Harvard University Press, 1953, copyright, 1953, by The President and Fellows of Harvard College. It is reprinted by permission of the publishers.

THE ONLY JUSTIFICATION for an extraneous foreword is the hope of drawing on one's good will with readers to secure their attention to an unknown author, or to assure them that a seemingly extinct volcano has again burst into flame. The crass absurdity that such could be the purpose of introductory remarks to the *Holmes-Laski Letters* precludes a misinterpretation of arrogance. When the public is offered two hefty volumes of correspondence neither revealing long-awaited secrets nor appealing otherwise to elemental curiosity, but preoccupied merely with things of the mind and the insoluble issues of man's spiritual quest, it may not be amiss to bear witness to the excitement these letters have stirred in one who has read every word of them.

This testimony is the more relevant since the public has already had two volumes of the *Holmes-Pollock Letters,* and since it comes from one who has read hundreds of unpublished

276

letters of Mr. Justice Holmes and Harold J. Laski to other correspondents. How is it possible, we naturally suspect, that these *Letters* should not echo what we have already read? How can a correspondence so copious excite the mind from first to last? With full awareness of the treachery of superlatives, it becomes necessary to say that this correspondence surpasses all others from the pen—and it was the pen—of these prolific and extraordinarily endowed letter writers.

One may ask in all soberness, was there ever another such correspondence? Consider its duration and continuity and range: high themes canvassed with enormous learning and a light touch, expressing deep convictions unmarred by intolerance, the exploits of two self-reliant adventurers in the world of ideas, passionately pursued but with gargoylish humor. Added to all this, are the striking differences between the two correspondents.

The outpour began with a bread-and-butter note from Laski, on July 11, 1916, following the first meeting of the two in the Justice's summer home at Beverly Farms, thirty miles north of Boston. This opening letter and the prompt, longer reply by Holmes foreshadow the essential characteristics of an exchange that lasted for close to twenty years— the last letter written by Laski on February 17, 1935, about a fortnight before the Justice's death. They found themselves drawn to one another at first sight by the magnetic attraction of two deep-plowing minds full of disinterested zest for the adventure of ideas.

Consider the situation of the two men who struck up at once this deep, lasting friendship on that July day, 1916, at Beverly Farms. By that time, through his writings—a famous little book, a few essays, and his opinions—Holmes had powerfully changed ways of thinking about law and had thereby rationalized law. A few months earlier, his seventy-fifth birthday had been celebrated as a national event. His fame transcended the boundaries of his own country. He was acclaimed the pre-eminent judge of the English-speaking world. Indeed, Judge Cardozo, no mean authority, was inclined to the view that Holmes was the profoundest intellect who had ever dispensed Anglo-American justice. The gifts which nature had showered upon him—the handsome face and distinguished presence, the noble voice and charming manner—were accentuated by his long, dashing career which enveloped him as though in a romantic aura.

Neither David Belasco nor Max Reinhardt could have contrived a more dramatic contrast than Laski and Holmes when their friendship began. Facing one of the most impressive personalities of his day was a frail stripling of twenty-three. More than half a century separated them. Until he spoke, Laski was not particularly noticeable. But it was not the first time that Laski struck fire in an old man who was the leader of his profession. When Francis Galton, the famous geneticist, discovered that the author of an article which had attracted his attention was "a schoolboy at Manchester, aged 17!!" he wrote: "It is long since I have been so much astonished. The lad probably has a great future before him and he will make a mark if he sticks to Eugenics. . . ."

The lad did not stick to eugenics after he went up to Oxford. Probably through the influence of Sir Ernest Barker, then a don at New College, the problems of politics, especially how liberty was to be achieved, became for the rest of his life Laski's dominant interest. He left Oxford at the outbreak of World War I. Having been rejected for war service because of his physique, he spent two years as a tutor at McGill. At the time of his visit to Holmes he had just come to Harvard, an obscure junior instructor in the Department of Government, piecing out an academic pittance with which to support his wife and child (he had married at eighteen), by much writing during the summer, for Herbert Croly's *New Republic*.

Short as was his stay at Cambridge, only four years, the qualities in Laski that produced "the shock of recognition"

between him and Holmes made a dent also on Harvard. Were
there not a cloud of witnesses, competent and critical, it would
not be credible that a young, unknown teacher could affect
so deeply the life of a great university in so brief a time. For
he taught his colleagues as well as his pupils, as do all great
teachers. In his case they were senior and distinguished colleagues. Professor Charles H. McIlwain, one of the glories
of Harvard both as scholar and teacher, said of him: "His
influence on students was greater than that of any other instructor I have ever known. His influence on me was profound. . . ." One more bit of evidence must suffice. It is
that of Professor Zechariah Chafee, Jr., the eminent legal
scholar and humanist: "There are few men with whom I
have disagreed so often, and fewer still with whom I have
passed so many happy hours and from whom I have learned
so much."

It is not surprising that an ardent spirit with such diverse
talents should have had his energy dispersed in many directions and his compassionate nature readily enlisted for all
sorts of causes and individuals. But the main stream of his life
was teaching. His central significance was that of teacher.
To that calling he gave all he had—his learning (Holmes,
writing to Pollock, called him "one of the very most learned
men I ever saw of any age"), his eloquence, his imagination,
his fantastic feats of memory, his dialectic powers, his ever-
ready kindness and generosity, above all, what has been
rightly called his "quite passionate interest in young people."
There can be few countries in the world where there is not
someone who will cherish for the rest of his days what Laski
meant to him as a teacher. Not often can the function of
teacher have been more completely fulfilled.

A temperament as swift as Laski's in reacting to any manifestation of injustice was bound, on occasion, to be betrayed
by an excess of zeal on the side of the angels. He was not
one of those, as R. H. Tawney said of him, who regard the
omission from the beatitudes of "Blessed are the discreet" a

regrettable oversight. The world suffers less from knight-errantry induced by a passion for liberty than from prudence dictated by self-regard. The letters of both men contain flippant and heretical passages that may offend some sensibilities. Judgments upon Holmes and Laski are bound to be drawn from these letters. But fair judgment can rest only on the correspondence in its entirety.

One more thing ought to be said. Good talkers are apt to embellish their tales and Laski's stories often gained in the telling. Indeed, at times he reinforced history by fancy. Some of his anecdotes remind one of Landor's *Imaginary Conversations*, except that they are gayer and more illuminating. More often, however, when his accounts seem to transcend common experience they do so because things happened to Laski that lay outside the experience of less extraordinary people. And if he appears to indulge in some tall tales about the great, he was in fact the intimate of men like Lord Haldane and John Morley and Lord Chancellor Sankey and eminent men on the Continent, in the United States, and in Asia. He did move in the center of affairs as well as among the notables in the world of learning.

Holmes and Laski were obviously men apart. Much about them was calculated to keep them apart also from one another. But the factors of divergence—antecedents, age, preoccupation, geography—were absorbed by the confluence of their feeling for one another and by the intensity and range of their intellectual interests.

Thus it came to pass that when Laski announced to Holmes, in the early stages of their friendship, his return to England, the Justice wrote: "I shall miss you sadly. There is no other man I should miss so much." And toward the end, as Laski kept up his flow of gay and sustaining letters, his venerable friend wrote: "One of the greatest pleasures of my waning life is a letter from you."

Eight

Sir William Holdsworth

(1944)

Sir William Holdsworth (1871-1944) was an eminent English law teacher and historian. This appreciation of Professor Holdsworth is reprinted from the February 1944 issue of the *American Bar Association Journal* (Vol. 30, p. 81).

ONLY A James Bradley Thayer, a Maitland or a Holmes would be qualified to appraise Holdsworth's achievements. But even one not an expert may avail himself of an opportunity "to lay a wreath, if only of dry leaves, upon his grave." We know what Maitland, the master of English legal history, thought of Holdsworth's work when only the ground had been broken for what became the mighty edifice. In his inaugural lecture, in 1888, Maitland deplored the fact "that no attempt has ever been made to write the history of English law as a whole." In 1903 appeared Holdsworth's first volume of such a history, to be followed, as then projected, by only one other volume. Maitland was able to say of it, "Mr. Holdsworth has done well: indeed he has done admirably well" (19 L. Q. Rev. 335). This was the highest of praise. While Maitland was bountifully generous, he was fastidious of truth in the domain of learning. In 1909 came the contemplated second volume, expanded into two volumes. Had Maitland survived their appearance he doubtless would have welcomed volumes two and three with one of his enduring essays. Fortunately, Pollock induced his friend Holmes to give the magistral judgment.

Mr. Holdsworth is telling us a profoundly interesting story. It is one of the most important chapters in the greatest human document—the tale of what men had most believed and most wanted. It is told with learning and scientific instinct, and the book is to be recommended equally to philosophers who can understand it and to practical students of the law (25 L. Q. Rev. 412, 414-15).

With the publication of the twelfth volume, in 1938, the end of Holdsworth's goal, one would suppose, had been reached. In view of the estimates that Maitland and Holmes placed upon what turned out to be merely the beginnings of Holdsworth's labors, it is not presumptuous to surmise how profoundly they would have rejoiced over the intricate and stupendous tapestry of learning which Holdsworth steadily wove for forty years. Considering the panorama of history which he unfolded—seven centuries of it—and the vast mass of materials that he had to digest, much of it dreary and recondite, only implacable industry could have encompassed the sheer volume of his output. But volume is the least significant aspect of scholarly work. Too often it is the enemy of scholarship. Holdsworth wrote and wrought with fidelity to those canons for responsible inquiry into legal history which Maitland had for all times set for students of English legal institutions.

A man's achievements are to be measured by subtracting from what now exists that which he has added to what preceded him. Holdsworth's twelve volumes have not merely added to the knowledge and understanding of law as it is administered throughout the world, in all the legal systems which are rooted in the common law as well as where English law, as in South Africa and India, has been grafted upon native institutions. A work like Holdsworth's is not merely a book. It is a process of intellectual reorientation. No longer can British history be written without due regard to the interplay between social and legal ideas. No longer can historic rules of law be considered without that fullness of understanding of their social context which Holdsworth has made possible. In short, Holdsworth earned the highest formal recognition which Great Britain makes of lasting achievement in the realm of the mind when he was given the Order of Merit.

Holdsworth magnificently proved that "the work is never done while the power to work remains." Not content with his twelve volumes, he labored on through the agonies of the war and eventually of personal bereavement. And thereby he has left us a rich legacy. For two more volumes, I believe, are still to come, part of the manuscript of which he sent across the ocean to this country for safety against contingencies. How one person was able to accomplish all this and yet engage in so many other activities, share so actively in the life at Oxford, and identify himself so much with the trials and joys of the young, it is difficult to comprehend. Especially puzzling is it to one who knew him as a gay companion and on several occasions at All Souls' drank port with him in the best traditions of the eighteenth century.

He as truly served civilization in a scholar's quiet way as did the son of his pride. Holdsworth dedicated his life to the promotion of the sway of law as against brute force and arbitrary power, to resist which Flight Lieutenant Richard Holdsworth, R.A.F., gave his life.

Nine

John Dewey

(1949)

John Dewey (1859-1952) was, of course, the distinguished philosopher and educator. On the occasion of his ninetieth birthday celebration on October 20, 1949, at the Hotel Commodore in New York City, Mr. Justice Frankfurter made these appreciative remarks.

THIS VAST ASSEMBLY has gathered to take note of the birthday of a mere professor of philosophy. To be sure, it is his ninetieth birthday. Nevertheless I suspect that only a handful of those present belong to the American Philosophical Society, and probably not many more are philosophers, technically speaking. Every shift of society and every calling is here represented—"Rich man, poor man, beggar man, thief; doctor, lawyer, merchant, chief." What brings us together? Not to do honor to John Dewey; that is beyond our power. Nor has he need, as even a great thinker sometimes has, of relief from the solitude of thought by encouragement. We are here to express our gratitude for what he has given us and to renew our faith in the ultimate reliance of civilized man, not upon passing fads and gadgets, but upon the things of the spirit. From John Dewey's presence we can draw new strength for our tasks of moral pioneering.

What has he given us? He has been one of those thinkers to the measure of whose thought men move who may never have heard of him. What he has written is to be found between the covers of more than a hundred volumes. But through them all—and my knowledge of their contents is proof of the educational potency of osmosis—there pulsates something beyond the business of professors of philosophy. There may be a vast difference between a professor of philosophy and a philosopher. One whose professional preoccupations are the eternal, unsolved problems of metaphysical speculation is great in any humanistic sense only if he transcends the bounds of his technical problems and fertilizes the thoughts of men to whom the terminology of philosophic inquiry may be a foreign language. Such a thinker makes every profession rethink its specialized problems. He has this effect because he is capable of sending galvanic rays of illumination through the particularized interests of fragmented thought. For he sees the organic below the surface of the discrete; he is capable of seeing it because of deep sympathy with the possibilities of life in all its fullness.

There is not a person in this room who could not, out of his own vision of life, give proof that such has been the impact of John Dewey upon his time—and happily it has been a long time. Let me summon a great witness. Speaking with the freedom of private correspondence, Mr. Justice Holmes thus expressed his feelings about John Dewey's work: "It is like shavings of jade—subtle—sometimes epigrammatic—emancipated—seeing the world and man as fluid. . . . It makes on me an impression like Walt Whitman, of being symphonic, and of having more life and experience in his head than most writers, philosophers or others. . . . There are moments that suggest that he could write well, but then comes obscurity. Still . . . to my fancy he gets closer to the cosmic wiggle than anyone else that I know in these days. . . . So methought God would have spoken had He been inarticulate but keenly desirous to tell you how it was." Again and again, in speech and letter, Mr. Justice Holmes expressed his homage with characteristic flavor, because he was a man who was exceedingly glad to pay without stint his spiritual debts.

Only very few of us were fortunate enough to have had John Dewey as a classroom teacher, but all of us went to school to him. Especially lucky have been those who have had the unpremeditated teaching of his conversation. My own sense of him is best conveyed by what was said of a famous Cambridge don of some three centuries ago: "I never got so much good among all my books by a whole day's plodding in a study, as by an hour's discourse I have got with him. For he was not a library locked up, nor a book clasped, but he stood open for any to converse withal that had a mind to learn. Yea, he was a fountain running over, labouring to do good to those who perhaps had no mind to receive it."

I am not concerned with the winds of philosophic doctrine. I am not competent, even were this the occasion, to define the strength and the direction of the gales that Dewey released. But this much, perhaps, I may venture without arrogance. Dewey's thinking is too pervasive to be confined within a cult or to be in the keeping of a school of possessive disciples. His philosophic outlook has not been imprisoned within a fixed system established by inexorable syllogisms. Life, with its exuberance and irony, has a way of making mockery of such systems. Dewey taught us to use all that is fruitful in experience to gain new experience in dealing with problems that too often defy the abstractions offered for their solution. Preoccupied though he has been with intellectual issues far from the crowd, he is a good embodiment of homespun American optimism, with his deeply rooted belief in the resources of the individual, provided only the conditions of society permit their unfolding. But his is an optimism enlightened and tempered by a humble awareness that man's untraveled road requires pertinacity of spirit and readiness to encounter the untried. His optimism is cautious and self-testing. His belief in the possibility of man is a source of energy, not an anodyne.

If I have caught the robust faith behind the varied expressions of John Dewey's thinking, it has seemed to me not unlike the testament of faith, making allowances for poetic license, left to his young sons by a poet who fell in the last war. "For man is omnipotent. There is no goal he can imagine in the realm of mind which he cannot reach sooner or later in the realm of matter. There is no force yet discovered which is strong enough to foil him: through his children he can overcome even the apparent finality of death. There is no fear so potent that it will forever deter him, nor any suffering so great that he cannot endure it for his spirit's sake. In him is every quality that he attributes to his gods: beauty, wisdom, omniscience, omnipotence, divinity."

Ten

Alfred North Whitehead

(1948)

Alfred North Whitehead (1861-1947), the eminent philosopher and mathematician, was called to Harvard University in 1924 after completing a brilliant academic career at Cambridge University and Imperial College in England. At Harvard he and his wife became good friends of Professor and Mrs. Frankfurter. After Professor Whitehead's death on December 30, 1947, Mr. Justice Frankfurter sent this letter to the New York *Times,* which published it on January 8, 1948.

FROM KNOWLEDGE GAINED through the years of the personalities who in our day have affected American university life, I have for some time been convinced that no single figure has had such a pervasive influence as the late Professor Alfred North Whitehead. Certainly so far as this applies to the country's oldest university, my statement will hardly be disputed. I should like to try to describe the nature of the ferment imparted by a thinker whose philosophic speculations were mostly beyond the capacity of those whom he touched.

That our universities have grave shortcomings for the intellectual life of this nation is by now a commonplace. The chief source of their inadequacy is probably the curse of departmentalization. Among students, as well as among teachers, there has been a tendency to regard courses as something which exist in nature, instead of artificial simplifications for the mastery of what are complicated organisms, whether of nature or reason or society. Professor Whitehead exerted powerful influence to break down this separatism in the various departments of the university.

From the time that he came to Harvard in 1924 he infused an understanding of interdependence among the various disciplines, to use the current jargon. For all who came within the range of his infectious personality, arid professionalism was quickened into exhilarating meaning and the universe expanded. Such was the quiet, almost shy magic of his qualities that his influence imperceptibly but quickly permeated the whole university.

The need for breaking down sterilizing departmentalization has been widely felt. Unfortunately, however, a too-frequent way of doing it has been, wittily but not too unfairly, described as the cross-sterilization of the social sciences. That is a tendency by which a difficult problem, say of the law, is solved by relying on the formulation of a dubious truth in some other field.

Professor Whitehead's insistence on understanding through realization of the interdependence of thought and ideas and institutions was quite otherwise.

He was fiercely on guard against the illusions of verbalization and did not confuse certainty with certitude. In short, he was tough-minded because he felt the universe as illimitable. He distrusted closed systems because they imprison the creative possibilities of insight and experience. He was relentlessly exacting of accurate responsible thinking, precisely because he knew that even the most rigorous thought cannot achieve fullness of comprehension.

It was not by courses or lectures that he ignited to deeper understanding and more beautiful visions the minds and feelings of hundreds of students, alike youngsters fresh from high schools and colleagues themselves eminent. He did this predominantly through informal and unpremeditated talk, mostly in his modest apartment, which gave even the most

timid freshman the sense of participation in an exciting adventure. Everything of distinction contributed toward these
unfailingly memorable occasions. Not to mention Mrs.
Whitehead would be to omit enveloping loveliness.

Professor Whitehead had a benign and beautiful presence,
a voice and diction that made music of English speech, humor
that lighted up dark places, humility that made the foolish
wiser and evoked the wisdom of the taciturn. For twenty
years Professor Whitehead exercised this great and radiating
influence. He did so at Harvard because he was there. He did
so beyond because he was what he was. People came to Harvard because he was there. People read his books who had
no background for understanding them. This partly explains
why he is said to be so hard to read. No one who is ready to
read serious books can fail to find luminous charm in his non-
technical writings, like his recently published *Essays* and his
Adventures of Ideas.

To dwell, however inadequately, on the qualities of a
teacher like Alfred North Whitehead is important if our
universities are important. They are important if the institutions specially charged with the accumulation of the intellectual capital of the world are important to a society. Who will
deny that Professor Whitehead was right in his belief that
the fate of the intellectual civilization of the world today is
to no inconsiderable extent in the keeping of our universities?
"The Aegean Coastline had its chance and made use of it; Italy
had its chance and made use of it: France, England, Germany
had their chance and made use of it. Today the Eastern
American states have their chance. What use will they make
of it? That question has two answers. Once Babylon had its
chance, and produced the Tower of Babel. The University
of Paris fashioned the intellect of the Middle Ages."

The awful question that confronts American universities
is: What are they doing with their power and their duty?

Eleven

Morris R. Cohen

(1949)

Morris Raphael Cohen (1880-1947), the distinguished philosopher and mathematician, taught at the College of the City of New York for many years. While studying for his doctorate in philosophy at Harvard, he roomed with Felix Frankfurter, then in his third year at the Law School. Their friendship continued for more than forty years. When Professor Cohen's autobiography, *A Dreamer's Journey*, was published posthumously in 1949, Mr. Justice Frankfurter reviewed it for the New York *Times* (March 27, 1949).

THIS IS a very moving book whose appeal transcends personal association. For Morris Cohen in his sixty-seven years carved out a career of pervasive influence and achieved a serene spirit, although he was handicapped by extreme poverty in early youth and the lifelong ill health which resulted from it. In his case frustration and suffering were transmuted into compassion for the common fate of man and served only to strengthen his native impulse to understand.

This is the life of a thinker. Barring minor excursions into the world of affairs, Morris Cohen analyzes in this book the influences that shaped his thinking, not about the problems and panaceas of the day, but concerning the ultimate inquiries into how men think about them. In short, he was a philosopher, conceiving philosophy as "simply stubborn thinking about problems in all fields of life's endeavor—thinking which

refuses to accept as final the common limitations at which
creatures of habit stop thinking." He identified philosophy
with "natural curiosity or wonder about the nature of the
world, things, life, knowledge, art, religion and morality as
roads leading to a common concern with perennial problems," turning that curiosity in upon himself and proving
that the adventures of the mind can be as exciting as the
deeds of soldiers and statesmen.

Such an accomplishment required rigorous objectivity in
looking inward, the candor of humility, a lambent wit that
sees man's efforts in their cosmic perspective, and a lucidity
of speech that can convey delicate and complicated ideas in
purest English prose. In Morris Cohen these gifts were happily fused. And since he applied these gifts in trying to account for himself, Morris Cohen not only fortified the human
spirit but also made a permanent addition to the slim volume
of literature that sheds light on the creative process.

Essentially Morris Cohen's life was given to contemplation—not as an evasion of life but as one of its deepest aspects.
His lasting significance may be that to an extraordinary degree he encouraged in others the habit of contemplation. This
he did as one of the greatest teachers of our time, and teaching like Morris Cohen's is as rare as it is precious. It is my
belief that he will endure not so much through his writings—
though I am the last to underrate those that I am competent
to judge—but in the minds of men and in the minds of generations to come. For he transformed the interests and outlook of thousands of students throughout the land to such an
extent that they then became the generators of new insight.

That this should be so is all the more striking because
Morris Cohen, powerful as he was, was happily not the powerful purveyor of doctrine. If he had a doctrine it was to be
critical of doctrines. It was an honest judgment and not a
flourish of rhetoric that made Mr. Justice Holmes write of
Morris Cohen, "I envy the youth who sit at his feet." And

what *did* the youth carry away from him for the rest of their lives?

When I started to teach philosophy in City College I found myself devoid of the gift of verbal fluency, and so I naturally resorted to the use of the Socratic method: teaching by means of searching and provoking questions. The head of the department, who was not similarly handicapped—in fact he was exceptionally gifted as a teacher—at first demurred.

"What do you do to make your students into fine fellows?" he asked.

To which I replied, "I'm not a fine fellow myself, at least not so much better than my students that I can venture to impose my own standard on them."

Never having discovered for myself any royal road up the rocky and dangerous steep of philosophy, I did not conceive it to be part of my function as a teacher to show my students such a road. The only help I could offer them was to convince them that they must climb for themselves or sink in the mire of conventional error. All I could do to make the climbing easier was to relieve them of needless customary baggage. This exposed me to the charge of being merely critical, negative or destructive. I have always been ready to plead guilty to that charge.

It seemed to me that one must clear the ground of useless rubbish before one can begin to build. I once said to a student who reproached me for my destructive criticism, "You have heard the story of how Hercules cleaned the Augean stables. He took all the dirt and manure out and left them clean. You ask me, 'What did he leave in their stead?' I answer, 'Isn't it enough to have cleaned the stables?'"

Knocking logical errors and comfortable illusions out of young people's heads is not a pleasant occupation. It is much pleasanter to preach one's own convictions. But how could I hope, in a few weeks of contact with my students, to build up a coherent worldview that should endure throughout their subsequent lives? . . . It seemed to me a more important service in the cause of liberal civilization to develop a spirit of genuine regard for the weight

of evidence and a power to discriminate between responsible and
irresponsible sources of information, to inculcate the habit of admitting ignorance when we do not know, and to nourish the
critical spirit of inquiry which is inseparable from the love of
truth that makes men free.

To me, this did not mean the old-fashioned liberation of the
mind from all traditional beliefs, but rather the supplying of students with new points of view that would enrich their outlook
and thus help them to attain intellectual independence. This in
practice meant attempting to teach future scientists, lawyers,
economists and citizens to think philosophically about the problems of science, law, economics and citizenship.

These quotations convey better than another's interpretation the task which Morris Cohen set himself as a teacher of
philosophy. Their homely flavor is characteristic of the book,
but they give barely a hint of the exhilaration, the excitement,
the stimulus to independent inquiry and responsible thinking
which he stirred in his students. I doubt whether in our time
any one equaled him as a wielder of the Socratic method, and
I speak as one who sat under some of its greatest masters.

I have said that in this book Morris Cohen accounts for
himself. But he cannot account for himself without accounting for his ancestors, and he cannot account for his ancestors
without accounting for a good deal of American history.
When President Franklin D. Roosevelt once observed, "We
are all immigrants," he uttered a truism of profound implications. The immigrants who, in fusion, have made the United
States, brought diverse gifts to the New World and created
diverse problems. As an essential part of the story of his mind
Morris Cohen expounds with tenderness the story, beginning
in the 'eighties, of the Russian-Jewish immigrants to whom
America beckoned as a means of escape from the cruel tyran-
nies of the Czarist regime.

Morris Cohen dwells lovingly on his formative years in

Neshweis and Minsk before he was brought to this country in his twelfth year, because that was part of the story of his journey "from the medieval to the modern age." He had to tell this story, partly in pietistic devotion but even more to make younger generations remember what they too quickly forget.

When he was chided by his son for neglecting what seemed "more important enterprises, like the volume on metaphysics, to indulge in the writing of an autobiography," Morris Cohen replied in a letter (included in the book) of which I can quote only a small part:

I have . . . for forty years nourished the hope of writing the story of my life as an illustration of the various forces which have met or found expression in my life, especially of currents which have molded Jewish history and which are vividly illustrated in the heroic struggles of my father and mother, under diverse conditions, to earn their daily bread and to bring up their children in decency. You, and the men of your generation, seem to have no conception of the magnitude of this struggle and the immense fortitudes which sustained it. I thus have a burning desire to do what so few people that I know can do, namely, outline the basic facts of the great epic—the odyssey, if you like—of the generation which cut its roots in the old home and crossed the ocean into a strange land without any resources other than their own unconquerable fortitude.

The book, therefore, not only gives insight into the making of a significant mind, it also gives another deep glimpse into the makings of America. It joins the company of Jacob Riis's *The Making of an American,* Booker Washington's *Own Story,* and Mary Antin's *The Promised Land.*

This autobiography is an effort, and a triumphant one, as was Morris Cohen's whole life, after things that are of "perennial value."

Twelve

Felix S. Cohen

(1954)

Felix Solomon Cohen (1907-1953), the son of Morris R. Cohen, was also a respected scholar and teacher of legal philosophy. His interest in law was not merely academic. As a lawyer for the federal government, principally in the Department of the Interior, he devoted much of his life to active protection of the rights of Indians. His *Handbook of Federal Indian Law* is the definitive work on the subject. The Winter 1954 issue of the *Rutgers Law Review* contained a symposium of articles in memory of Felix Cohen, and to it Mr. Justice Frankfurter contributed this foreword (Vol. 9, p. 355).

FELIX COHEN'S LIFE was incomplete—he died at 46—but not unfulfilled. Certainly it was not unsuccessful, if the measure of success for a thinker is to give substantial samples of his best. The predominant devotion of Felix Cohen was to law and he dealt with enduring problems of law. Being enduring, they were not essentially novel, but being enduring they remain always fresh. It would not honor the memory of one whose modesty and passion for truthtelling would disdain praise beyond the truth to claim for him seminal contributions to the law. Over the course of centuries these have been more than rare. Indeed, since continuity with the past is a necessary ingredient of law, significant contributions are largely made by adaptation of past to present, by formulation of a generalization immanent in discrete instances, by absorption of new insights into the nature of man, by re-

296

sponses to new needs of society. If law is not to stifle life but to serve as one of the powerful means for releasing its potentialities, law must be subjected to a constant critical scrutiny in order to be freed from outworn entanglements with the past.

And so the enduring problems of law raise ultimate questions about its sources and its sanctions, the accommodation of present and past and future, the limits of effective legal action, the interplay of the subjective element in any judgment and the objective criteria by which it professes to be guided, the relation of law to morals, the mode of bringing unconscious influences and inarticulate assumptions to the surface, the means for ascertaining the validity of what are deemed to be relevant juristic criteria. He who persuasively confronts those whose concern is law with the duty of facing such questions, who does not himself flinch from their complexity nor from the necessity of seeking answers though recognizing the elusiveness and impermanence of all answers, joins the company of the relatively few who build their permanent share in the coral reef of the law.

Felix Cohen belongs to this select company. Very early he gave proof of his understanding of the range and depth of the great issues that underlie the illusory simplicity with which legal problems are ordinarily stated. For him the presuppositions of legal rules were not a measure of their validity. The rules had to be justified by validation of their presuppositions. But his inquiring spirit accepted the universe in which he lived. He did not reject claims of practicality that were parochial in order to embrace theories that were utopian because empty. The opportunity to express grateful esteem for a valiant and high-spirited thinker who was not above the battle of life is not to be turned into an occasion for scholarly appraisal of his work. Suffice it to say that for me Felix Cohen's *Handbook of Federal Indian Law* affords the means for appreciating his qualities as man and scholar and jurist.

Certainly when he embarked upon the undertaking which culminated in the *Handbook,* the Indians were probably the most neglected, because least powerful, of our minority groups. Only a passionate desire to vindicate our democratic professions would have led anyone to undertake the forbidding task of bringing meaning and reason out of the vast hodgepodge of treaties, statutes, judicial and administrative rulings, and unrecorded practice in which the intricacies and perplexities, the confusions and injustices of the law governing Indians lay concealed. Only a ripe and imaginative scholar with a synthesizing faculty would have brought luminous order out of such a mishmash. He was enabled to do so because of his wide learning in the various fields of inquiry which are relevant to so-called technical legal questions. Learning would not have sufficed. It required realization that any domain of law, but particularly the intricacies and peculiarities of Indian law, demanded an appreciation of history and understanding of the economic, social, political and moral problems in which the more immediate problems of that law are entwined. It is, I think, fair to say that this interplay between reflective thought and proper regard for actualities characterizes the body of his writings.

He cared deeply for the professed aims of a democratic society. His was a compassionate nature and he yielded to it with passion. But it may be said of him as was said of another that passion was behind his judgment, not in front of it. Convictions had to justify themselves at the bar of reason. Intensity of feeling did not prove reason.

> Memory fades, must the remember'd
> Perishing be?

Memory of Felix Cohen will not fade in the many to whom he imparted something of his own gift for zestful living. In the great anthropological document that is the law his contribution will not perish.

Thirteen

Joseph B. Eastman

(1944)

Joseph Bartlett Eastman (1882-1944) dedicated his life to public service. He was appointed to the Interstate Commerce Commission in 1919 and served as its chairman for numerous years. Appointed Director of the Office of Defense Transportation in December 1941, he held that office until his death. He was widely regarded as the exemplar of a public servant: able, industrious, and modest. Mr. Justice Frankfurter noted the significance of Joseph B. Eastman's career in this letter to the New York *Times*, published March 17, 1944.

THROUGH HIS APPOINTMENT of Judge Thomas M. Cooley as its first chairman, President Cleveland started the Interstate Commerce Commission off with a great tradition. To indicate as does your editorial today that no man contributed more distinction to that commission than did Joseph B. Eastman is not to be unmindful of the services of other distinguished commissioners—men like Lane and Prouty. But Eastman's career had a significance beyond his pre-eminence in the field of his specialty. And on that I should like to say a word.

The main issues confronting our society—the mastery of unemployment involving the wise direction of the processes of production and distribution, the well-being of agriculture, the conduct of public utilities, the control of disease and crime—are deeply enmeshed in intricate facts. Merely to analyze these issues requires a vast body of technical knowledge.

Such analysis is only a preliminary to exploration of possible remedies. In a world more and more dominated by technological forces, government must have at its disposal the resources of training and character—men equipped to understand and to deal wisely with the complicated issues to which these technological forces give rise. We are more than a century removed from Jacksonian days of versatile improvisation.

Without a permanent and professional public service, highly trained, imaginative, and courageously disinterested, the democratic aims of our society cannot be achieved. Such a body of public servants is indispensable, no matter what social and economic policies may express the popular will in the executive and legislative branches of the Government. Of this need, Joseph B. Eastman symbolized the best fulfillment. He not only furnished striking proof of the extraordinary gifts which the Government attracts. His reappointments to the Interstate Commerce Commission, by Presidents of varying outlook, prove that disinterested capacity will find effective support even from those who suffered adverse rulings. For Eastman's reappointment to the commission was strongly urged by railroads whose views on vital issues he rejected.

One of the most genial Presidents remarked that "government after all is a very simple thing." The truth, of course, is that no enterprise is more complicated than modern government. No enterprise is more in need of skilled and devoted service and a large measure of continuity in that service. That can only come if men of high talents and character and disinterestedness are attracted to government. More than fifty years ago Theodore Roosevelt said, "The merit system is the American system, the unaristocratic system; and no system could be less American and more undemocratic than the patronage system which it supplants." It is right that government should not even pretend to compete in salaries by which private enterprise tempts. The satisfaction of government service lies on a different level. But it is wholly wrong to expect right standards of public service from officials whose salaries are too low to enable them to meet the minimum standards of cultivated life. It is even more disastrous that public service, except in the highest offices, should lack public esteem. The tide of opinion should be for and not against public administration as a career for talent. Otherwise the public cannot expect the professional training, the detached judgment, and the moral courage necessary for the conduct of intricate public affairs by men who are not subject to the scrutiny and do not enjoy the glamour of public office.

Eastman's public service is a just cause for pride. It ought also to make us ponder on the needs of our public service and the conditions for its adequate fulfillment.

Fourteen

Augustus L. Richards

(1953)

Augustus Loring Richards (1879-1951) was, like Felix Frankfurter, a member of the Class of 1906 at the Harvard Law School. An outstanding member of the New York bar, he never held public office. This memorial written by Mr. Justice Frankfurter for the Fiftieth Anniversary Report of the Harvard College Class of 1903 (p. 676) tells, however, of the unique and invaluable public services rendered by Mr. Richards during World War II.

COMPARISON OF ADVOCATES to actors is not a novelty. The fragility of their fame is another thing they have in common. Except in the rare instances where the art of actor or advocate is preserved in the amber of great literature, those who play their part on the stage of the theater or on the private stage of the bar do not survive beyond the memory of their contemporaries. And when the distinguishing significance of a mere lawyer—a lawyer, that is, who has not conveyed his qualities through the opportunities of public office or expressed himself within the covers of a book—is the ardor and pungency of his personality, it is almost a foredoomed enterprise for one not gifted with poetic imagination to try to create an image of him for those who did not know him.

Such is the problem in any effort to make vivid one's conviction that Gus Richards was one of the extraordinary men of our time. He was a subject made to order for the kind of biographic essay in which the English excel—writers like Walter Bagehot, Lytton Strachey, G. M. Young, or Algernon Cecil. They do, I suppose, because succulent, odd characters make a livelier appeal to the English than to us. Gus Richards was an odd character. Not that he departed in outward ways from the beaten path of many a Massachusetts lad. The biographical details of his life will be found in the admirable "Memorial of Augustus Loring Richards," written by his partners, in the *Memorial Book of the Association of the Bar of the City of New York*, 1951. It was not one of those appreciations of the dead written with a dead hand. It lives.

The bare facts can be quickly retold. Richards was born in Belmont, Massachusetts, November 15, 1879, and he died January 8, 1951, in New York City. He was the son of David J. Richards, '76, and Esther Loring Richards, '75, of the Wesleyan Academy in Massachusetts. Gus was earthy by temperament, a trait reinforced by his upbringing on a farm. Gus had the benefits of the exacting life of a farming family in Massachusetts sixty-odd years ago. In his home, he also breathed the atmosphere of deep cultural and religious interests. He had already the habit of reading when he went to the Boston Latin School. There he won prizes for excellence in classical studies and in modern studies, and doubtless there he stocked his mind with the riches of English literature, especially the King James version of the Bible, Shakespeare, and the New England poets. These were riches on which he drew heavily as a lawyer and in his polemic private correspondence. Even more important, this avid early reading in imaginative literature stimulated his own imaginative faculties, particularly enabling him to interpret the feelings and motives of others, especially those unlike himself. From the Latin School, Gus went to Harvard College on a scholarship and paid his way both through the college and through the Harvard Law School by scholarships and tutoring in English and Latin. He graduated among the first in his class, and his commencement part, "The Boy in Robert Louis Stevenson," is still worth reading, we are told by those competent to judge.

His law school record was creditable enough, but he was not the only member of the Law School Class of 1906 to illustrate that the school's examination system, fair as I then deemed it and now deem it, was not an infallible means for discovering intrinsic legal excellence. For I had no doubt from my talks with Gus that the stuff of a first-rate lawyer was in him. He abundantly proved it in practice.

Gus was at once one of the most fearless and one of the most modest of men. He was so respectful of what he deemed to be the qualities implied by law review rank and of his failure to achieve it, that it required a good deal of persuasion for him to follow his desire to try his luck at the New York bar. Quite on his merits he obtained a clerkship in the firm of Hughes, Rounds & Schurman. He became a member of the firm in 1916 and remained with it, in its various transmutations, until his retirement from active practice in 1941. Thus he was a partner of Charles Evans Hughes during the years when the later Chief Justice was such a dominant figure at the New York bar, and continuously with Charles Evans Hughes, Jr. Gus Richards's qualities as a lawyer may be briefly summarized by saying that both the Hugheses gave enthusiastic proof that Gus Richards was their worthy partner.

To Richards a litigation was an intellectual campaign. He was a legal strategist of the first order. He realized, as lawyers not always do, that judges, no less than juries, must be infused with the conviction that your side of the case represents justice. Gus Richards had rare talent in digging below the surface. Where others saw only an ordinary transaction, he was relentless in pursuing trails opened up by his fertile mind. This combination of indefatigable industry and legal imagination, with felicitous command of language, made him a formidable opponent who seldom failed to register victories.

But the distinctive qualities of Richards found perhaps their most striking employment after his retirement from active practice. The reason for his retirement bespeaks the character of the man. The invasion of the Low Countries by the Nazis set Gus afire. He loathed tyranny because he was dedicated to the spirit of man. The war in Europe became his war. Roosevelt had no stronger supporter than Richards in his efforts, before Pearl Harbor, to give every possible aid to the Allies "short of war." Richards said that for him to continue to do business as usual when civilization was at stake was like balancing one's checkbook while the building was on fire. "At least I could help a little bit," he said, "to hold the ladder against the building while the firemen were climbing up to arrest the fire and save the occupants." And this he did with uncommon originality, devotion, and power.

It is a long story, but the short of it is that Gus Richards constituted himself a Sixth Column to fight those whom he regarded as the Fifth Column—those who overtly or covertly resisted President Roosevelt's efforts, those who by complacency or timidity or hostility were retarding or resisting, as he conceived it, our contribution to the Allied cause and thereby throwing weight on the side of the dictators. He had retired to his farm at Remsen, near Utica, New York, once owned by Baron von Steuben and for him redolent with ancestral and Revolutionary associations. From there he conducted a one-man campaign against the Isolationists, the America-firsters, the Bundists, the Chicago *Tribune*, the Colonel Mc-Cormicks, the Hamilton Fishes, *et omne genus*. How did he do it? By the simple and splendiferous device of sending to members of Congress, to newspapers and their proprietors, most deftly worded telegrams in answer to utterances which he regarded as deleterious to the overriding national interest. Only a lawyer as skillful as Gus, and one who could draw deeply on the resources of English literature for the apt quotation and the striking phrase, and at the same time was ready to spend himself and his money on a great cause, could have conducted what may without hyperbole be called a fabulous campaign.

The campaign told. His victims smarted under the thrust of his pen which gained in force because, with apparent ingenuousness, he not only signed these communications but gave his address, Remsen, New York. It required more than imagination and pertinacity and passionate concern for a man to carry on this enterprise as Gus carried it on all during the war. It required, as I have said, a lawyer of great skill. For only one as knowledgeable as Gus could have been as piercing as he was in some of his telegrams to many a potent figure in our public life and at the same time stay this side of the dangers of libel action.

In all this he was not a Don Quixote. He had deeper psychological insight than those who were amused by what they regarded as futile antics. Gus proved once more that the constant dropping of water gradually does wear away a stone. These persistent, clever assaults not infrequently got under the skin of his victims. They were made to realize that they did not have the field to themselves. They became self-conscious and to that extent the strength of their strokes was somewhat blunted. Moreover, he did not merely go after his enemies. He realized that it is equally important to encourage your friends. And many a telegram from Richards gave strength to voices on behalf of the Allied cause, not excluding that of the President himself.

These communications of Richards constitute a unique aspect of the war literature. A set of them, in a series of stout volumes, is in the Franklin D. Roosevelt Library at Hyde Park. They will, one ventures to believe, be important to future historians. It will help them to recreate the atmosphere of the pre-Pearl Harbor period, as well as of the war years. Political action and nonaction grow out of atmosphere. Without an appreciation of atmosphere the past is apt to be falsified or rendered as caricature; atmosphere evaporates unless recreated by the pen of imaginative, perceptive historians.

Much has been left unsaid of the public good done by this wholly private person—of his gift to the State of New York of reclaimed land containing two million trees, now known as Steuben Memorial Forest, of the founding of Steuben scholarships for college education, of occasional suggestive writings out of his deep knowledge of the history of the American Revolution. In all these enterprises he was joined both in thought and in execution by his wife, Alice Butler Richards, with whom he had the happiest companionship for thirty years.

As for his many acts of kindness, his extraordinary fidelity as a friend, his manifold generosity—they are the private possession of his many, many beneficiaries. When he died the world was left much poorer in courage and kindness, in whimsy and wisdom.

Fifteen

Robert P. Patterson

(1952)

Robert Porter Patterson (1891-1952) was Secretary of War from 1945 to 1947, having resigned his position as a judge of the United States Circuit Court of Appeals in 1940 to become Assistant Secretary of War. He was a student in the first class taught by Professor Frankfurter at the Harvard Law School, and the friendship then formed continued throughout his life. After Judge Patterson was killed in an airplane crash, Mr. Justice Frankfurter wrote this letter to the New York *Times*, which published it on January 27, 1952.

IT IS NOT listless obedience to the ancient saying about the dead which spontaneously brings to mind terms like "gallant," "dedicated," "noble," in thinking of Robert P. Patterson's life. Perhaps you will allow one whose friendship with Patterson began in his student days at the Harvard Law School to give some indication of the aptness of such characterizations.

Patterson combined qualities that made him a leading man in a Harvard Law School class conspicuous for ability, and also enabled him to have a distinguished record on the field of battle. In spite of his outstanding scholarship, he never showed the slightest trace of pedantry and never indulged in mental gymnastics. He never seemed confused or baffled or tired when working excessive hours or when dealing with new, complicated situations. Simplicity and directness and force were the traits of his mind, and on occasion he showed the defects of these admirable qualities. These traits were only in part intellectual. Character and mind did not dwell apart in him. Thus he was free from hampering doubts and inhibitions which afflict to some extent even good men, in matters carrying responsibility and calling for decisions which would recoil upon the actor in case of error.

This clarity of mind and disinterestedness of purpose led to decisions of wisdom for his own happiness and the country's good. Perhaps the most outstanding quality of the man was a total lack of self-regard. He sank himself in whatever task was at hand with complete obliviousness of the effect upon himself. And when a choice of tasks was to be made he invariably chose the less self-indulgent, and the larger duty.

In his early practice he never had the slightest concern about what is called "getting credit." Although his growing family was dependent on his modest earnings, he left the alluring promises of practice to become a federal judge. His training and character had so disciplined his passionate nature that he became one of the eminent judges of the land with every right to look forward to an eventual seat on the supreme bench. This prospect he promptly surrendered when Colonel Stimson asked him to be his assistant secretary of war. Particularly the younger generation of professional men were moved by his example. Their actions are influenced not by noble sentiments but by valorous conduct. Between Stimson and Patterson there was an interplay of understanding and trust, the want of which may be fatal in the conduct of war, but no less conducive to disaster in times of peace. It was characteristic of Patterson that he was eager to engage in the immediate hazards of war. He regarded World War II as his from the beginning, and only the impact of Secretary Stimson's personal authority over Patterson prevented him from resigning his office in 1944 to take a commission as an infantry officer once more.

He was a fighter and therefore sometimes fought need-lessly. But he was also Mr. Great-Heart. As such, he was one of those rare men to whom other men become easily and tenaciously attached. The affection of his colleagues on the bench equaled their respect for him as a judge. His troops adored him. Even in that period just after World War I when one of the popular sports was "panning" officers, they made this man, who had been awarded the Distinguished Service Medal for extraordinary heroism in action, the head of their regimental association. In particular encounters his refusal to compromise what he deemed to be the obvious right often irritated those who did not see with his excluding clarity. But irritation never lingered long. It was impossible to know him even passing well without having one's judgment determined by the purity and selflessness of Patterson's character.

It is idle to try to dissemble one's feeling of the cruel waste-fulness of his death. But the manner of his life ought to be-come part of our national heritage.

Sixteen

Emory R. Buckner

(1941)

Emory Roy Buckner (1877-1941) was considered one of the greatest trial lawyers of his generation. He was a student at the Harvard Law School in the class behind Felix Frankfurter's, and they formed a friendship which was maintained and fortified through the years, particularly when they served together as Assistant United States Attorneys under Henry L. Stimson. Mr. Buckner attained eminence at the New York bar as a member of the celebrated firm of which Elihu Root was counsel; and in 1925-1927, he was United States Attorney for the New York district. After his death Mr. Justice Frankfurter wrote this letter of appreciation which appeared in the New York *Times* for March 14, 1941.

I SHOULD LIKE to add a footnote to your admirable editorial on Emory R. Buckner in the *Times* this morning.

To his friends—and few men could have left truer attachments behind him—the death of so gay and gallant a spirit means an irreplaceable loss. But the central achievement of his professional life has a significance that deserves to be cherished in public memory.

Nature gave Buckner extraordinary professional endowments. The uses to which he put them were his own superb accomplishment. The greatest of these uses was the way in which he put into practice his uncompromising conception of the function and standards of a prosecutor. His was an instinctive ethical nature, but one whose comic spirit precluded the taint of self-righteousness and the dullness of moralizing.

This strong impulse for right and justice was early confirmed and disciplined through his apprenticeship under
Henry L. Stimson as United States Attorney for the Southern
District of New York. Buckner's genius for the forum at once
manifested itself there. He was happiest and most effective
when his great gifts of advocacy were in the service of the
public.

As an Assistant United States Attorney, as one of the assistant district attorneys of New York County, as counsel for the
Aldermanic police investigation, as United States Attorney,
and as special prosecutor of municipal malefactors, Buckner
displayed uncommon energy and skill in the successful prosecution of subtle and complicated crimes, against powerful
opposition.

But what is much more important is that in all these prose-
cuting offices Buckner realized that he who wields the instruments of criminal justice wields the most terrible instruments
of government. In order to assure their just and compassionate
use, a prosecutor must have an almost priestlike attitude toward his duties. Buckner practiced this attitude without
deviation.

The quality of this public service is all the more shining in
a man so zestful of life, so companionable, so tolerant of the
foibles and even of the laxities of others as was Buckner. His
pure and rigorous standards in the enforcement of law should
serve as an example long to be cherished and one by which
to judge others who are entrusted with the responsibilities of
criminal justice.

Seventeen

Arthur D. Hill

(1947)

Arthur Dehon Hill (1869-1947) was an illustrious member of the Boston bar for more than half a century. He was counsel for Sacco and Vanzetti in the last stages of the unsuccessful legal struggle to save them from the death chair. In this letter to the Boston *Herald* (which published it on December 2, 1947), Mr. Justice Frankfurter related the circumstances in which Mr. Hill accepted the assignment.

THROUGH VARIOUS IMPORTANT SERVICES, Arthur D. Hill proved himself a notable citizen. But he deserves especially to be remembered for his significant contribution to civil liberties. As good a test as any of a civilized society is the treatment accorded to those accused of crime. The more fair-sounding the provisions of a Bill of Rights, the more it constitutes merely mocking rhetoric unless its professions are translated into the daily administration of justice so that the lowliest of creatures may have ample opportunity to prove their innocence. Nothing is farther from my mind than to stir the dead embers of a tragic controversy. But I think it is important for the traditions of the law and of this Commonwealth now to make public the circumstances under which Arthur Hill became counsel for Sacco and Vanzetti in the final stages of that affair.

The time had come when Mr. William G. Thompson had exhausted his energy in his powerful devotion to the cause of the men, and yet appeal to available legal process had not come to an end. The men were entitled under due process not to go to their death until every avenue of relief afforded by law had been pursued. It was at this stage that I was asked if I would try to enlist Mr. Hill's legal services to undertake a final effort on behalf of the men, hopeless as it seemed, by appeal to the federal law. I saw Arthur Hill, told him the situation and, more particularly, that if he undertook this thankless task it would have to be solely as an exercise of the public profession of the law, for it would have to be done without a fee.

Without hesitation he made an answer that deserves permanence in the history of the legal profession. This is what he said: "If the president of the biggest bank in Boston came to me and said that his wife had been convicted of murder but he wanted me to see if there was any possible relief in the Supreme Court of the United States and offered me a fee of $50,000 to make such an effort, of course I would take the retainer as would, I suppose, everybody else at the bar. It would be a perfectly honorable thing to see whether there was anything in the record which laid a basis for an appeal to the federal courts. I do not see how I can decline a similar effort on behalf of Sacco and Vanzetti simply because they are poor devils against whom the feeling of the community is strong and they have no money with which to hire me. I won't particularly enjoy the proceedings that will follow but I don't see how I can possibly refuse to make the effort."

Eighteen

William DuBose Sheldon

(1943)

William DuBose Sheldon (1913-1943), a member of the Class of 1938 at the Harvard Law School, had qualities of character that endeared him to all his friends, including Mr. Justice and Mrs. Frankfurter. He entered the Navy in 1942 as an ensign, and his tragic death the following year led the Justice to write this letter, which appeared in the Washington *Post* and the Washington *Evening Star* in their issues for March 26, 1943, and in the *Harvard Alumni Bulletin* for April 10, 1943.

THE FRIENDS of Lieutenant William DuBose Sheldon, U.S.N.R., who died March 10 from illness contracted at Guadalcanal and at other South Pacific engagements, will welcome the tribute paid him by the commanding officer of the Pacific Fleet Bombing Squadron, because in that simple account they will recognize the authentic Bill. He had all the gentler qualities—loyalty, modesty, high courtesy, regard for the tender places in life—to a degree unusual in so young a person, and an unselfishness remarkable in a person of any age. In him selflessness came from a deep insight into the essential tragedy of life and a deeper dedication to its mitigation. But in Bill Sheldon these gifts of gentleness were united in rare measure with sterner qualities, likely to be missed by those who knew only his quiet voice, his shy hesitating manner, his finely sculptured face, and delicate physique. With time one became aware of deep reserves, of a strong, even stubborn will, and a maturity far beyond his years. He was one of those whom William James called "the once born."

Ever since his student days he was a leader of men, affectionately called "Uncle Bill," and behind that name exercising a moral authority over his contemporaries which they rejoiced to recognize. Gifts of character are rarer than gifts of mind, and the sources of such moral sway as Bill held over men are not easy to fathom. If I may venture an explanation, Bill possessed such moral authority because he had moral superiority without moral snobbery. The clarity of his mind achieved its full powers because the motives of his actions and judgments were swept cleaner of dross than is true of most men.

The Greeks had such as Bill Sheldon in mind when they said the good die young. No one saw more clearly than he the moral issues of this war, and he felt his life belonged to his country not as to a devouring state but to an organized way for leading civilized lives. It was like Bill to make his decision to be a part of the war swiftly, silently, and alone. As it was like him to endure, after conspicuously gallant service in combat, the vicissitudes of illness far from home and friends, without letting them know. That is hard for his friends to bear now, but it was characteristic. He kept his troubles to himself.

If I have said anything exaggerated or false, if I have been guilty of the sentimentality which so easily overtakes one in the first shock of loss, I ask Bill's pardon. There is no swifter way to bury the dead. And Bill is someone to think back upon, to measure one's self by, to cherish in death as in life.

Nineteen

Guido Pantaleoni, Jr.

(1947)

Guido Pantaleoni, Jr. (1900-1943), was a student of Professor Frankfurter at the Harvard Law School, from which he was graduated in 1923. In the midst of an illustrious career at the New York bar, he felt the cause of the war so strongly that he volunteered for overseas duty with the Office of Strategic Services. He was killed in action in Sicily on August 8, 1943. On November 29, 1947, a corner of the Harvard Law School Library in Langdell Hall, Cambridge, was dedicated to his memory. On that occasion Mr. Justice Frankfurter made these remarks.

ALL OF US, even those who are not attached to any formal religion, have need of that which silent prayer satisfies. It is the need of gathering together one's inner resources. This is not an occasion for elegy. We are here not to memorialize Guido Pantaleoni, but to invigorate our weakness from his strength, to fortify our purposes from his vindication of them. For "what survives is the resistance we bring to life, not the strain life brings to us." The average life is finished but incomplete, and too often hardly begun. Guido's life though unfinished was complete. And it was complete at each stage of its progression.

The daily bustle of existence crowds out ultimate questions which cannot today be evaded if our coming together here has any deep-felt meaning. What is life for? is a question we may shrink from attempting to answer. But not to have it force itself with frequency upon our attention bespeaks spiritual torpor. The test of any theory about life is in the quality of those who exemplify it. What satisfies me as a working theory Mr. Justice Holmes has best put into words, and Guido exemplifies it as fully as did Holmes:

The rule of joy and the law of duty seem to me all one . . . [t]he joy, the duty, and, I venture to add, the end of life. I speak only of this world, of course, and of the teachings of this world. I do not seek to trench upon the province of spiritual guides. But from the point of view of the world the end of life is life. Life is action, the use of one's powers. As to use them to their height is our joy and duty, so it is the one end that justifies itself. Until lately the best thing that I was able to think of in favor of civilization, apart from blind acceptance of the order of the universe, was that it made possible the artist, the poet, the phi- losopher, and the man of science. But I think that is not the greatest thing. Now I believe that the greatest thing is a matter that comes directly home to us all. When it is said that we are too much occupied with the means of living to live, I answer that the chief worth of civilization is just that it makes the means of living more complex; that it calls for great and combined in- tellectual efforts, instead of simple, uncoordinated ones, in order that the crowd may be fed and clothed and housed and moved from place to place. Because more complex and intense intellec- tual efforts mean a fuller and richer life. They mean more life. Life is an end in itself, and the only question as to whether it is worth living is whether you have enough of it.[1]

Guido had enough of it. He always felt the passion of life to its top. What is more noteworthy, Guido means more life for all of us whose lives he touched, if only in passing. Such driving energy as Guido's is apt to be self-aggrandizing and destructive of others, at least of their feelings. In Guido's case it was tender and gay and energizing of others. He makes

[1] Holmes, *Speeches* (1934), p. 85.

us believe in the joy and the duty of high action, because he never cramped his life by the imprisoning bounds of mere prudence. He often, and finally, went beyond what is termed "the call of duty" because he responded to the call of joy. He would have had to deny his ardor for life not to give it, if necessary, in order to live it.

And that sense of the wonder and the glory of life lay at the bottom of that interest in him of which, like an inextinguishable flame, the Pantaleoni Corner will be a perpetual reminder. For to him "civil liberties" was not some reformer's vagary or a busy lawyer's outside hobby. "Civil liberties" summarizes his sense of the variegated range of the mystery of life and the conditions necessary for its enjoyment. He knew—none better—that in the house of life there are many mansions. He wanted free access to his mansion. He no less wanted access to the mansions of others to be free, for their sake and for his. But he knew that without some ordering freedom becomes chaos. He also knew that order can escape the brutal rule of tyranny only if it derives from that most exciting of all collaborative enterprises we know as democracy. He knew, in short, that freedom rests on those intricate arrangements for self-rule which is law.

This place then, this school of his devotion, dedicated as it is to the study of how men may fruitfully govern themselves, is the most fitting place for him to gaze, with participating ardor, down upon an endless procession of youth, like himself, zestful and generous, who in turn will look up to him and find inspiration for a tender and full and rich life.

Twenty

Stanley M. Silverberg

(1954)

Stanley Marvin Silverberg (1919-1953) served as Mr. Justice Frankfurter's law clerk during the annual term of court which began in October 1943. An honors graduate of the Harvard Law School in 1942, his brilliant and promising career was abruptly, tragically terminated when he died, the victim of a rare blood disease, in New York on November 13, 1953. This obituary sketch was written for the *Memorial Book of the Association of the Bar of the City of New York* (1954, p. 80).

WHATEVER WAS MEANT by the Greek saying that the good die young, it can hardly be denied that the premature cutting of the thread of a gifted life has its special poignancy. This ruthlessness of fate is mitigated in the case of those who express themselves in some enduring form of art or science. Poets and composers and mathematicians whose lives are cut short live on through their poems and scores and formulas. Advocates pursue a more impalpable calling. Though advocacy serves the deepest interests of man, the art by which it does so is for the most part ephemeral. Rare instances of oratory may become part of literature, though even these suffer from the vicissitudes of fashion. For the rest, the response to excellence in advocacy is in the memory of the profession and in the oral tradition handed down from generation to generation of lawyers. An almost indispensable condition for such recognition is time, long years at the bar. That condition was denied Stanley Silverberg, who died at thirty-four, and this makes his career all the more notable.

Much was crowded into the mere decade of professional life that was vouchsafed him. The year after his graduation from law school Stanley Silverberg spent with Judge Learned Hand, on the Court of Appeals for the Second Circuit. At Stanley's funeral Judge Hand bore testimony to the distinguished qualities which he manifested at the very outset of his career. After his fruitful year with Judge Hand, Stanley became my law clerk during the October term, 1943. For me it was the nurturing of a stimulating, prized friendship; for him it was the full utilization of the opportunities for maturing reflections afforded by intimate observation of the Supreme Court's functioning. The shrewd eye of the then Solicitor General, Charles Fahy, spotted Stanley's worth and annexed him, after his year with me, to that ablest single group of barristers in the country, the Solicitor General's Office. There, Stanley Silverberg grew from strength to strength. From the first he showed that the stuff of the advocate was in him; and by the time he left the government, when the Supreme Court adjourned in June 1952, had fashioned himself into an accomplished practitioner of the art of persuasion. When he appeared at the lectern, erect and handsome, with an agreeable voice, serene rather than self-confident, tactful but firm, and always master of his case, the Court increasingly was assured of an argument that gave pleasure as well as enlightenment. He respected the traditions of the Supreme Court as a tribunal not designed as a dozing audience for the reading of soliloquies but as a questioning body, utilizing oral arguments as a means for exposing the difficulties of a case with a view to meeting them. He held up his share of the probing process, and members of the Court were kept alert to observe the responsibilities of the questioner. It is fair to say that in a few short years Stanley Silverberg had attained a stature as an advocate matched by few lawyers coming before the Court, including the most eminent and experienced members of the bar.

Lawyers vary greatly in the adjustment that has to be made in going from public work to private practice. Even those who came to public office from long private practice find the return to it difficult. This has been true of some of the ablest lawyers. It could hardly have come easy for so sensitive and artistic a nature as Stanley's to transfer from the self-disciplining responsibilities of the Solicitor General's Office and the intellectual and artistic demands of Supreme Court arguments to the time-sheet exactions and client preoccupation of a large private law office. In time such qualities of mind and character and personality as were Stanley Silverberg's were bound to make themselves felt at the New York bar. It was denied him to run the course. But to his wife, Shirley, and to his two young children, Margaret Rose and David Jesse, he leaves the heritage prized most by our profession. By full loyalty to the best standards—intellectual and moral—of the law he enhanced them. Short as was his life, he pursued and achieved the ambition which alone is untainted by petty vanity, "to hammer out as compact and solid a piece of work as one can, to try to make it first rate, and to leave it unadvertised."

Twenty-one

Adolph C. Miller

(1953)

Adolph Caspar Miller (1866-1953) was a professor of economics whom President Wilson appointed to the Federal Reserve Board, upon which he served until 1936. A common interest in music and the arts led to a lifelong friendship with Mr. Justice and Mrs. Frankfurter. After his death the Justice wrote this letter to the Washington *Post*, where it appeared on February 16, 1953.

SINCE HIS DEMOCRATIC FAITH was not sentimental, Jefferson realized—no one more so—that, through a process of permeation, the quality of society is largely determined by few people. Particularly is this true of a community as preoccupied as Washington with ephemeral events, passing personalities, and the exigent needs of crises. Such a community needs especially to be nourished by men of intellectual depth and philosophical detachment. The death of Adolph C. Miller, therefore, has seriously diminished the cultural and spiritual influences of Washington. He infused private lives with his own high standards and his feeling for the arts, our public affairs with his disinterestedness and courage.

A man of wide reading and avid learning, he knew the difference between knowledge and wisdom. He did not accept slogans or time-honored premises as commandments handed down on Sinai. He was constantly alert to question the validity of premises which, if faulty or incomplete, could not be rescued by drawing impeccably logical conclusions from them. With these bracing qualities of independence and insight, Dr. Miller invigorated the Washington atmosphere for forty years. Who is to say that this was less important than his contributions to economic science and their application by him during his long membership on the Federal Reserve Board?

As such, he served under five Presidents of varying temperaments and political outlook. With at least three of these he was on intimate personal terms; they drew upon his counsel in good season and bad. To all he gave that rarest aspect of devotion to the presidential office—courageous candor. To each he told, with surgeon-like truthfulness, exactly what he believed, however unwelcome his analysis and explication of complex issues may have been, and of course always with exquisite courtesy.

Adolph Miller lived a full life. But the lives of all who knew him, and even of those who did not know him, are emptier for his passing.

Twenty-two

Florence Kelley

(1953)

Florence Kelley (1859-1932) was a lawyer, the daughter of Congressman William D. ("Pig Iron") Kelley of Pennsylvania. Her social sympathies were deeply stirred by the conditions she discovered as chief inspector of factories for the state of Illinois (1893-1897), and her experiences there led her to found the National Consumers League, which she directed until her death. She became acquainted with Felix Frankfurter through their interest in minimum-wage legislation. In 1953 a biography of Mrs. Kelley entitled *Impatient Crusader*, written by Josephine Goldmark, was published by the University of Illinois Press. Mr Justice Frankfurter wrote this foreword.

THE PAGES THAT FOLLOW give an account of the life of a woman who had probably the largest single share in shaping the social history of the United States during the first thirty years of this century. Any such limitation of time regarding influence of a vital force like Florence Kelley is artificial. During that period hers was no doubt a powerful if not decisive role in securing legislation for the removal of the most glaring abuses of our hectic industrialization following the Civil War. But we owe her an even deeper and more enduring debt for the continuing process she so largely helped to initiate by which social legislation is promoted and eventually gets on the statute books.

The domestic problems of our country after the Recon-

struction period may be said to have revolved in the main
around the responsibilities of wealth to commonwealth. Those
were the problems that were Mrs. Kelley's concern, and, for
her, wealth was not shorthand for plutocrats. It merely implied the utilization of the labor of others for profit. Fly-by-
night subcontracting in tenement houses created situations as
disregardful of human dignity and as responsible for stunted
childhood as mighty steel mills or enormous textile factories.
And in her view it was equally true that enterprise, both
petty and gigantic, may, if unchecked by legislation, deny
children the rights of childhood and exploit economic needs
of women not because of man's inhumanity to man but because they "know not what they do."

There are two kinds of reformers whose chief concern
has been that earning a living shall not contradict living a
life. One type is apt to see evil men behind evils and seeks
to rout evil by moral fervor. Florence Kelley belonged to the
other, the cooler and more calculating type. Not that she was
without passion. But passion was the driving force of her
mind, not its substitute. She early realized that damning facts
are more powerful in the long run than flaming rhetoric, and
that understanding is a more dependable, because more permanent, ally, than the indignation of the moment. No painstaking natural scientist in his laboratory worked more faithfully to verify an experiment than did Mrs. Kelley in digging
out and assaying the much more elusive, the far less verifiable
data of the sociologist. By the toilsome and heartbreaking exploration of the actual conditions in industry, particularly
insofar as they affected the employment of children and
women, Mrs. Kelley discovered the truth, and by her indefatigable pen and eloquent tongue gave it power.

She was like a general in making the truth prevail over the
forces of darkness—the darkness not of evil but of ignorance.
She went about winning cohorts, men and women whose
consciences she could ignite, and whose minds she could edu-

cate to serve as constructive guides to their consciences. She realized that a few people who cared and who knew why they cared would serve as infectious forces in influencing their environment. So commonplace has telling social investigation become in our day, such progress has been made in securing a quantitative basis for removing social abuses, that it is hard to realize how much we owe to the pioneer efforts of Florence Kelley and the co-workers whom she won to her causes. It is not the function of these few introductory words to summarize the exciting story of Florence Kelley's undaunted efforts to eliminate what she helped to reveal as the ugly concomitants of our stupendous industrial development —child labor, unconscionable hours of work, particularly for women, exploitingly low wages, a shockingly high rate of infant and maternal mortality, neglect of safeguards against occupational diseases. I may, however, give assurance that it is an exciting story.

Without haste and without rest this great general enlisted for the duration of her life to prevent the economic forces of society that were designed for the well-being of man from making inroads upon his well-being. Possessed of a deep understanding of the processes of government, she saw that it is not enough to deal with evils to which modern industry gives rise by episodic crusades. From the beginning of her work as a chief inspector of factories for Illinois she realized the importance of effective administration and all that it implies—a system of alert oversight, a permanent, trained, nonpolitical inspectorate, reliable statistics, illuminating reports as the basis of continuous public education. And as she went from Chicago to New York and from New York everywhere throughout the United States, with the National Consumers League and its local affiliates as the instruments of her inspiring leadership, she translated her ardent democratic faith into practical terms and definite, realizable aims. She based her efforts for legislative reforms on wide popular support, the support of a public educated to be responsive to its responsibility, and asserting it not with the ardor of rhetoric but with the impact of hard fact.

It was the same combination of scientist and humanitarian in Florence Kelley that gave her victory in 1912, after six years of effort in partnership with another notable woman, Lillian D. Wald, in seeking the establishment of the United States Children's Bureau. Today it is difficult to understand the resistance to the establishment of this scientific bureau that was to do for ameliorating knowledge regarding child life in the United States what the Department of Agriculture had long ago done for knowledge about pigs. Today when the Children's Bureau is as much taken for granted as is the Bureau of Animal Industry, one can hardly recall, except as something very funny, the attacks that were made on the early publications of the Bureau which proved our high infant mortality rate as compared with that of other countries, and particularly on the disclosure of the vast disparity in the death rates among infants in different sections of the same cities.

It is good that all this should seem like a foolish or weird dream of the past, but it is not good that similar absurd and destructive attacks should be made against equally wholesome measures in our day.

This book ought to be read by all who are immediately concerned with problems of government and by all whose duty it is to enlighten the public. Florence Kelley's life imparts a sense of perspective, it helps us to realize that the familiar is not the necessary. The story also fills one with hope. Florence Kelley spoke of herself as "the most unwearied hoper" in the United States. Newton Baker said of her: "Everybody was brave from the moment she came into a room." Her courage is contagious even from the printed page. The story of her life also carries two indispensable lessons for a democratic society, humility and tolerance: humility in not assuming that our own narrow views, however much we may cherish them, represent eternal truth rather than beliefs derived from a limited experience; tolerance toward differing views of fellow Americans whose motives may be no less pure than our own and whose aim may be the national welfare no less than ours.

To write as lifelessly as I have written about Florence Kelley is to write about her as though she had been merely an institution. The least self-regarding of people, she dedicated her life to the well-being of others. Yet such is the power of personality that she remains in the memory of all whose lives she crossed as one of the most vivid of experiences. She was an inextinguishable flame. From time to time, at different periods, nature in her mysterious ways concentrates in producing a group of remarkable people. Florence Kelley was one of a galaxy of wonderful women with whom she worked—Jane Addams, Julia Lathrop, Lillian D. Wald, Grace and Edith Abbott, Alice Hamilton, among others. Florence Kelley seemed at the time, and remains in memory, the most salient, salty character of them all.

This book is the life of an extraordinary woman by a remarkable woman. In her own exquisite way Josephine Goldmark, a younger co-worker of Florence Kelley, belonged to the galaxy I have mentioned. I wish I could express in more adequate words my feelings of gratitude to Florence Kelley and Josephine Goldmark for the examples they afford of high purposes pursued with gaiety not unmixed with passion, pursued with consecrated devotion not tainted by self-righteousness.

Twenty-three

Monsignor John A. Ryan

(1939)

John Augustine Ryan (1869-1945) was director of the Department of Social Action, National Catholic Welfare Conference, for many years. A common interest in the promotion of social legislation, particularly minimum-wage laws for women, led to the formation of his friendship with Felix Frankfurter. At a dinner honoring Monsignor Ryan on the occasion of his seventieth birthday, given in Washington on May 25, 1939, the Justice made these informal remarks.

SEVERAL THINGS CONTRIBUTE to my pleasure in coming here in honor of a man who, despite all appearances to the contrary, is regarded as venerable, since he has attained the high mark of Biblical expectancy. Monsignor Ryan's contribution to human welfare none can gainsay. Happily, his work as a Christian teacher has been recommended by a personality in which social zeal, aggressive integrity, and homely simplicity have been enhanced by an almost coercive charm.

He belongs to a church which has had a varied experience in human history. It has survived both poverty and prosperity, outlived alien and hostile philosophies, and throughout has shown that adaptability to changing conditions which is the index of an extraordinary vitality. It has been the distinction of Monsignor Ryan as a teacher of theology to apply dogmas avowedly conservative to the solution of problems affecting the welfare of the masses in ways that have gained him gen-

eral recognition as a foremost liberal. Central to his thought
have been the moral dignity of the individual and man's effort
toward enhancing social security. It has not been his lot to
enjoy the detachment and serenity which we associate with
the life of a scholar. But perhaps it will be permitted one
outside his faith to suggest that the practical pursuit of Monsignor Ryan's convictions has been strengthened by the
thought that in promoting his conception of social justice
he was faithfully carrying out the commission his church gave
him to preach.

Many are here tonight who do not subscribe to the authority of those dogmatic principles which have supported and
energized John Ryan in his teachings. Perhaps they salute
him with more conscious gladness because, from different
starting points from theirs, Dr. Ryan has reached conclusions
of whose wisdom and fruitfulness this is a celebration. The
members of his own church must find an additional satisfaction in feeling that he is an illustration of a cherished Catholic
principle that the ancient church is ever new. And so we
find those high in the authority of his church, his colleagues,
and his disciples take special pride in him at a time when he
has been steadfast in his active devotion to those universal
claims of humanity which have been so flagrantly denied by
great temporal powers.

We confidently wish that Monsignor Ryan will carry on,
unmindful of the clock, for many years, and that on the
troubled and uncharted seas which the world now sails, his
wisdom may point out stars for the course and his kindness
may bring comfort to the weary mariners. And may the tribute of this dinner be remembered by him as testimony of
our gratitude and as proof of a life greatly lived.

Twenty-four

Katharine Ludington

(1953)

Katharine Ludington (1869-1953) was an outstanding leader in the movement for woman suffrage in the United States, and held state and national offices in the League of Women Voters. Her friendship with Felix Frankfurter began in Washington during World War I, when he and her youngest brother, Arthur, were housemates. This tribute to Miss Ludington was written by the Justice for the *Connecticut Voter*, published by the League of Women Voters of Connecticut, and appeared in its issue for April 1953.

A LIFE DEVOTED UNSPARINGLY to the public good into the ninth decade inevitably leaves a deep imprint. But Katharine Ludington leaves behind her a vivid memory much more for her personality than for any particular thing she did. She was that rarity—a distinguished presence. She was that when she was merely a private person. Indeed, she came of a tradition in which the distaff side of the family was destined for a wholly private role—generous in spirit and broadminded within the limits of a protected life. The world of Edith Wharton's New York was the world of her interests until World War I changed also her world. But the war was merely the occasion, not the cause. Logically enough, it was a profound private grief that changed the course of her life.

It was, I believe, the early death of her beloved youngest brother, Arthur, that transmuted the direction of her energies. Arthur was the type of person much more indigenous to England than to this country. He was a gentleman, in the enduring as well as in the limited sense of the term, motivated by a feeling for public service. In him public service took a most disinterested form. It meant serving the public, not holding office. As a private citizen he worked on difficult public problems, private investigation, and writing, and in association with various professional or civic bodies. In our society one is deemed an odd stick who cannot be tagged as holding this or that office, or belonging to this or that profession. One was stumped when asked what this private scholar and this private public servant was "doing." It took me some time before I hit upon a formula for answering the perennial question, "What does Arthur Ludington do?" It was: "He makes a profession of citizenship." Can one not so characterize Katharine Ludington's career?

Upon his death in 1914, K. L. took over Arthur's interests, and very conciously I suspect, and thereby his sense of civic obligation and public direction. Of course this did not happen overnight; but progressively and with surprisingly quick success she accomplished a striking readaptation of personality. All the distinction of the private Katharine Ludington she took into her public life. Naturally, suffrage became her immediate preoccupation, and I can only surmise the amount of self-discipline it entailed for her to assimilate the coarseness and even the brutality which, for the first time in her life, she must have experienced in some aspects of the opposition to woman suffrage. From the perspective of the present such opposition seems almost funny. It was not funny then. But she was not a single-track suffragist. Very early she was aware that the vote was not an end. The vote was the instrument of democracy, and democracy was the arrangement of society by which the inborn qualities of men and women were to be given opportunity for the fullest fruition.

She therefore very quickly acquired alert interest in the social-economic issues of our time. She was equally alive to the realization that if the carnage of war was not to be merely carnage, measures must early be taken to set in train forces for securing a decent recuperative peace. Above all, she realized that indispensable to the wise solution of public problems and the furthering of the public good is debate. It was one of the deepest articles of her faith throughout her long public life that "acts are foredoomed to failure when undertaken undiscussed." And so at that charming little house in New York, 56 West 10th Street, and even more during the summer and fall months at the Lyme house, and in her favorite picnic spots in the environs of Lyme, there was talk—copious, free-flowing, ardent, but tolerant talk, by all sorts of friends of hers and friends of friends. Sometimes she kept the disputants to the main theme when talk became too dispersive or too frivolous. But she did so always in ways to remind one of the old saying, "Manners maketh man." She had the kind of manners, simple dignity and genuine cordiality, that also reminded one of Matthew Arnold's "Morals are three-fourths manners."

Her public life thus became a continuous progression. The suffrage movement inevitably led to the National League of Women Voters, and by sheer force of her personality and her intrinsic contributions, K. L. became one of its national officers and thereby was projected into national political affairs. By imperceptible stages she moved from the world of Edith Wharton to the contemporary days of Carson McCullers. Outwardly she and her surroundings remained the same. But she took in, in her shrewd and tolerant stride, the great shift in the political scene from the days of Grover Cleveland to those of Franklin D. Roosevelt even as she watched with shrewd and sometimes skeptical interest the enormous shift from her own days as a portrait painter to the daring innovations and even incomprehensibles of our day.

I am afraid that the intimations I have given are too meager to convey to those who did not know K. L. the qualities that made her so distinguished a personality and so powerful an experience in the lives of many. Those who knew her do not need another's vivification of her image. The unbroken ties of comradeship for more than forty years—the many, many joys together, the deepening of friendship through shared sorrows, the benefactions of her imagination in the service of friendship—all those aspects of personal relations that make for affection and admiration are of that private world which even her preoccupation with public life kept sweet and inviolate.

Twenty-five

John G. Winant

(1947)

John Gilbert Winant (1889-1947) was America's wartime ambassador to Great Britain. Felix Frankfurter became acquainted with Mr. Winant when the latter was Governor of the State of New Hampshire. After Mr. Winant's death an editorial appearing in the Washington *Post* (November 5, 1947) stated that his "virtues were of the heart. He was inarticulate in speaking and in writing; he had no gift for administration; he dreamed of a place for himself among the highest, yet he had no quality of leadership. His ambitions, in other words, were far greater than his attributes." These observations impelled Mr. Justice Frankfurter to write this letter to the *Post*, which published it on November 6, 1947.

ONE DOES NOT HAVE to accept *de mortuis nil nisi bonum* as a maxim of wisdom to find your November 5 remarks on John G. Winant not merely ungracious but strangely imperceptive.

He was no administrator, you say. Granted he was not. It is demonstrable, I believe, that the relatively few presidents who are securely part of our national tradition were poor administrators. This does not imply that poor administration is a virtue. It does indicate that the valuable significance of a man may outweigh administrative deficiencies.

Winant was inarticulate, you say. Facility does not often come from the depths, and halting speech may be—as it was in Winant—part of an inner struggle to convey a groping vision with sincerity.

Winant was not among the thinkers. How many statesmen or nonstatesmen are? But there was something authentically American in his effort to give political expression to spiritual striving. It is that which made the British people find in Winant strength and succor at a time when they were called upon to summon all their spiritual resources against overwhelming material power.

At a decisive hour in the history of civilization he proved once more the truth of Emerson's insight, that "the last lesson of life, the choral song which rises from all elements and all angels, is a voluntary obedience, a necessitated freedom. . . . Honor and fortune exist to him who always recognizes the neighborhood of the great, always feels himself in the presence of high causes."

Twenty-six

Lord Lothian

(1940)

Philip Henry Kerr (1882-1940), the 11th Marquess of Lothian, was the British ambassador to the United States from August 30, 1939, until his death on December 12, 1940. His friendship with Felix Frankfurter began during World War I when the former was secretary to Lloyd George, then Prime Minister of Great Britain. Lord Lothian was widely respected in the United States as a discerning observer of the American scene. At the request of the Washington *Post*, Mr. Justice Frankfurter wrote this tribute to Lord Lothian. It appeared in the *Post* on December 15, 1940.

IN THE LIBRARY of the new federal court for the prospective Dominion of India there is a set of Farrand's edition of the records of the Constitutional Convention of Philadelphia. These noble volumes Lord Lothian carried from this country to India. The episode affords a key to the late ambassador's feeling about this country's significance to a civilized organization of the world. A federal system for the states and provinces of India with its three hundred millions of people of diverse tongues and conflicting religions was his dream for India, and America was his appeal to experience for the validity of the dream. Such also was the solid hope he drew from our history for the accommodation of the jangling interests of Europe almost from the moment he left Paris, heartsick over the shortcomings of the Versailles Treaty. That fusion of imagination and purpose which made a union of the thir-

338

teen states has been the deepest inspiration of his public outlook for the last twenty years.

Not for a moment did Lord Lothian forget that inspiration
after war was loosed upon the world and he himself became
one of the dominant figures in its prosecution. Ships and planes
and munitions were for him but the terrible and ephemeral
means by which a world was to be relieved of dominance by
force and was to gain new opportunities for enhancing the
worth of Lincoln's common people.

For that is what Lord Lothian really cared about—that the
compassionate faith of Lincoln in the moral worth of every
individual should become the dominant faith of the world,
a faith achieved through works. He had a strong historic sense
and one had to see him at his ancestral Blickling to realize how
deeply history nourished him, how much a part of him his
ancient countryside was. He equally responded to the fresh-
ness and vitality of this country—to its optimism, its camaraderie, its diversities—because history fed and did not imprison his own youthful spirit. Thus it was that at a most
sensitive period in the relations between his country and ours,
presenting as severe a test as could be encountered by an ambassador, he enlisted the respect and the increasingly warm
friendship not only of those with whom he had dealings but
of the country, to which he spoke from time to time with
candor and courage.

This achievement of Lord Lothian's was not due to any
technical equipment or diplomatic skill. It flowed from the
fact that as a frequent visitor to this country and an unostentatious traveler on its highways and byways he acquired
a spontaneous love for the United States and was able to speak
its language because he shared its ultimate aspirations. In his
own person he proved how shallow and paltry are the surface
differences that divide men when mankind is confronted with
a challenge to all that unfettered reason and daring imagination have achieved.

Twenty-seven

Lord Inverchapel

(1951)

Archibald John Kerr Clark Kerr (1882-1951), 1st Baron Inverchapel of Loch Eck, was a British career diplomat who served his country with great distinction for more than forty years in posts all over the world. After a two-year period of service as ambassador to the United States, he retired in 1948 and resumed his farming activities in Scotland. His friendship with Felix Frankfurter, then a law officer in the War Department, began in 1911 when he was on the staff of Lord Bryce, the British ambassador in Washington. The friendship continued through an active correspondence and was renewed when Lord Inverchapel came here as ambassador in 1946. After his death in 1951, Mr. Justice Frankfurter wrote this letter to the London *Times*, which printed it on July 14, 1951.

MAY ONE OF THE oldest of Lord Inverchapel's American friends draw on the hospitality of your columns to bid an affectionate farewell to that tender and gay and stouthearted spirit?

It tells much of his generous nature and of his quality of detachment that we had hardly exchanged greetings on his arrival in Washington as ambassador, when he said: "It should have been Eustace," meaning Lord Eustace Percy, his admired associate in the Bryce embassy.

It was a different Archie Kerr who returned to Washington as ambassador and it was a different Washington. The otiose

American capital in the days of Lord Bryce, a sideshow, almost, of American life compared with New York, had become, in large measure, the hurly-burly center of a distraught world. And Archie Kerr had in the meantime assimilated the significance of the revolutionary awakening of Asia, and had mastered at least the enigmas of Soviet Russia.

These experiences had nourished his imagination and deepened his sensitiveness to the claims of human dignity everywhere and in all shifts of society. And so he heeded little the surface sides of Washington, perhaps too little in view of the interplay of extrinsic and intrinsic in Washington.

For Archie Kerr the United States was never an exhilarating zoological garden. He relished and almost shared, because he deeply understood, the divers manifestations that American vitality and optimism take. He did not mind, also because he understood, that they were not always subtle or felicitous.

He cared more for the authentic anonymous American, old and young, with whom he readily struck up acquaintance wherever he went and to whom he played charming host at the embassy, than for the formal leaders of society. With all his subtlety, he did not always conceal this. At bottom, in these choices his integrity and an ingrained shyness asserted themselves. In his public appearances he was inclined also toward dealing with weighty themes obliquely, for fear he might betray his disdain of pomposity or make a show of feeling.

But those of us who heard his beautifully phrased but almost chokingly articulated leave-taking from his American friends are not likely to forget the experience. The manner in which he withdrew to his beloved Scotland when the time came for leaving the public stage, on which he always retained a private face, was a fitting climax for an endearing character.

Twenty-eight

Hume Wrong

(1954)

Humphrey Hume Wrong (1894-1954) was a distinguished Canadian diplomat who served as ambassador to the United States from 1946 to 1953. He returned to Ottawa to become Under-Secretary of State for External Affairs, only to die shortly thereafter. This letter in tribute to him was sent by Mr. Justice Frankfurter to the London *Times*, which published it on January 28, 1954.

WITH ITS CONCENTRATION of politics and consequent maneuvering for place and power, Washington is a beehive something less than edifying. In this environment Hume Wrong exercised a permeating influence for good. He did so primarily because he was a man of rare goodness. But such goodness too often fails of the impact that his made because it is not combined with his intellectual qualities and sagacious judgment. One felt the edge of his mind when one came close to it, but it was effectively disciplined not only by the enduring impress of the best of Balliol, but also by his own academic tradition and practice.

Partaking as he did in the process of decision making, in problems as difficult as any that confronted the acumen of statesmen at the highest level, his qualities of character and intellect were reinforced by a gentle humor which enabled him to reduce or divert the inevitable friction of personalities.

342

By having a cool view of problems enveloped in an atmosphere of suspicion and fear, he was uncommonly well equipped not to overlook considerations relevant for judgment.

In the social life of Washington the warm and sincere hospitality presided over by Hume and Joyce Wrong was social life at its most engaging. It thereby promoted those civilized ends which true diplomacy serves. Unbeknown to his friends, Hume may have worn himself out. But he never appeared worn; he was never stale. Looking back one now can see that he did not appear to be a tired man because he was buoyed up by a strong though unostentatious sense of duty. In Hume Wrong's case the cliché "the world is poorer for his going" is a truth.

Twenty-nine

Sir Willmott Lewis

(1950)

Sir Willmott Harsant Lewis (1877-1950) was Washington correspondent of the London *Times* from October 1920 until his death on January 4, 1950. At the invitation of the British Broadcasting Company, Mr. Justice Frankfurter delivered this tribute to Sir Willmott in a broadcast to England, January 5, 1950.

IN SIR WILLMOTT LEWIS the style was the man even unto death. From a gay luncheon he went peacefully to sleep forever. Thus his exit was like his performance, decisive and complete. There was no waste, no ambiguity, no tapering off. His dramatic quality was not an artifact. It was a rich nature's response to the complexity and mystery and drollery of life. A critical but not a cynical nature, a fondness for his fellows despite their frailties, a deep sense of the august march of history, a disciplined gift for pithy and lucid writing, enabled him to discharge with distinction his great public function for a quarter-century.

Public function, not public office. In both the United Kingdom and the United States the press has profound constitutional importance, for the business of the press is promotion of truth and wisdom regarding public matters by furnishing the basis for their understanding. Since the reporting of events and the elucidation of their meaning are the task of correspondents, they may fairly be said to exercise a function not unlike that of judges in ferreting out the truth from treacherous evidence and presenting it in fair balance and with clarity.

Especially is this the task of one who is charged with informing the British people regarding American affairs through the most influential medium of the British press. The Washington correspondent for the *Times* is not only a source of vital information for British readers of what goes on in America. Inevitably, through fruitful personal relations, or the want of them with those who influence American thought, he serves as an important hyphen between British affairs and their effective understanding in the United States.

Nimble as was his wit and skeptical as was his mind, Lewis never forgot that he was exercising his faculties in the service of a truer understanding among English-speaking peoples, one with another. He was wholly true to the truth-seeking and truth-speaking functions of a journalist. Of course the position of the Washington correspondent of the *Times* is one of great influence, but not necessarily for good. Willmott Lewis's influence was, I believe, overwhelmingly for good. Only wide reading, much reflection, detachment of spirit, and sympathetic understanding of the complexities of America could have written the dispatches that came from his pen during all those years in Washington. On occasion he would write short essays on complicated American problems of constitutional law, like the two pieces that he wrote by way of background to the so-called Court fight in 1937, which could not be improved upon by an American specialist. The light of one who was born to charm has gone out, and the Washington scene will be much the poorer without him. But he has set journalistic standards that can be departed from only at the peril of true understanding even among peoples who know each other as well as do the British and the Americans.

Thirty

Thomas Mann

(1945)

Thomas Mann (1875-1955), the renowned author and winner of the Nobel Prize for Literature, came to live in the United States after the Hitler regime was established in Germany. At a dinner held on June 25, 1945, at the Waldorf-Astoria Hotel, New York, under the auspices of the Nation Associates, honoring Dr. Mann on the occasion of his seventieth birthday, Mr. Justice Frankfurter saluted him in these words.

TRUTH NOTORIOUSLY HAS a hard time of it. Ancient wisdom admonishes against speaking ill of the dead, and our Puritan tradition constrains us from offending the modesty of the living. I would offend more than Dr. Mann's modesty, if I ventured, assuming I were competent to do so, a critical appreciation of the place of Thomas Mann in the history of creative literature and more particularly of his place in the noble line of great German writers, who spoke not with the tongue of provincialism but with the enduring speech of those who are unbounded by time and space. He feels, I have no doubt, that the times are too anguishing, and the scale of events too vast, for personal glorification. Dr. Mann has a significance that transcends his person and for the moment, perhaps, even his contributions to literature. For it so happens that Dr. Mann symbolizes events and principles that can

346

hardly fail to remain forever among the great stories in the destiny of man.

I take it we are here tonight because civilization is nourished by instructive examples. The intellectual and spiritual history of Thomas Mann could easily be translated into a good part of the history of the Western world for the period that spanned the two World Wars. This is not the time, and I am not the person, to hazard such an ambitious attempt. But Dr. Mann's sympathy and tolerance will forgive me for the few observations that I am tempted to make.

One does not have to be a Vansittartite to believe that the Hitler regime did not come like a thief in the night, that Nazism had a long, much too long, nurturing. The empire of the Hohenzollerns was also a menace to mankind, in that the controlling forces of Germany wanted Germany to be the sun and not merely have a place in it. They sought power to consign others to darkness. But the pre-Nazi Reich at least was a *Rechtsstaat:* it was under the rule of law. To be sure, the law was full of faults and unjustifiable rigors; yet there was a rule of law, and it was fairly enforced. The Third Reich abolished the rule of law, and when the Führer after the June 1934 purge unashamedly declared, "I am the supreme law of Germany," he merely avowed what every little Führer in his little domain practiced. Where there is no rule of law, the rule of terror, of which we have had such gruesome details lately, inevitably follows. But it falsifies history to believe that the terror was first introduced in '33. The fact of the matter is that the terror began after World War I. I need remind you only of the succession of political assassinations—Rosa Luxemburg, Liebknecht, Erzberger, Rathenau. There were manifestations of the terror on a less dramatic, but perhaps more insidious scale. The truth of the matter is that the forces which eventually seized control of Germany proceeded to destroy the internal enemies before they undertook to tackle their external foe. These lawless forces assumed, as they

often do, the habiliments of patriotism. They called themselves, and were called, *vaterländisch*. And many were silent
who disapproved the means, because the ends which were
promoted were seemingly nationalistic. Another factor contributed not a little to these destructive, anti-rational forces in
Germany. It was the fragmentation of democratic-minded
opinion under the Weimar Republic. Government became
partly deadlocked and partly corrupt through the multiplicity
of parties in what was deemed to be a mathematically attainable representation of the various shades of opinion, the differences among which were negligible compared with the
difference between a state under the rule of law and a lawless
state.

But events outside Germany were not without influence
upon what unfolded within. I believe it to have been of considerable significance that Nazism went from strength to
strength until finally it reached power at the same time that
the faith in democracy in the great Western nations became
less and less vigorous, the democratic philosophy more and
more questioned. I shall speak only of some tendencies in
this country between the two World Wars. One heard in
increasing volume praise of "efficiency" as against the inevitable waste of words—for democratic government is fundamentally rule by persuasion, which means words. It is not
pleasant reading now to turn to the praise of Mussolini as a
"good European," even by those who saw no inconsistency
between their devotion to the democratic faith here and their
support of Mussolini abroad. One heard much shallow talk
about the need for concentration of power; and equally shallow sneers against the doctrine of the separation of powers.
These enthroners of the god "efficiency" forgot that the wise
founders of this country were not unaware of the claims of
efficiency in government when they consciously sought to
avoid arbitrariness of government by guarding against undue
concentration of authority in any one organ of government.

The founders were mindful of the eternal dilemma confronting democracy of which Lincoln was so aware when he asked, "Must a government of necessity be too strong for the liberties of its people, or too weak to maintain its own existence?" Worst of all there was gradually inculcated a distrust of and an indifference to politics. One heard a good deal of talk about the importance of adjourning politics. Nothing could have played better into the hands of Fascist forces. The adjournment of politics is precisely what Fascism is. Thus, an eminent educator in our Babylonian era thanked Heaven that his university students were studying politics less and less. And when, at the time of the Spanish Civil War, Archibald MacLeish summoned scholars to an understanding of what was at stake, he was advised by another educational leader that civilization must be nourished in the ivory tower, and that scholars should not take sides in purely political conflicts. As though the untrained and undisciplined response of mankind to social problems is democracy! As though the operations of democracy can be left to chance!

Precisely because a democracy is a government of the people or is a sham, citizenship is the most important office in a democracy.

And no citizen exercises a more important function in a democracy than does a poet, for the poet is concerned with the abiding issues of life. The poet, beyond anyone, must rescue us from the dominance of the moment. Poets thus shape public events by shaping the movement of ideas—the thoughts and aspirations of men which are the cause and not the effect of public events. In the deepest sense it is true that poets are the real legislators of the world. What determines action is not facts, but the feelings of worth aroused by them. These feelings are aroused not by abstract logic but by imagination. And imagination is the poet's instrument.

The direction of these remarks, by which I have poorly expressed what is in the minds of all of you, points to the

historic example which Thomas Mann has so luminously furnished. He first thought that he could be nonpolitical. He
too believed that there could be a divorcement between art
and politics. Happily he soon saw that society was indivisible.
And so he confirmed and acclaimed the earlier insight of
Tolstoi. But even after he dissociated himself from the evil
rulers of Germany and challenged their wrath, he hoped to
maintain his honorable ties with the German past by exiling
himself; and he "thought to keep silent." Perhaps he will
permit me to say that he had for years lived in exile in his
native land long before he left it physically. Soon he found
that it was not possible for him to be silent. He realized that
there is only one way in which a poet can keep silent when
his feelings are stirred: by silencing forever the poet in him.
As a lasting example to all poets who in the future may be
tempted to think that they may keep the word without utter-
ing it, Thomas Mann chose not to be silent. He spoke, as
nature endowed him to speak.

And by crossing the ocean and casting his lot among us,
Dr. Mann has reinforced another truth. That truth pertains
to us, and not to him. It is the inner truth of America. Not
the least part of the heritage left by Franklin Roosevelt, especially to his own people, is the reminder that "we are all immigrants." There are humorless folk who are under the delusion that merely because some of these came here on earlier
ships their descendants have superior virtues. To make Ameri-
canism turn on blood instead of on completeness of devotion
to the spirit of the Declaration of Independence, the Second
Inaugural, and the Four Freedoms, is to come dangerously
near the abyss into which Nazism finally fell. To differentiate
between *Mayflower* descendants and the Sidney Hillmans,
the Charlie Polettis, the Commander Stassens, the Al Smiths,
the Booker Washingtons, the Wendell Willkies, is to sap the
the most precious force in the American fellowship—regard
not for the accidents of birth, but for the inherent moral

worth of the individual. The essence of the democratic faith is the equal claim of every man to pursue his faculties to the humanly fullest—for his sake, but no less for the sake of society. Nature is the greatest of democrats. She endows men with the noblest gifts, heedless of genealogy. Greatness always remains a mystery—but what is more fitting than that Lincoln should gradually but securely have become the uncontested symbol of America.

Thirty-one

Chaim Weizmann

(1944)

Chaim Weizmann (1874-1952) was the first President of Israel. A distinguished chemist who, as head of the British Admiralty Laboratories during World War I, was responsible for many discoveries in the field of chemical warfare, Dr. Weizmann was a living fusion of science and statesmanship. The initial tie between him and Felix Frankfurter was their interest in Zionism, but a warm friendship developed between them which continued to the end of Dr. Weizmann's life. A volume of essays in tribute to him, edited by Meyer W. Weisgal, was published in 1944 by The Dial Press, Inc., under the title *Chaim Weizmann*. Mr. Justice Frankfurter contributed this foreword.

HEINE USED TO SPEAK of God as the Great Aristophanes. It surely is 'a manifestation of providential irony that the civilized world should find a fitting occasion to express its esteem for Chaim Weizmann at the precise moment when Adolf Hitler awaits his doom. I do not mean the obvious juxtaposition of Weizmann as the symbol of Jewry and Hitler as the spearhead of fiendish anti-Semitism. The antithesis between the two men goes far deeper. Hitler's anti-Semitism is not an isolated prejudice or even a vein of bigotry which in less virulent form has possessed men, often unwittingly, whose purposes and feelings otherwise could not be called uncivilized. Hitler's anti-Semitism is the most obvious and immediate

352

expression not merely of antirationalism but of a challenge to the whole blend of forces that constitute the process of modern civilization. In short, Hitler's challenge is against that vast stream of history of which the Greek and Hebrew influences have been the greatest tributaries.

Dr. Weizmann strikingly represents the confluence of these ethical and intellectual forces because he is at once an East European Jew and a Western scientist. This is not the place to embark upon an analysis of the range of issues so conveniently oversimplified and too often distorted by being called "the Jewish problem." Their explosive implications even for societies most deeply attached to the democratic faith arc today too tragically patent. Several contributors to this volume have sought to bring understanding of conflicts that can leave no sensitive nature without a troubled heart. But in addition to these concerns of government and peoples a personal problem is presented to every Jew outside of Palestine—and we now know that by a hostile world a person will be treated as a Jew even though his family has belonged to a Christian communion unto the third or fourth generation. Dr. Weizmann has shown once more and for the whole world to see that neither full devotion to the country of one's allegiance nor the esteem of the Gentile world call for truculence or timidity from a Jew. If only he be secure in the citadel of self-respect a Jew will walk erect, with humility as becomes every human and with fortifying but quiet pride as becomes every inheritor of a great past.

Dr. Weizmann was endowed by nature with charm and gift of tongue and wisdom that is wrapped in humor. But it is not by these endowments alone that he has secured hold over masses of men as well as of such cool and skeptical minds as Lord Balfour and General Smuts. "If you will it, it is no mere dream," said Herzl, the founder of modern Zionism, about the re-establishment of Palestine as the Jewish homeland. In that faith Dr. Weizmann has lived. It is his unrelenting effort to realize that faith that has had such a contagious influence for thirty years.

But the purpose of this faith was not at all "to turn back the clock of history." A Jewish Palestine for Dr. Weizmann means creation not restoration. Weizmann the scientist has outstripped the imagination of Kipling the poet. For Weizmann, rooted as he is in Eastern religion and Western scientific culture, proves that not only may East and West meet; they may become fused in a single person. And Dr. Weizmann would be the first to insist that there is nothing unique about such fusion.

It is characteristic of the movement which he is leading that hardly before the guns had been silenced in Palestine during the last war and before an influx of immigration was possible, Dr. Weizmann laid the cornerstone of the now flourishing Hebrew University on Mt. Scopus. Thus, by assuring systematic and unfettered inquiry, an indispensable condition for a civilized society was attained.

The fire of youth in Dr. Weizmann's spirit is still overwhelmingly in the service of the great cause of achieving harmonious relations between the Jew and the world—for the world's sake and to assure inner serenity for the Jew. The forces which he is seeking to bend to good will and reason do not easily yield to imaginative statesmanship. But he is not balked by intrinsic difficulties nor by the timidities of shortsighted prudence. It is as true now as it was in the days of Euripides that the worldly wise are not wise. Dr. Weizmann is a dreamer—the dreamer of one of those dreams which become reality when men have the good sense and vision to make them so.

Thirty-two

Rabbi Stephen S. Wise

(1949)

Stephen Samuel Wise (1874-1949) founded the Free Synagogue of New York in 1907 and was its rabbi until his death. He was extremely active in Zionist affairs, and served as president of the American Jewish Congress. His friendship with Felix Frankfurter grew out of their interest in Zionism. A memorial meeting in honor of Dr. Wise was held in Boston on May 25, 1949, and to it the Justice sent this message.

STEPHEN WISE WAS such a vital force that for all of us life feels much less alive without him. It is foolish to single out one dominant trait in so dynamic a personality. But if I had to fasten on one quality above all others in Dr. Wise I should say it was moral courage—that rarest ingredient of character. It was moral courage that made him so sensitive to injustice, whoever the victim and whoever the perpetrator. It was moral courage that made him so fearless in the espousal of causes to promote goodness in every direction, and since he felt deeply he put no restraints of prudence upon his eloquent tongue. When he spoke, he spoke out—behind his loyalties was passionate conviction. And it was moral courage that made him inwardly harmonious, however discordant the world outside.

There was nothing parochial about him. His espousal of Zionism and of the collaboration of the nations of the world for peace was not only consistent with burning devotion to his own country. These causes were for him manifestations of his American patriotism. For he was devoted to the United States not merely as a geographic term but as a nation dedicated to principles which should be vindicated for all peoples everywhere. Because he so strikingly embodied moral courage, the moral resources of the world will be the poorer without Stephen Wise unless, in gratitude for his services, we are true to his significance.

Thirty-three

Alfred E. Smith

(1944)

Alfred Emanuel Smith (1873-1944) was the Democratic candidate for President in 1928. He served as Governor of the State of New York for four terms, during which he became acquainted with Felix Frankfurter, then a professor at the Harvard Law School. This reminiscence of Al Smith was related by the Justice in a letter to the New York *Times*, which published it on October 7, 1944.

ONE EPISODE IN Al Smith's life can now be told, and it deserves perhaps not to go unrecorded.

Early in 1929 some sixty leading members of the Harvard faculties, who had supported Governor Smith for president, dined him as an expression of their esteem. To voice their sentiments the group selected as distinguished a mind as was then in active service at Harvard—Professor Alfred North Whitehead. The learning with which he compared Al Smith's statesmanship to the latter's most appropriate analogue among Roman emperors heavily overdrew not only on Al's learning but also on that of most of his colleagues. But it was done with such felicitous charm that Professor Whitehead's remarks were freed from the slightest taint of pedantry and communicated only warmth of feeling and delight of mind.

When Al rose in response, the contrast between the two men could not have been more striking—the contrast between the exquisite product of centuries of refined cultivation and the child of Oliver Street who had outgrown the bounds but not the humanity of his origins. Their voices, their diction, the quality of their humor—everything about these two men seemed antithetic except their regard for the dignity of the common man and their appreciation of the awful difficulties of governing a modern society.

After a characteristically unpompous word of acknowledgment, Al launched into an hour's talk that held the gathering in the vise of his personality and of his unrivaled powers of exposition. Ironically expressing wonder at what he could say worthy of an academic company, he said that he decided to speak on the "weaknesses of the government of the State of New York." He picked that topic because "we have got to understand the weaknesses of government in order to know how to build strength against them."

It was an altogether fascinating performance, and its quality can perhaps most pithily be gathered from an observation by Professor Whitehead. Since the occasion has passed into history, he will forgive me for quoting him without leave. As Al sat down, Professor Whitehead whispered to me: "How Aristotle would have enjoyed this address! Why shouldn't Harvard make Al Smith Professor of Political Science?"

Thirty-four

Franklin D. Roosevelt

(1945)

Franklin Delano Roosevelt (1882-1945) nominated Felix Frankfurter to be an Associate Justice of the Supreme Court on January 5, 1939. As Governor of the State of New York (1929-1933), Mr. Roosevelt had occasionally called upon Professor Frankfurter for advice. When he became President in 1933, he offered the solicitor generalship to Mr. Frankfurter, but the latter declined. This tribute in memory of President Roosevelt, written shortly after his death, appeared in the *Harvard Alumni Bulletin* for April 28, 1945 (Vol. 47, p. 449).

"WHEN A GREAT TREE falls, we are surprised how meagre the landscape seems without it. So when a great man dies. We may not have been intimate with him; it is enough that he was within our view; when he is gone, life seems thinner. . . . The happiest of us hardly can hope for a destiny so complete and fortunate as that which has just been fulfilled. We shall be fortunate enough if we shall have learned to look into the face of fate and the unknown with a smile like his." Said of another, this was prophetically true of Franklin Delano Roosevelt and the world that mourns him.

Writings about Napoleon fill sizable libraries. Roosevelt will claim an even larger share of history as long as the civilization endures that he helped to save. Fluctuations of historic judgment are the common lot of great men, and Roosevelt will not escape it. What history will ultimately say, it is

359

for history to say. Only one thing is certain: he will remain among the few Americans who embody its traditions and aspirations.

But if history has its claims, so has the present. For it has been wisely said that if the judgment of the time must be corrected by that of posterity, it is no less true that the judgment of posterity must be corrected by that of the time. Franklin Roosevelt cannot escape becoming a national saga. It is right that this should be so, for such sagas guide and sustain the high endeavors of a people. But the saga must not swallow up the man, whose vivid friendship gave hope to millions though they never knew him, and whose death brought a sense of personal loss to millions who never saw him. This deep identification with his fellow men must be saved from the impersonality of immortal fame.

This identification with his fellow men was Roosevelt's profoundest characteristic and the ultimate key to his statesmanship. He was a democrat in feeling and not through abstract speculation about governments. When he said, "we are all immigrants," it was not a phrase but a feeling. And this feeling was not merely gregariousness in a setting of charm. It was not an undiscriminating love of his kind. His friendliness was so inclusive that his discriminating and often uncanny perception of men's qualities was a less apparent trait. He was keenly aware of men's frailties and follies. But he identified himself also with their follies and frailties, and so escaped the corrosion of cynicism.

This permeating friendliness represented true feeling. But equally true were deep recesses that were accessible hardly to anyone. From the time he was a boy, according to his mother, he had the self-sufficiency and the strength that come from a reserved inner life. Thus, while to outward view he was usually debonair and had a gaiety at times easily taken for jauntiness, he had a will of steel well sheathed by a captivating smile. His optimism was a phase of this resoluteness.

For too many people optimism is an evasion, a Micawber's hope that something will turn up. In Roosevelt, optimism was not an anodyne, it was an energy—an energy to spur his resourcefulness, a force that gave creative energy to others. An official not given to idolatry was once heard to say, "After talking with the President for an hour, I could eat bricks for lunch."

There were thus fused in him, and to an extraordinary degree, qualities indispensable for leading his people out of a period of deepening economic and moral deterioration by invigorating the forces of democracy. The same qualities fitted him to serve as a symbol of hope for liberty-loving people everywhere, in resisting a seemingly invincible challenge to civilization. Franklin Roosevelt's sophistication gave him understanding of men; his simplicity gave him trust in them. His understanding enabled him to govern; his trustfulness made him the exponent of democratic government.

Public men, like other men, are moved by major and minor motives, and the art of government has its own logistics. Moreover, instead of being "after all a very simple thing," as one of our Presidents so tragically misconceived it, government is a very complicated enterprise, and democratic government the most difficult. Undoubtedly there were surface deviations and inevitable tacking from time to time in the course Roosevelt pursued. But one cannot read the first study about Mr. Roosevelt as a public figure, written in 1911 by that discerning journalist, W. A. Warn, without realizing that during the thirty-five years of his public life he steered a consistent course—the course of his dominant impulses. When Roosevelt first came to the presidency, he could not escape the truth of Burke's dictum that we must reform in order to conserve. Events demanded a leader of social reform, and Franklin Roosevelt had the prepared mind and temper for it.

When Roosevelt became President, disillusionment about Europe, strong belief in disarmament rooted in idealism, preoccupation with domestic problems, and the prevalence of influential opinion in favor of economic nationalism, combined to produce a good deal of blindness concerning the extent to which the fate of this country was bound up with that of the rest of the world. A strange juxtaposition of history brought President Roosevelt and Hitler to power at the same time. By the law of his nature Franklin Roosevelt from the first felt revulsion against Hitler and his cohorts as individuals, and hostility to the resurgence of barbarism which they represented as a system. He clearly saw that the new barbarism, if unchecked, would be a menace to civilized society, not excluding that of the United States.

The function of statesmanship is to endeavor to forestall untoward events or to prepare adequately against them. The President had to do both at the same time. He worked with might and main to avert a war which was bound to be infinitely more destructive and agonizing than the last one, and to avert it by saving, and not surrendering freedom. Politics in a democracy means a continuous process of education. But education does not always mean exposition, and certainly not shouting. It involves much incubation. Not least of the arts of statesmanship is that of correct timing, of knowing what to say and when. The President was confronted with illusions highly creditable to men of good will, but steadily rendered invalid by Hitler. He was also confronted by pressures of every kind, of which democracy is an amalgam. And in his own political household he must often have encountered hesitation rather than encouragement. But there came a time when he could no longer doubt that he had to shift from the task of social reform to war leadership, in order not only to maintain our spirtiual heritage but to assure opportunities for further progress as a free society.

There came a moment when President Roosevelt was convinced that the utter defeat of Nazism was essential to the survival of our institutions. That time certainly could not have been later than when Mr. Sumner Welles reported on his mission to Europe. Certainly from the time that the fall of France seemed imminent, the President was resolved to do everything possible to prevent the defeat of the Allies. Although confronted with the obvious danger of attack by the Axis upon us, there came that series of bold and triumphant measures which Mr. Churchill authoritatively summarized in his moving speech, on April 17, 1945, to the House of Commons—the shipment of arms to Great Britain, the stab-in-the-back speech, the base-destroyer deal, lend-lease, the smoothing of the difficult ways of the Allied purchasing missions, the encouragement of Mr. Willkie's trip to England, the assistance in a hundred ways of British economic warfare, the extraordinarily prompt and cordial support of Russia. Moreover, while engaged in this series of complicated moves, he so skillfully conducted affairs as to avoid even the appearance of an act of aggression on our part.

And so, in the hour of national disaster on that Sunday afternoon after Japan had struck, when the President gathered about him his Cabinet and his military chiefs, the most experienced statesman among his advisers, after watching the President's calm and resolute control of the situation, could say to himself, "*There* is my leader."

His silver voice is stilled but the pitch he struck in others will gather volume. While his death comes as a cruel and monstrous loss, the creative energy which his life released throughout the world will continue, and, one is justified in believing, will even enhance his influence. He now joins the select company of those whose "home [is] in the minds of men, where their glory remains fresh to stir to speech or action as the occasion comes by. For the whole earth is the sepulchre of famous men; and their story is not graven only on stone over their native earth, but lives on far away, without visible symbol, woven into the stuff of other men's lives."

The ultimate mysteries of life are merely renewed. They remain the same. Franklin Roosevelt knew this well and he chose to express it at the Harvard Tercentenary Celebration in the words of Euripides:

> There be many shapes of mystery.
> And many things God makes to be,
> Past hope or fear.
> And the end men looked for cometh not,
> And a path is there where no man sought.
> So hath it fallen here.